*Concepts that
Distinguish
Judaism*

The B'nai B'rith History of the Jewish People
was first published during the years 1959–1964
as the B'nai B'rith Great Book Series.
The present edition, in five volumes,
has been selected to be part of the B'nai B'rith Judaica Library.
The Library is sponsored by the
B'nai B'rith International Commission on Adult Jewish Education
in an effort to promote a greater popular understanding
of Judaism and the Jewish tradition.
The volumes in the series are:

Creators of the Jewish Experience in Ancient and Medieval Times
Creators of the Jewish Experience in the Modern World
Concepts that Distinguish Judaism
Great Jewish Thinkers of the Twentieth Century
Contemporary Jewish Thought

The B'nai B'rith History of the Jewish People

GOD · TORAH · ISRAEL

CONCEPTS THAT DISTINGUISH JUDAISM

Edited with introductory notes by
Abraham Ezra Millgram

Annotated bibliographies by
Steven T. Katz

B'nai B'rith Books
Washington, D.C.

Jerusalem • London • Paris • Buenos Aires • East Sydney

Library of Congress Cataloging in Publication Data

Concepts that distinguish Judaism.

Bibliography: p.   Includes index.
1. Judaism—Doctrines—Addresses, essays, lectures.
I. Millgram, Abraham Ezra, 1901–
BM601.C62 1985   296.3   85-72299
ISBN 0-910250-00-6   ISBN 0-910250-01-4 (pbk.)

Dedicated to
the memory of

Rosa (Mrs. Maurice) Weinstein ז״ל

ויהללוה בשערים מעשיה

"Let her works praise her in the gates."
(Proverbs 31:31)

Contents

The Jewish Vision of God and Man

A Tradition in Transition

Introduction

The towering achievement in publishing by the B'nai B'rith International Commission on Adult Jewish Education has been, to this date, the B'nai B'rith Great Book Series edited for four volumes by Simon Noveck and for the fifth by Abraham Ezra Millgram. These books, as Rabbi Noveck described, presented "the inner-content of Jewish tradition, the great personalities and thinkers, the ideas, beliefs and religious movements of Judaism." In short, they are a *History of the Jewish People.* The nearly fifty scholars, teachers, and rabbis who contributed original essays to these volumes were a preponderant majority of the great interpreters of Jewish civilization at mid-century. Twenty-five years after they began to appear, the freshness and vigor of each essay is undiminished.

The continuing demand for each of the volumes by colleges and universities, synagogues and day schools, is being met by this revised edition. The essays are presented as they originally appeared, though for greater clarity the volumes themselves have been retitled and the series renamed. It was my belief that this new edition would enjoy a greater utility if each of the essays were supplemented by annotated bibliographies that reviewed the literature relevant to the subjects of the essays. Three distinguished scholars and teachers have joined me in the preparation of these bibliographies: Steven T. Katz of Cornell University, Reuven Kimelman of Brandeis University and Arthur Kurzweil, the noted author and lecturer. Each of us benefitted as students from this series, and the opportunity to enhance its value has brought us much satisfaction.

The American journalist George Will recently wrote of the growing rootlessness of our lives, our failure to connect to our past and our neglect of our legacy of a shared and valuable civilization. He was addressing himself to the inadequacies of the American educational system as it teaches the essence of Western civilization, but his point applies with a special urgency to the demands of a sound Jewish education. He chose, quite fortuitously, a Biblical example to illustrate his argument:

> In 1940, a British officer on Dunkirk beach flashed to London a three-word message, "But if not..." It was instantly recognized as a quotation from the Book of Daniel, where Nebuchadnezzar commands Shadrach, Meshach and Abednego to worship the golden image or be thrust into the fiery furnace. They reply defiantly; "If our God whom we serve is able to deliver us, he will deliver us from the fiery furnace, and out of thy hand, O king. But if not, be it known unto thee, O king, that we will not serve thy gods, nor worship the golden image which thou hast set up."

The message from Dunkirk is stirring evidence of a community deriving cohesion, inspiration and courage from a shared history. The question this story raises is how many of us today could either receive or transmit such a message from the rich legacy of Jewish civilization?

B'nai B'rith International through its Commission on Adult Jewish Education is sponsoring the republication of these volumes in the belief that they can play a large role in stimulating a desire to learn about Judaism, Jewish history and Jewish civilization, and that of themselves they are superb examples of the living Jewish tradition.

The joy of being a Jew is not derived from books. It is a product of a rich family life wherein Judaism radiates a happiness and contentment that passes beyond the ability of language to describe. It is the product of partaking of the company of other Jews. Yet for the connectedness of one Jew to his religion and peoplehood there is a need for the passion to be grounded in understanding and knowledge. These essays can play an important part in awakening and satisfying a desire to learn and comprehend.

There is nothing obscure in these volumes. They have been written with an enviable clarity, and they will inform the non-Jewish reader as fully as the Jewish reader. In presenting these volumes to the public, B'nai B'rith looks forward to a full engagement of the ideas presented therein with the wisdom and curiosity of men and women everywhere.

The B'nai B'rith Commission on Adult Jewish Education continues to enjoy the support, advice and commitment of its founder Maurice A. Weinstein, and the then B'nai B'rith International President who worked diligently to establish the Commission's work at the center of the B'nai B'rith—Philip M. Klutznick.

This new edition has benefitted from the encouragement of B'nai B'rith International President Gerald Kraft and key members of the Board of Governors. Mr. Abe Kaplan, the immediate past chairman of the Commission, and Dr. A.J. Kravtin, the current chairman have been effectively energetic in promoting this work. Executive Vice President Dr. Daniel Thursz and Associate Director Rabbi Joel H. Meyers provide the leadership and environment necessary for a Jewish educational program of quality to flourish, and within the Commission my patient secretary Mrs. Edith Levine does the same. My collaborator on this project has been Mr. Robert Teitler, a devoted B'nai B'rith member and a creative publisher.

Michael Neiditch, Director
B'nai B'rith International Commission
on Adult Jewish Education

Washington, D.C.
July 24, 1985
5 Av 5785

Foreword

Several times daily the Jew declares the unity of God. In this concept the Jew senses a unity that pervades all life. It is the foundation of nature, of humanity and of the moral law. Albert Einstein's lifelong search for a formula to express the unity of all existence is said to reflect in part his Jewish heritage. It was his way of proclaiming the unity of God.

This book attempts to delineate and define the Jewish way of life, its nature and uniqueness. Paradoxically, its organization of subject matter seems to contradict this concept of unity. The book deals with three distinct broad areas of Jewish concern. To be sure, this tripartite pattern has often been justified by a statement attributed to the *Zohar:* "The Holy One, blessed be He, the Torah and Israel are one." But this quotation is to the best of our knowledge aprocryphal. Ideally Judaism should be treated as an integrated whole, an absolute unity, without beginning or end. But how is one to plan and organize a book for finite human beings whose every life experience has both a beginning and an end? The unity of Judaism must necessarily be divided into several parts which together represent its totality. One part of the book focuses on the people of Israel; another deals with the concept of Torah in its broad sense; a third part wrestles with the faith as taught to Israel in the Torah; and the final section attempts to bridge the tradition with modern life. This segmentation is obviously a surgical operation, but it has advantages which compensate for the seeming distortion.

We might have started the book with any one of the three broad areas. We might have begun with the concept of God, the Creator of man and the Giver of the Torah to Israel. Or we might have started with the concept of Torah which, according to the Rabbis, was the master plan for the creation of the world and man. Equally cogent is the logic of starting the book with Israel, for Israel is the most tangible reality, the bearer and embodiment of Judaism. The last of these approaches was chosen because the people of Israel represents a known concept, an immediate reality, while for many readers the concepts of God and Torah are relatively remote and abstract.

Although the writers are all committed to Judaism as a way of life, the nature of their Jewish commitments is far from identical. Among the contributors are Orthodox, Conservative, Reform and secularist Jews, widely known as clear thinkers, lucid writers and authentic students of the panorama of Judaism. Each theme was developed by its author in his own separate way. The result is a book with varied emphases, ranging from those of the ultra-tradionalist to the ultra-modernist. The differing viewpoints and emphases render the book challenging and thought-provoking, especially for discussion groups which can be guided to investigate the diverging viewpoints and their philosophic foundations.

There is also some overlapping of subject matter, inevitable when several people write independently. The counterparts were not eliminated in order to preserve the unity of the individual essays. Besides, repetitive elements are often the proverbial blessing in disguise, treating the same subject from different viewpoints and giving the reader new insights and deeper understanding.

The reader will find that the approach of the writers is generally expository. There is no attempt "to win converts to the faith." This is in line with the book's goal, which is to shed light on the central concepts of Judaism and to stimulate intelligent thinking on their relevance to modern life.

The Publications Committee of B'nai B'rith's Commission on Adult Jewish Education rendered valuable help for which the editor is deeply indebted. He is especially grateful to its Chairman, Dr. Oscar I. Janowsky, and to Drs. Eugene Borowitz, Ira Eisenstein, Norman Frimer and Harry Orlinsky, committee members, who read manuscripts in the early stages. This distinguished group along with Rabbi Morris Adler, Chairman of B'nai B'rith's Commission on Adult Jewish Education, and Mrs. Lily Edelman, Director of B'nai B'rith's Department of Adult Jewish Education, helped immeasurably in the initial planning of the book and the selection of the writers, and especially in evaluating the final manuscript and submitting valuable suggestions for its improvement.

ABRAHAM EZRA MILLGRAM

Jersualem, Israel
December, 1963

ISRAEL,
PEOPLE OF THE
COVENANT

More than three thousand years ago Israel's total annihilation was triumphantly announced by Pharaoh Merneptah. On the column of victory in his Temple of the Dead is inscribed, "Israel's . . . seed exists no more." Paradoxically, this is Israel's introduction on the stage of history.

Pharaoh Merneptah was the forerunner of numerous others, among them rulers of vast empires, who said: "Come, and let us cut them off from being a nation; that the name of Israel may be no more in remembrance" (Psalms 83:5). During the first and second centuries the Romans crushed the Jews mercilessly; in the fifteenth century Israel was swept out of the Iberian Peninsula; in our own generation the Nazis slaughtered the Jews by the millions.

The classic justification of these tragic events was articulated by Haman to Ahasuerus: "There is a certain people," said he, "scattered abroad and dispersed among the peoples in all the provinces of thy kingdom; and their laws are diverse from those of every people; neither keep they the king's laws; therefore it profiteth not the king to suffer them. If it please the king, let it be written that they be destroyed" (Esther 3:8-9). Similar words have been uttered in different eras by the spokesmen of many nations such as Apion, Torquemada, Chmielnicki and Hitler.

But Israel succeeded in confusing and perplexing its enemies not merely by its miraculous survival, but by its remarkable vitality and creativity. Though few in number and dispersed throughout the world, Israel has succeeded in exerting a profound and decisive influence on the totality of mankind. The message of Israel's prophets still speaks clearly and emphatically to the heart of mankind; the religious offspring of Judaism—Christianity and Islam—stir the emotions and convictions of hundreds of millions of men and women. In every continent, the unique and substantial contributions that Judaism has made to Western civilization have stamped its character everlastingly on life patterns.

The paradox of Israel deepens considerably if we permit the Bible to define and clarify the nature of this singular people. We discover that Israel is alternately blessed and cursed, exalted and denounced by its own spokesmen. They are called "the seed blessed of the Lord" (Isaiah 65:23), and elsewhere they are denounced: "Therefore have I made thee a reproach unto the nations and a mocking to all the countries" (Ezekiel 22:5). Similarly Israel is dignified by God as "the branch of My planting, the work of My hands wherein I glory" (Isaiah 60:2), and is denigrated as a "sinful nation, a people laden with iniquity; a seed of evil-doers, children that deal corruptly" (*Ibid.* 1:4).

No wonder there are so many conflicting concepts and images of the Jew and of the Jewish people. The Jews are admiringly called by some "the chosen people" and "the people of the Book," and are denounced by others as "stiff-necked," doomed everlastingly to wander over the face of the earth as punishment for rejecting the divinity of Jesus.

Superimposed on the historic confusions about Israel is the advent of modernity and its violent impact on the Jew. Whereas modernity came to the nations of Western Europe gradually, as a process spanning several centuries, it came to most Jews as a sudden confrontation between the medieval ghetto and nineteenth- or twentieth-century modernism. With lightning speed the Jew was catapulted out of the tight, narrow ghetto into the broad, wide world. Moreover, modernity challenged some of the fundamental assumptions of Judaism and caused many revolutionary reactions among Jews. As a result the once homogeneous, though hardly harmonious, Jewish community has been split apart and fragmented into diverse and radically differentiated segments, parties and sects.

It is therefore not at all surprising that questions are raised. Who is a Jew? What makes one a Jew? What have the wide variety of Jews in common? Can one still speak of a Jewish community? Is there any future for the so-called community of Israel outside the Land of Israel? We obviously need an authentic image of Israel—the ideal and the real. This first section aims at shedding light on some of these perplexing questions.

1. The Jewish Image of the Jew

ALFRED JOSPE

W H E T H E R Judaism still represents a vital and distinctive orientation to life and the world and can still speak to the deepest needs of modern man is a question which has long troubled some of our best minds.

It troubled Franz Rosenzweig, one of the most creative and provocative Jewish thinkers of our time and the author of a profound book on Jewish theology, *The Star of Redemption*. The son of a wealthy businessman, brought up without any contact with Jewish values and experiences, in his youth concerned only with art and music, a first-rate Hegel scholar and historian, utterly disinterested in Jewish life and affairs—what made this man write a book on Jewish theology?

A letter he wrote in 1909 gives us a clue. One of his cousins, also born to Jewish parents, had become converted to Christianity. Rosenzweig's parents wrote their son how shocked they had been by their nephew's defection, which they considered a disgrace. Rosenzweig answered that he himself had advised this step. Hans, the cousin, had felt in need of a living religion, something which his parents had completely failed to give him. Under these circumstances, was it not better to acquire a religious identification belatedly than not at all? "Because I am hungry, must I, on principle, go on being hungry? Does principle satisfy a hunger? Can being non-religious on principle satisfy a religious need?" Can a man who searches for deeper values and more enduring loyalties be satisfied to be a Jew merely by the accident of birth, by carrying an empty label that is of use only for legal purposes—the marriage or death certificates? "Confronted with the choice between an empty purse and a handful of money, shall I choose the empty purse?" We are really Christians in nearly every respect; our country is Christian, as are our schools, the books we read, the entire culture which forms us. Judaism is a dead religion, unable to quench the thirst of the seeker after a living faith.[1]

Later, Rosenzweig was to discover the meaning of Jewish distinctiveness. But when he wrote this letter at the age of twenty-three, Judaism was theologically dead and meaningless to him. Numerous persons have shared this feeling: Israel's time is past. There is nothing distinctive which it still can say to the Jew or the modern world.

Sidney Hook, the contemporary philosopher, reaches the same conclusion, not on theological but on sociological and philosophical grounds. He feels Jews differ so completely in the articulation of their faith, their background, history, ancestry, culture, language and political aspiration that the quest for any formula to express what Jews may have in common is fruitless. Every criterion breaks down in the face of the multiplicity of facts concerning the beliefs and behavior of those who call themselves Jews or are so called by others. Hence, the only statement that can be made about a Jew is that he is "anyone who for any reason calls himself such or is called such in any community whose practices take note of the distinction." [2] Professor Hook realizes that the bond, which, for him, unifies the Jewish group is merely something negative—the experience of prejudice and social exclusion which, he feels, is common to all Jews and sets them apart from others; but he denies that there is any other bond that holds Jews together. Judaism possesses no distinctive ideals, beliefs or values which are generally accepted or can be decribed in positive terms.

This conclusion is shared by many, among them the sociologist Melville Herskovits, who was the first to define the Jew as "a person who calls himself a Jew or who is called Jewish by others";[3] Jean-Paul Sartre, the French existentialist, who defines a Jew as "one whom other men consider a Jew"; and the poet Karl Shapiro, who, in the introduction to his *Poems of a Jew*, says that "no one has been able to define *Jew*" for "being a Jew is the consciousness of being a Jew, and the Jewish identity, with or without religion, with or without history, is the significant fact."

Even so deeply committed a Jew as the late Kurt Lewin, the social psychologist, felt it difficult, if not impossible, to find a convincing positive rationale for the continued existence of the Jewish group. He knew that categories such as religion, race, nation or ethnic culture were inadequate to define the Jews. Surveying the sweep of Jewish experience, he found it was not easy to see "why such a group ought to be preserved as a separate unit, why it has not entirely given up its will to live, and why the nations have refused to grant the Jews a full assimilation." [4] Nevertheless, he recommended that the Jewish group accept the fact of its underprivileged minority status and try to make the most of it. Even though Judaism may not possess distinctive theological or cultural values, there is psychological value in membership in the Jewish group. Every person must have a sense of belonging for the sake of his emotional well-being, and it is far better to be a member of a persecuted minority than to be a marginal man who is doubly uprooted. The best armor against prejudice is self-respect. Hence, an early build-up of a clear and positive feeling of belongingness to the Jewish group is one of the few effective things that parents can do for the later happiness of their children. [5]

The difficulty is that the remedy which Lewin prescribes is the very malaise from which Jews suffer. He counsels them to accept their membership in the Jewish group for the sake of their emotional adjustment, when the source of their trouble is their very doubt whether membership in the Jewish group is spiritually meaningful and socially desirable. Lewin, too, is unable to offer a positive rationale for the maintenance of Jewish distinctiveness.

Many other attempts have been made to define the meaning of Jewish existence; yet all point to the same fact: the Jewish people has usually been an enigma to its own adherents no less than to outsiders. To John, in the Fourth Gospel, the Jews are of the devil, while for the Talmud they are as indispensable to the survival of the world as the winds. To the German historian Heinrich von Treitschke, who lived around the turn of the century, the Jews are the ferment of decomposition, an element of unrest and change in civilization, while for Judah Halevi, the medieval Jewish poet, Israel is the heart of mankind by its special propensity for religious insight and experience.[6] To sociologist Max Weber, the Jews, because of their lack of power and persistent insecurity, have to be classified as a pariah group, while even so rational a thinker as Abraham Geiger, German Reform leader, claimed that Jews have a special genius for religion.[7] To the poet Heinrich Heine, Judaism, as he once quipped with more bitterness than irony, was not a religion but a misfortune, while other Jews throughout the centuries have found strength in Isaiah's dictum that the Jewish people is a light unto the nations, God's witness and spokesman in an idolatrous world. To British historian Arnold Toynbee, the Jews are merely a fossilized relic of an ancient Syriac civilization, while to philosopher Alfred Whitehead the Jews are very much alive and their survival is largely due to the fact that they are probably the most able race of any in existence.[8]

A bewildering maze of contradictory definitions and claims! Who is right? How should the evidence be read? What is the historic image the Jews have had of themselves? What is their vision of themselves, their view of the meaning of Jewish existence, their concept of the role of Jews in history?

The Jewish Value Stance

The Jewish image of the Jew is embodied in what has been called a "value stance," [9] a specific attitude toward life and the world.

Man basically has only two possibilities to establish a relationship to the world. He can accept or reject it. Both world views exist. One is embodied in the way of Judaism, the other in the way of an Eastern religion, Buddhism.

As Leo Baeck has pointed out, Judaism demands moral affirmation of man's relation to the world by will and deed and declares the world to be the field of life's tasks. Buddhism denies this relation; man is to devote himself to self-meditation and without volition. The one is the expression of the command to work and create, the other of the need for rest. The one works for the Kingdom of God in which all men may be included, the other leads to the desire to sink into nothingness and to find deliverance from the ego. The one calls for ascent, development, growth, the steady march toward the future; the other preaches return, cessation, a future-less existence in silence. Judaism, therefore, is ultimately the affirmation of an active, creative relationship to the world, Buddhism the denial of such a relationship.[10]

But there are various ways in which life and the world can be affirmed. The Greeks, for instance, also affirmed them, but in a wholly different way from that of the Jews. Socrates accepted death even though he was innocent by his own definition of justice. He refused to escape when his friends wanted to make it possible because he accepted and affirmed the higher authority of the state. The state cannot exist when law is set aside. Defiance would result in chaos.[11]

Compare Socrates' attitude with that of the prophet Nathan, who castigates David's defiance of justice in his affair with Bathsheba; with Elijah, who denounces Ahab for his murder of Naboth; with Isaiah's denunciation of the religious and political leaders of Jerusalem because of their corruption; with Jeremiah's fearless and flaming indictment of the religious hypocrisy and moral depravity of his generation and its government. The Greek thinker gives passive assent to the existing social order even though it may be evil. The prophet is a challenger of the social order precisely because it is evil. For the one, government imposes laws which cannot be challenged. For the other, government itself stands under the judgment of the law and must, if necessary, be challenged in God's name. One the teacher, who wishes to influence man's minds and thoughts, the other the firebrand, the prophet, who wishes to judge the social order. For the one the highest virtue is that man *think* correctly, the intellectual apperception of reality. For the other, the highest virtue is that man *act* correctly, the moral penetration of reality.

For this reason, the value stance of Judaism also differs profoundly from the world view of Christianity which insists that the highest virtue is that man *believe* correctly. The verse in the Book of Habakkuk (2:4) which Paul quotes in the first chapter of his *Letter to the Romans* became the cornerstone of the new religion: "The just shall live by His faith." The difference between Judaism and Christianity emerges from their different views of the nature of man. For Christianity, man is sinful from birth, incorrigible; no matter how hard he may try, he cannot overcome sin and achieve salvation through his own efforts. For Judaism, man can and does sin, but must not. Created in the image of God, he has the capacity for growth, love and compassion, for doing what is right and good. Therefore Christianity insists that though deeds are important, the indispensable condition of salvation is faith in Jesus as the Christ; that ultimately nothing has to be done, nothing to be fulfilled; that after the works are done, salvation is achieved not by the merit of one's deeds but by the acceptance, in faith, of the officially formulated correct form of belief. Judaism proclaims that ultimately it is man's acts which matter and not his notions or thoughts, which may well be erroneous or mistaken. God's nature and thoughts are beyond human grasp, but His commandments are "neither hidden nor far off."

While Christianity preaches the redemption of man from this world of sin through his faith, Judaism urges the redemption of this world from sin through man's actions.

The Election of Israel

The Jewish value stance toward life and the world is the context, the frame of the picture. The details of the picture reveal the image Jews have had of themselves as Jews.

This image has several dominant features. One is the concept that Israel is the "chosen people," a concept which permeates much of Jewish literature and thought, its folklore, prayers and liturgy. Even though Moses Maimonides, the medieval Jewish philosopher, did not include it in his Thirteen Articles of Faith, the concept of "election" has always been deeply embedded in the Jewish consciousness. When a male Jew is called to the Torah, he recites the traditional blessing, *asher bahar banu mi'kol ha'amim*, praising God "who has chosen us from among all other nations." When Jews recite their daily morning prayer they say the benediction, *she'lo assani goy*, thanking God "that He has not made (us) gentiles." When they pronounce the benediction over the Sabbath wine, they declare that God has chosen and sanctified Jews from among all other peoples in the same way in which He has distinguished between Sabbath and weekday. When Jews make *Havdalah* on Saturday nights, they recite the traditional *ha-mavdil*, glorifying God for setting Jews apart from all other peoples just as He set apart the sacred from the profane and light from darkness.

Few of Judaism's teachings have been so misunderstood as this concept of the "chosen people." George Bernard Shaw, comparing it to the *Herrenvolk* concept of the Nazis, castigated the Jews for the arrogance of their claim to racial superiority. H. G. Wells considered the concept a hindrance to world unity. Protestant theologians persist in describing the God of Judaism as a tribal deity interested only in protecting His own people, and not as a God concerned with the whole of mankind; and avowed anti-Semites cite this as proof for their claim of a Jewish conspiracy to dominate the Christian world. The concept has even been rejected by some Jewish thinkers, especially Mordecai M. Kaplan and the Reconstructionist movement, as an anachronism, a concept that belongs to a thought world of the past and is incompatible with the equality and dignity of all men and the demands of democracy. The assumption by any individual or group that it is the chosen and indispensable vehicle of God's grace to others is utterly untenable for modern man.[12]

What then did the Jews mean when they spoke of themselves as the "chosen people"? How did they understand the meaning of their election?

For Jewish tradition, the Jewish people is not merely one of many peoples; it was selected by God as His peculiar treasure. Israel's place and role in the world are part of a divine plan which manifested itself first in the early days of the world's existence when the Creator of the Universe bestowed His blessings upon the patriarchs as reward for their faithfulness and love and promised that their children and all future generations would continue to receive His blessings because of "the merits of their fathers."

Centuries later, at a particular time in the cosmic drama and at a particular place, Sinai, God revealed Himself anew when He made His will known to the entire Jewish people. His will is embodied in a particular document, the Torah. It reveals not only the conduct which is to govern man's life but also the instrument which God has chosen to make His will known to the rest of the world. This instrument is the people known as Israel. Israel is God's "chosen people."

But why did God single out this one people, the Jews, for His purposes? The rabbis and thinkers of the past were not unaware of the difficulties which the concept of "election" involved. Maimonides and others with him stated that all that can be said is that God so willed it. It is impossible for man to understand why God should have revealed His will to one particular nation. The fact, however, is that He did. Man can do nothing but acknowledge the fact, for he is not God and cannot hope to fathom the secrets of divine providence.[13]

Other scholars and thinkers sought to find positive reasons for Israel's claim to election. Two bipolar, diametrically opposed streams of thought and argument developed. For some rabbis, the people of Israel merited and continues to merit election because of its special service and faithfulness to God. Jews were the first ones to proclaim God as the Supreme King at the shores of the Red Sea (Exodus 15:18). They were the only ones willing to accept the yoke of God's Kingdom at Mount Sinai when all other nations refused God's gift of the Torah.[14] Their special faithfulness merits their special relationship with God.

But just as much or more emphasis is placed by Jewish tradition on the opposite point of view—that God chose the Jews for reasons of His own; that election is not based on merit but represents an act of grace on the part of God; that God's love for Israel is not given as a reward but offered freely despite the shortcomings of the Jewish people. Quoting Hosea's statement (14:5), "I will love them freely," the Midrash conceives of God as saying: "My soul volunteered to love them though they are not worthy of it." And the Tanna of the School of Elijah proclaims:

> Blessed be He who chose Israel from among all the nations and made them verily His own and called them children and servants unto His name . . . and all this because of the love with which He loves them and the joy with which He rejoiced in them.
>
> *(Tanna d'be Eliahu,* p. 127)

Whatever "reasons" could be found—whether the traditional Jew felt he was "chosen" because of some special merits of his own or of his fathers, or because of God's freely offered though unmerited love—he firmly believed that the Jewish people had been singled out by providence to receive God's law and to serve as the faithful guardian of the divine will and message until all men would accept them. Yet this concept of the "chosen people" is not exclusivist and does not imply the rejection of the rest of mankind as inferior. Even though the Jews claimed a monopoly of God's revelation, they never claimed to be superior to the rest of mankind by reason of birth, blood or race. Anyone can become a Jew by embracing Judaism. A person who converts to Judaism becomes a *ben Avraham*, a "son of Abraham," by entering into Abraham's covenant. Rabbi Meir said that Adam had been created from dust which had been collected from all corners of the earth so that no nation could claim the distinction of being better or having cradled mankind. Some of the greatest rabbis are said to have been descended from converts to Judaism. Indeed, according to Jewish tradition, King David, from whose house the Messiah would come, was a direct descendant of Ruth, the Moabite.

Judaism clearly acknowledges that men can be blessed with salvation even though they are outside the Sinaitic covenant. A special calling is demanded but no exclusiveness of salvation is proclaimed. Traditional Judaism insists that "the righteous of all nations have a share in the world to come (*Midrash T'hillim* to Psalm 9:17) and that man should first lead a good life and then ask God for religious truth.[15] As Morris Joseph puts it, "Israel's election does not give him a monopoly of the divine love." [16] For Judaism, all human beings are God's children and have an equal claim upon His care and solicitude. The divine test of a man's worth is not his theology or descent but his life.

In the same way, the protection of the law was extended to every inhabitant of the country, Jew and non-Jew alike. In the words of Numbers, "Ye shall have one statute both for the stranger and for him that is born in the land." Jews have always been particularly sensitive to these problems for, as the Bible and Jewish observances constantly remind them, they themselves had been strangers in Egypt, and the memory of that experience had burned itself into their consciousness. Because they knew what oppression of minorities meant and what it could do to the soul of the oppressed, they hated oppression and wanted to make sure they would never succumb to its practice.

What the concept of election has meant in Jewish life, in positive terms, is illustrated by a story of the Rabbis. The ancient rabbis once asked: Why did God choose Israel? Because all other nations refused to accept the Torah. Originally, God had offered it to all nations of the world. But the children of Esau rejected it because they could not reconcile themselves to the commandment "Thou shalt not kill." The Moabites declined the offer because they felt they could not accept the commandment "Thou shalt not commit adultery." The Ishmaelites refused because they could not square their habits with the commandment "Thou shalt not steal." All of them rejected the Torah; only Israel was prepared to accept it.

The story makes a crucial point. Think of ancient Israel: an insignificant little people in the vast spaces of the Near East. It could have been like all other peoples of the area, content to live in some forgotten corner of the world, working, procreating, building houses, struggling with nature to wrest a living from it, and gradually fading away from the arena of history.

And yet, in this very people, there suddenly blazed forth the conviction that it is not enough just to exist; man must live for something. Therefore, this people is different from the peoples in whose midst it had been living. Something gives meaning to its life, through which it becomes articulate about the meaning and purpose of its existence. For the first time in the history of mankind, national difference becomes transformed into moral and spiritual distinctiveness.[17]

Here we can grasp the full meaning of "election." It is in the idea of his "election" that the Jew becomes conscious and articulate about what he conceives to be his task and role. He becomes conscious that he possesses a truth that separates him from other groups. And he declares that this difference is not only justified but valuable and important. Hence, election is the living certainty of a religious community that it possesses a truth which distinguishes it from all other peoples, but which addresses itself to all of mankind. It is a unique and vital possession which gives Jewish existence a sense of purpose and direction.

The Concept of the "Covenant"

This truth which distinguishes the Jew from all other peoples is embodied in the concept of the "covenant," the second feature in the image which Jews have of themselves as Jews.

The Hebrew term for covenant is *b'rit*, a covenant or agreement between God and Israel by which Israel accepted the Torah. This acceptance implies two fundamental notions. First, the agreement between God and Israel is bilateral. If God selected Israel, Israel consented to be elected. If God chose Israel, Israel, in turn, chose God. As Israel Zangwill once put it, a chosen people is at bottom a choosing people.

Secondly, if the concept of *election* signifies the consciousness that the Jew possesses a truth which sets him apart from others, the concept of the *covenant* signifies the consciousness of what that truth is. It is Torah. It is the Law of Sinai. It is the acceptance and affirmation of God's design for man's life, the consciousness of what God demands of man—of what man must do to make His truth alive regardless of the hardships or obligations it may entail. The covenant is man's response, *Hineni* —"Here I am"—to the voice that calls; it is the acceptance of the obligation inherent in election.

The concept of the covenant has numerous connotations in Jewish tradition and literature. After the flood, God enters into a compact with mankind through Noah, in which God pledges that He will never again destroy the human race, and man in turn pledges to abide by the fundamental moral laws in dealing with his fellow men. The term is used again when God enters into a covenant with Abraham, and calls upon him to train his descendants to keep the ways of the Lord, while God pledges Himself to bless Abraham and his descendants and multiply their seed.

The prophet Hosea defines the covenant as an act of love between God and Israel, symbolizing their bond of partnership in which man is given a share in the never-ending process of creation and the redemption of mankind through love and faithfulness:

I shall betroth thee unto Me forever.
I shall betroth thee unto Me with right and justice, with love and
    mercy.
I shall betroth thee unto Me in truth, and thou shalt know the
    Lord.   (Hosea 2:19-20)

The most significant expression of the covenant idea, however, can be found in Chapter Nineteen of Exodus:

> Now then, if you will obey My voice and keep My covenant, then ye shall be a peculiar treasure unto Me above all other people. For all the earth is Mine. And ye shall be unto Me a kingdom of priests and a holy nation. (Exodus 19:5-6)

These two verses point to the two major convictions embodied in the covenant relationship between God and Israel. One is the profound and basic Jewish belief that the earth is the Lord's. He had promised the land to their forefathers; He had liberated the people from Egyptian bondage; He had guided them through the perils of the wilderness until they reached the land He had promised them. But the land itself belongs to God. He has given it to the people in fulfillment of His part of the covenant. But Israel can never claim absolute possession of it. That possession depends on the faithfulness with which it fulfills its part of the covenantal relationship.

And the obligation which God has set before Israel in the covenant is defined in the task to become "a kingdom of priests and a holy nation." Election is not a divine favor extended to a people but a task imposed upon it. It does not bestow privileges; it demands service. It is not a prerogative but an ethical charge, not a claim but an obligation, not a divine title for rights but a divine mandate for duties. The obligation is to live in accordance with the word and spirit of Sinai, to serve God in thought and act, to sanctify life and render it significant, to avoid cruelty, diminish evil, and purify man's hands and heart. Election means to become the prophet and if necessary the suffering servant of the Lord, to be heir to and perpetuator of the spirit of the men who entered the arena of history not as soldiers, statesmen or builders of empires, but as prophets of the ideal society, as the legislators of the priestly and sanctified life, as the visionaries of justice and human reconciliation, as the challengers of evil and the singers of hope, as rebels against paganism and cruelty, as the supreme architects of the religious life.

More, not less, is expected of Israel by virtue of the covenant. People who are ignorant of God and His will, men who have never been taught what truth and justice are, may be forgiven impiety and sin. But Jews cannot be forgiven so easily—Israel has a special commitment to God. When Israel fails, it commits a *ḥillul ha'shem*, a desecration of the divine name. Failure to live up to the ideal will be punished. Hence the prophet Amos warns the people in God's name, "Only you have I known of all the families of the earth. Therefore I will visit upon you all your iniquities" (Amos 3:2).

The Jewish people understood and defined their experiences in terms of this covenant relationship. Faithfulness was rewarded, defection punished. Therefore, even the destruction of the Temple, the people's exile and suffering, the persecutions and expulsions of the Middle Ages could not shatter the image Jews had of themselves. Destruction and exile were a national disaster but not completely unforeseen. They were part of the divine plan, foretold in the admonitions of the prophets. They were the punishment that was bound to come upon those who had violated the covenant and strayed from the path of God. Severance from the land did not imply severance from God. The Jew was persecuted not because God had abandoned or rejected him, as the victorious nations of the world claimed; God still loved him but wanted to chastise him into obedience and return. He suffered because he was not equal to his moral task.[18] In the words of the prayer book, "because of our sins were we exiled from our land." Other people sinned too, and would receive their punishment in due time. Israel, however, was the covenant people of whom God expected more than of others. Suffering was defined as punishment, and punishment in turn was a call to duty. Exile was God's call to return to the faithfulness inherent in Israel's role as the "chosen people." The acceptance of punishment opened the gate to redemption and return to the land.

But suffering was, for the Jew, not only a judgment on himself but also a judgment on the world. It was not only a punishment for sin, a proof of his own shortcomings and imperfections; it was also a sign that the world itself was still unredeemed, that evil was still rampant, that God's community of love and peace was still unrealized and would so remain as long as the peoples of the world continued to reject the God who had made man, and served the gods they had fashioned for themselves. The Jew began to realize that those who do not suffer are not always innocent, that worldly successes or failures are not the ultimate measure of things, that a man or nation which disavows the use of power is almost certain to be worsted in the pressures of life, that might is not necessarily right, and that suffering is not necessarily evidence of divine rejection but the price one may have to pay for loyalty to ideals in an unredeemed world. As Yannai, an early medieval Hebrew poet, put it:

> Not everyone who is loved is loved
> Not everyone who is hated is hated
> Some are hated below, and loved above . . .
> Hated we are for You we love, O Holy One! [19]

Israel's unbroken love of God, the Jew's dedicated fulfillment of his responsibilities under the covenant, was the only road that would ultimately lead to the redemption of man and the social order. The suffering of the Jew was the constant reminder that man's work was not yet completed and hence a call to all men no less than to the Jewish people to resume their never-ending task to do God's will.

The Messianic Concept and the Mission of Israel [20]

The conception of life as a moral task and the never-ending quest for perfection is the third and perhaps most characteristic feature of the Jewish image of the Jew. It finds its highest expression in the concept of the Messiah.

Jewish Messianic thinking is rooted in one of man's profoundest needs, his concern with the future. We hunger for certainty. We want knowledge of that which is to come. But it is in the nature of things that there can be no such certainty or knowledge.

For this reason some nations of antiquity, living through eras of crisis and catastrophe, despaired of the future and turned their vision to the past. The present was chaotic, the future dark. Therefore, they yearned for a renewal of the past which they felt was the embodiment of all goodness and happiness. Hesiod and Ovid, for instance, in their descriptions of the five successive ages and races of man, began with the Golden Age, when man lived happily and painlessly on the fruits of the untilled soil, passing away in dreamless sleep to become the guardian angels of the world. They ended with the Iron Age, the most degenerate of all, in which the authors themselves lived. The past was good, perfect and ideal. The present was evil, the future dark and foreboding.

In contrast to these attitudes, the Jew did not evade the problem posed by the future. He never placed perfection in the past but instead projected it into the future. Of course, the Bible starts with perfection: the first man, Adam, must necessarily have been happy and perfect until his fall. Yet this idea has never played a significant part in Jewish thought. What is important is not man's descent but his ascent, not his past but his future. Jewish thinking looks for happiness, virtue and perfection, not to a past Golden Age, but to the future, to "the end of days," a favorite phrase of the prophets.

This projection of perfection into the future is an integral part of Jewish thinking, and has been called the most striking and characteristic feature of the religion of Israel. It originated in the Bible, whose pages constantly echo this challenge to work for human perfection until it will ultimately be established on earth. This trend in Jewish thinking can be summarized in a single word—Messiah.

There are two views of the Messiah in Jewish tradition. The one has come to be called the *man*, the personal Messiah. The other is called the *time*, or the Messianic era. The one is a man, the other an age. The one is a son of the house of David, the other an epoch in the history of Israel and the world. The one is a Jew, the other a time yet to come.

The concept of a personal Messiah has its inception in the historical experiences of the Jewish people and the dreary political conditions in ancient Israel. The patriarchs had had to leave their native countries and wander in foreign lands. Then followed the Egyptian slavery with its memories of oppression. And even after the people had entered the Promised Land, they were not secure. They suffered the humiliation of frequent defeats and ultimately the loss of national independence.

It was only natural that a people with such a past and present should long for a future in which there would be an end to suffering, for a political redeemer who would unite the people and establish a strong nation able to withstand all enemies.

It was only in the reign of David that the popular longing for such a redeemer was satisfied. Under David's leadership, the people grew powerful, establishing a kingdom that reached from the borders of Egypt to the gates of Damascus. The glory of this kingdom and of the man who had wrought this miracle caught the imagination of the masses. David became the ideal Jewish king, the great national hero and redeemer. He had inaugurated a state of national glory. People hoped it would last forever—a hope that was strengthened by Nathan's prophecy that the throne of David would be established forever.

It was at this time that the Messianic ideal took shape in the minds of the Jewish people. In its inception, the Messiah was a political, a national ideal. He is the person who will bring relief from oppression, end the nation's disunity and insecurity, and establish a stable national government that will last forever.

But the Messiah is conceived not merely as a political liberator; he will also bring about the spiritual regeneration of the people. This is the second ingredient of the Messianic concept. While the Messiah was originally a national savior, a compensatory ideal conceived in times of national distress, a symbol of the indomitable will of the people to survive, he now also begins to personify the spiritual values and religious ideals to which the people of God should be dedicated. Gradually, the Messiah is conceived not only as the king but as the ideal king, the perfect ruler who will establish not only a stable government but one based on righteousness and justice.

This hope runs through the fabric of all the prophetic books and the Psalms. But it was Isaiah who crystallized it when he spoke of a new king who, endowed with the divine spirit, would arise from the house of David to establish peace and equity in the land, who would usher in the time when tyranny and violence would no longer be practiced on God's holy mountain and when the land would be full of the knowledge of God as the waters cover the earth (Isaiah 11:9).

The Messianic idea, at this stage of its development, was still particularistic. When the prophets spoke of the Messiah king, they meant a king who was to rule over Israel. When they spoke of the need for justice and perfection, they did not envision a utopian world state based on justice and perfection. They demanded that the people of Israel practice justice in the land of Israel. The Messiah was still a national concept. He was the redeemer of Israel, not the redeemer of the world.

The development of the Messianic concept could not, however, stop at this point. This is the third and most important stage in the development of Jewish Messianic thinking. The prophets had proclaimed the one God who created man and the world and who demands righteousness. But if there is only one God, can He be merely the God of one people, of Israel? Is He not also the God of all peoples, of mankind? The prophets had preached that Israel had been appointed by God to practice righteousness, stamp out evil, establish the good society. But should evil not be eradicated and righteousness be practiced wherever men live? The prophets had proclaimed the moral law. But is there one moral code for one people and different moral codes for other peoples? The moral law is universal law. Justice and righteousness are indivisible. God's demands are directed alike toward all men.

It is in this thought that Jewish Messianic thinking finds its consummation. Driven by its own inner logic, it widens into genuine universalism. It is at this point that the concept of mankind emerges for the first time in Jewish and, indeed, in Western thought. If there is one God who created the world and fashioned man in His image, all men are His children. If there is one God, there must be one mankind. And if there is one mankind, there can be only one truth, one justice and one religion to which not merely Israel but all men are called and which cannot find its historic fulfillment until all men are united in it.

Thus, the Messianic concept receives an entirely new direction. Deutero-Isaiah, Micah and other prophets no longer speak of the personal Messiah of the house of David, the individual who will become king and establish a reign of righteousness and peace for Zion. They speak of the new life which is to arise upon earth. The concept of the *one man* retreats behind the concept of the *one time*. The personal Messiah gives way to the "days of the Messiah," in which universal peace and brotherhood will be established and all mankind will be united in the service of the one God.

Israel's Mission

The people of Israel, however, has a special task in helping to fashion the Messianic age. Having conceived of the one God for the one mankind, Israel has as its mission to be the bearer and guardian of this truth until it will be accepted by all the nations of the earth.

I, the Lord, have called thee in righteousness, and will hold thine
hand and will keep thee for a covenant of the people, for a light
of the nations, to open the blind eyes, to bring out the prisoners
from the prisons, and them that sit in darkness out of the prison
house.   (Isaiah 42:6-7)

Thus the prophets proclaim that Israel itself has a Messianic
role in world history. They speak to Israel, but they speak
of the world and the nations. Israel is to be the servant of the
Lord. As God's servant, Israel will suffer and will be persecuted
because injustice, oppression and evil will continue to exist. But
Israel's suffering will not be meaningless or in vain. By its very
existence, Israel will be the symbol of protest—against oppression, injustice, idolatry, darkness and evil. Ultimately, the time
will come when Israel will be vindicated, when its trials will be
rewarded, when the world will know that "from the rising of the
sun and from the west there is none beside Me," when men will
mend their ways and a new heaven and earth will be established
—a day when "the Lord shall be king over all the earth," when
"the Lord shall be one and His name be one" for all peoples
(Zechariah 14:9).

Jewish Messianic thinking, thus defined, has a number of
fundamental implications.

First, the concept of a universal God is inseparably associated
with the concept of a universal religion. If the God of Israel is
the God of all nations, the faith of Israel must ultimately become
the faith of all nations. God desires the homage of all men. Prophetic Judaism envisions the ultimate universal acceptance of
Israel's universal God.

There is a radical difference between this prophetic notion
and the kind of interfaith statements which are in vogue in many
parts of the world in our time. The prophets do not say that all
religions are more or less the same and that the differences between them do not matter because "we all worship the same God
though we approach him in different ways." They do not claim,
as Count Zinzendorff, founder of the Moravian Brethren Congregation, did two centuries ago, that all religions are only
variants of the one central kernel which all have in common.
They do not argue, as Lessing did in his parable of the three
rings, that the sons of the king should respect each other and
live in peace with one another because none of them can be sure

who has received the genuine ring. They do not assert, as Rosenzweig did, that both Judaism and Christianity are equally authentic ways to God, the one leading through the son to the Father, the other leading directly to the Father. And they certainly are diametrically opposed to that popular kind of contemporary interfaith religion which proclaims that one religion is just as good as the other and that Christianity is the best religion for the Christian while Judaism is the best religion for the Jew. Contrary to all these approaches, the prophets, and especially Deutero-Isaiah, confidently express the hope that the time will come when Judaism will have become the religion of all nations.

Second, the Messianic Age will not come solely through the grace of God; it requires the labors of man. It does not signify an announcement of something which will ultimately descend to the earth from some other world. It will have to be merited and earned by man. It arises, in Leo Baeck's words, out of the very depths of the significance of life: it is the demand and the certainty of that which every person and every generation must do so that God's will and through it man's life be fulfilled.

Third, the Messianic Age is of this world, not of a world-to-come. It is a historic task and possibility, not an eschatological expectation. It is to happen here on earth and not in apocalyptical times, after the end of time. It is the great goal toward which mankind must work and move here in this world of time and space.

Fourth, Messianic thinking implies that man is not merely an object of history. He is also the subject of history. He is not merely driven by a blind fate. He can shape and create his own future. Hence, the central core of the Messianic concept is the conviction that history is not blind. It has direction and a goal. And wherever there is a goal, the future is no longer something to be dreaded. The future is not what *will* be, but that which *should* be. It is a task entrusted to man, a command to shape his life and make the historic process the instrument of the realization of that which is good.

It is in these thoughts that the Messianic ideal reveals its deepest meaning and significance as the central feature of the image which Jews have of themselves and of the meaning of Jewish existence. Man's life on earth is not a blind groping in darkness.

It is not a succession of unrelated accidents, devoid of point and purpose or, in Macbeth's words, "a veritable tale told by an idiot, full of sound and fury, signifying nothing." Life has meaning. History has direction. There is a goal and purpose to man's endeavors. And this purpose can be fulfilled by the man who learns to listen to the voice that calls—*election;* who responds by saying *Hineni*—"Here I am"—*covenant;* and who, accepting his role in the Messianic drama, becomes God's partner in the never-ending task of creation.

FOR FURTHER READING

BUBER, Martin, *Israel and the World* (New York: Schoken, 1985). A wonderfully rich collection of many of Buber's most telling essays on the relationship between Israel and her neighbors and on Judaism's inner self-understanding.

HESCHEL, Abraham Joshua, *God in Search of Man: A Philosophy of Judaism* (New York: Farrar, Straus & Giroux, 1956). A moving evocation of the Jewish spirit by a major Jewish theologian. Lyrical as well as logical, it is a classic work.

JACOBS, Louis, *A Jewish Theology* (New York: Behrman House, 1973). A representative, learned summary of what Judaism teaches on almost all basic theological matters.

KAPLAN, Mordecai, M., *The Religion of Ethical Nationhood* (New York: Macmillian, 1970). An important statement on Jewish political and ethical values by one of the great Jewish thinkers of our age.

PLAUT, Gunther, *The Case for the Chosen People,* (New York: Doubleday, 1965). A moving defense of Judaism and its classic self-understanding by a distinguished Reform scholar.

URBACH, Ephraim, *The Sages* (Jersualem, Magnes Press, 1975). The outstanding contemporary presentation of rabbinic views on central theological matters, e.g., covenant, Torah, mitzvot.

2 . *People and Land of Israel*

ABRAHAM S. HALKIN

F r o m its early beginnings, the land of Israel, then known as Canaan, was an integral part of the hopes and realities of the people Israel. In His first appearance to Abraham, God instructs the patriarch to go forth "unto the land that I will show thee." The growth of his seed into a large nation, promised then and on other occasions, was linked from the start to that particular land and confirmed in a formal covenant.

Canaan became the Promised Land. Abraham, Isaac and Jacob, while they sojourned there or traveled through it, or even when they were forced to leave its confines, were assured that this land would become the possession of their offspring, who would hold it forever. When Jacob, in response to a summons from Pharaoh, left Canaan with his family because of the severe famine which raged there, God reassured him: "I will go down with thee into Egypt; and I will surely bring thee up again."

Through the encounter between God and Moses at Mount Horeb, the Hebrew group was welded into a unit with a goal and purposeful future. Moses was appointed leader of that people with the task of redeeming the Hebrews from bondage and bringing them to the land "flowing with milk and honey." The Pentateuch contains an account of the Exodus and the giving of the Torah, the most decisive religious event in the history of the people Israel. The remainder of the narrative relates their wanderings through the wilderness until they reached the eastern bank of the Jordan. In their course, they conquered the Trans-Jordanian territories of the Amorites, who had refused them peaceful passage.

Under Joshua the Israelites conquered Canaan and made it the land of Israel. The subsequent vicissitudes of victory and defeat in battle, subjugation and independence, triumphant domination and slow disintegration fill the pages of the Bible's historical books. All events, as well as the steady decline of later days, were explained by the authors of these chronicles in the light of the relations between God and His people. Behavior pleasing to God brought success and prosperity; adversity was the consequence of disobedience. In both instances the role of man's efforts and arms was of slight importance.

When Assyrian imperialism and ambition reached the limits of western Asia and threatened the states of Israel and Judah (Eighth Century B.C.E.), a group of men known as the classic prophets arose to continue the religious interpretation of events. Motivated by the Assyrian threat plus the growing complexity of the international political and military situation, those divinely-inspired individuals formulated a new evaluation of the relation between God and the people Israel. They became obsessed with the realization that the sin of Israel was profound and that the ensuing disaster would be so grave as to include devastation of the land, capture of Jerusalem and even exile of the inhabitants to distant countries. The only possibility of escape lay in repentance, sincere change of heart. The wrong for which the Israelites had to atone grew out of their failure to live up to the high moral standards of the prophets. The Israelites were guilty of not being sufficiently righteous, pious or earnest.

In view of the extreme difficulty of attaining the heights required by God, the prophets were pessimistic regarding prospects for the future. They appealed for repentance with passion, but had difficulty persuading themselves that it would be realized. When Hosea and Jeremiah dreamed of a confession of guilt by the people coupled with the will to start anew, they quickly followed with the sober reflection that such dreams were ephemeral.

All the prophets, however, looked forward to an eventual settlement of accounts between God and His people, and the inauguration of a new era, the end of time, an age-to-come when individuals would no longer sin. They would be endowed with a "new heart," with no cravings other than to do right. Peace would prevail; the state of exile would end; the Jewish people—including the Ten Tribes who suffered exile in 721 B.C.E.—

much earlier than Judah, whose catastrophe came in 587—would be gathered back to their own land. A reign would set in of righteous living, prosperity and peaceful co-existence even between man and beast.

This prophetic expectation of restoration to the Holy Land and its rebuilding became a cardinal tenet of Jewish thinking. It assumed the role of a sustaining hope throughout the centuries. The partial return in 537 B.C.E. effected by Cyrus, the great Persian king, after he subdued Babylonia, soon made it clear that the prophets' predictions were not to be realized. The difficulties encountered by the approximately 42,000 returnees stood in sharp contrast to the Second Isaiah's rhapsodic prediction of events which were to follow the fall of Babylon. All the glorious visions still remained unfulfilled. About 520, during political disturbances in Persia, the prophets Haggai and Zechariah seem to have anticipated an early change in the situation of Judea which could bring to fruition their hopes and those of their predecessors. The conditions in the small province within the Persian realm remained unchanged and hopeless. The people were almost forced to conclude that the unquestionably true consolations uttered by the prophets still awaited fulfillment.

The Messianic Hope[1] and the Land

From about 200 B.C.E., a more formal conception of what is known as the Messianic age began to develop.[2] It expected a number of events to happen, all based on predictions by the prophets: the ingathering of the exiles; renewal of the productivity of the soil and the expansion of its capacity to support all the arriving population as well as the countless outsiders yet to join the fold; recognition by all peoples of the truth of Judaism's creed and principles; inauguration of a life of righteousness and social relations without malice or evil; universal peace, eliminating all weapons and all fear of war. This grand image of the future, which grew in color and intensity as the sorrows of the Jewish group multiplied, centered increasingly around a divinely-endowed and divinely-appointed individual who would serve as the instrument through whom God would realize these changes. He would be the Messiah, the annointed by God—a scion of the royal house of David, who would consummate the ultimate triumph in the struggles preceding the glorious epoch, and would rank as the dominant ruler in the world.

This hope served as the antidote to Israel's interminable exile and dispersion. During the centuries when Jews were victims of discriminatory regulations, diverse disabilities, persecutions, riots, slaughter and expulsion, they found solace in the knowledge that they were enduring all this suffering only to be recompensed by a greater glory which was to follow. They were confident that their relations with God, even if temporarily under a cloud, were closer than those of any other people, and that their lot would ultimately change for the good.

At all times these hopes have formed part of the religious creed of the Jew. A constant feature of his liturgy is the rehearsal of the Israelites' exile coupled with their ultimate expectations. His prayers abound in pleas to God to hasten the day of redemption, to gather His people Israel from the lands of their dispersion to their homeland, the land of Israel. Poets, philosophers and moralists have joined in singing the glories of that future, pleading for its early arrival, and reciting the marvelous features of the Holy Land in the Messianic age-to-come.

In times of difficulty the pleas became more poignant, the cries more heartrending, the protests more trenchant. In their sorry state the factor of amazement was added. Jews asked wonderingly how God could tolerate the haughtiness and insolence of their overlords, why He allowed their foes to taunt His people about the folly of clinging to their faith and how low their fortunes had fallen.

They could not comprehend the patience and long suffering of their Lord who permitted such insults to go unchallenged. Yet they remained steadfast. Of course, there were deserters. Even in relatively quiet periods some left the fold for one reason or another; and in days of persecution many more took the decisive step of abandoning their brethren. Some of the converts, either out of revenge or to still their consciences (or perhaps as the result of a new missionary zeal), actually turned against their former religion and its adherents. But those who remained loyal sought to explain and understand; they clung to their faith and hope, resolved to lead the life which would please God and thus bring on the days of redemption and ingathering.

In critical periods excitement would grow. In times of upheaval—the riots of the First Crusade and the protracted wars between Christendom and Islam, the occurrence of earthquakes and other natural calamities—expectations would soar. The approach of the "calculated end," the time of the Great Change, imagined from hints in the Book of Daniel or other works, was viewed—with both fear and hope—as proof that the Messianic woes were about to be initiated. These were the tribulations ascribed by tradition as prefacing the Messianic age. Men arose who claimed to be either the Messiah or his forerunner. Jewish chronicles have preserved a long list of such would-be saviors. Frequently, even after disappointment had extinguished the belief in early consummation, some adherents continued their faith in the leaders, consoling themselves with the explanation that the real Messiah would appear in due time. The unsuccessful pretenders were dubbed false Messiahs, yet they were "false" only in the sense that they did not achieve their objective; not all were deliberate deceivers or charlatans.

Clearly, it was faith in God and hope of redemption which infused the Jewish people with the will to survive and with an unflinching belief in their eventual return to the land of Israel. In order to evaluate the full import of this central article of faith in the life of the Jews, it is important to examine some of its results and consequences.

Undoubtedly the continued stay of the Jews in their various places of residence left its mark. Over the centuries they not only made peace with not living in the Promised Land but they also developed attachments to the places where they happened to be living. They cultivated relations with people and neighborhoods, they cherished memories connected with those places, their mores and patterns. Under these circumstances it is only natural that they adjusted their allegiance to the dream of future removal from the region in which they were domiciled and of restoration to the Jewish homeland. Their history as a people was one long record of exile and dispersion and of rituals and ceremonies to commemorate those disasters. They believed that predictions of the glorious future in their own land of Israel would be fulfilled, but no one knew when. It would be difficult, however, to maintain that most Jews were ready to respond to any and every summons to abandon their homes, familiar surroundings and activities for the unknown shores of the homeland, notwithstanding the happiness of being in that hallowed place. The history of Jewish attitudes during the last 2500 years bears out this reluctance.

In the light of this, the numerous liturgical compositions and other literary creations which plead for redemption and ingathering of the exiles must be judged in accordance with conditions. During persecution and other severe trials, such entreaties were drenched in tears and pervaded by a mood of deep yearning. On the other hand, in liturgical expressions of other more serene periods, the utterance of hope seems conventional and the prayers lack fire. Not that they are false or insincere; but they do not move the reader with the force of an outcry; they do not speak with the voice of a spontaneous outburst.

It is also in place to point to another effect of Jewish religious commitment. From the earliest times, authoritative voices in Jewry have always laid great emphasis on the decisive role of God and the relative unimportance of man's effort in determining the political fate of the Jewish people and their land. The Bible and rabbinic literature have taught that the people themselves can do little other than lead a righteous life, which may move God to act in their favor. The fortunes of the people and the land are entirely in His hands. Indeed, this negation of man's power led to statements in rabbinic literature which condemn as sinful efforts initiated by the people to re-establish political life.

The Jew has thereby been relieved of the task of exerting himself to regain what he had been taught to believe was his homeland. He has thus been aided in adjusting to life as a resident of his locality with no particular consciousness of alienation, except in occasional situations of difficulty and persecution. Although as a people Jews were aliens—their chronicles record little interest in the political fortunes of the lands they inhabited or in their potentates—they have reflected in their individual daily lives all the vicissitudes of normal human fate.

Moreover, acceptance by Jews of the doctrine that return to the land of their fathers and the ensuing new life rested ultimately upon God's will led to a certain unreality about the hope for the future. The land of Israel was converted into "the Holy Land" and Hebrew into "the Sacred Tongue." The Messiah became an almost divine creature, coupled with the concept of a celestial Jerusalem and a celestial Temple introduced as the city and sanctuary of the Messianic age. Even though a sober thinker like Maimonides dismissed as figures of speech many of these fantasies transforming the nature of the Holy Land, the vast majority, influenced no doubt by the general mood of "the Age of Faith" and parallel concepts in the dominant religions, came to expect a miraculous turn of events at the end of time.

The prevalence of Messianism in Jewish thinking has been fundamental to Jewish survival. The ultra-Orthodox and ultra-fanatical Neturai Karta, repugnant as their hostile activities in the recent history of the State of Israel may be, are no less in the tradition than those Jews engaged in the rebuilding and development of Israel in fulfillment of the age-old dream.

The Growth of Zionism

Zionism, whose crowning success is the establishment of the State of Israel, is the modern manifestation of the old concept regarding return to the land of Israel. Its theoreticians were of the Westernized Jewish communities, its causes grew out of developments in modern Europe and its impetus came from philosophies expounded in modern times. Zionism is a response to challenges with which modern Europe confronted Jewry.

At first, the transition of the Old World from medieval to modern times augured well, producing beneficial changes in the Jewish situation. Chief among these was the acceptance, and even respect, which the Jewish middle class—consisting of merchants, bankers and skilled financiers—began to enjoy in the growing mercantile and capitalist society of Central and Western Europe. As the European economy developed industry and commerce, both Jewish capital and financial talent were eagerly sought, which led to a rapprochement with non-Jewish society. It resulted in livelier intercourse between gentiles and the wealthier Jews and the latter's entry into previously restricted towns and areas. This in turn led to the growth among Jews of an interest in the culture of the new environment, with a concomitant neglect, and sometimes disdain, of their own Jewish world and heritage. By the time of the French Revolution, the considerable number of such assimilated Jews living in Germany and the lands west of it, forced a re-examination of their civil and political status. The question of recognizing Jews as citizens with full rights was now discussed in parliaments and cabinets of several countries. Their full acceptance, known as the Emancipation, began with the adoption of resolutions by the French National Assembly in 1791, and continued in other countries with varying tempo, all through the nineteenth century.

Across the Atlantic, in America,[3] acceptance and acculturation proceeded almost from the beginning of Jewish settlement. The rapid decline of religious practice among Jews, their growing ignorance of Hebrew and the Jewish traditions, and the disturbingly high incidence of conversion and intermarriage combined to call attention to the fact that Judaism was in the throes of a crisis that could prove fatal.

Programs to avert the danger were not slow in coming, generally seeking to provide the most practical or most effective means of observing and understanding Judaism under the changed circumstances. Efforts to "save" Judaism were abundant, from proposals to relinquish almost the entire body of Jewish religious practice and retain only its "eternal verities," its moral and philosophic teachings, to proposals defending the maintenance of every commandment of Orthodox law with a modern reinterpretation of their significance.

The Zionist movement came to the rescue, contending that radical answers were needed to stem the tide. Its point of departure was that all previous programs failed to diagnose the real issue. The emancipation achieved by Jews greatly improved their economic and political condition, but at the same time weakened their loyalty to their faith and culture. But it is a mistake, said the Zionists, to assume that the Jew's position in society would be normalized by redefining his obligations to his faith or by relieving him of his ritual burdens. Such assumptions fail to consider that the entry of Jews into general society has not eliminated or even reduced the disease of anti-Semitism. On the contrary, it has provoked a more virulent form of hostility, which makes it clear that they are most unwelcome when seemingly most acculturated. It also drives home the lesson that anti-Semitism is an ineradicable disease, an inescapable concomitant of Jewish and non-Jewish co-existence. Then, too, in modern society the factors making for flight from Judaism are more potent than are the efforts to thwart it.

If Jews were not to assimilate and eventually disappear into the general society, the only alternative was to emigrate to a land of their own. In the Zionist view, Jews who wanted to continue to be Jewish had to create a home in which to live and function as a sovereign people. Even a thinker like Ahad Ha-am (1857-1927),[4] who regarded "the plight of Judaism" more alarming than "the plight of Jewry," maintained that a Jewish state was necessary in order to create a center of Jewish culture which might stimulate a renaissance of Jewishness in the Diaspora.

Zionism is a product of the modern situation, its emphasis on national status paralleling the awakening of nationalism among other minorities in the late nineteenth century. The plan of action conceived by its founder, Theodor Herzl (1860-1904),[5] to negotiate with heads of states was in line with the diplomacy of that period. Convinced that the Jewish question was as much a matter of concern to the world as to the Jews, he exerted all his energy to bring the problem and its solution before authorities in various governments. Like Leo Pinsker before him, Herzl did not insist on Palestine. He viewed the need for a Jewish homeland as so pressing that the choice of the particular territory was not a primary concern. Of course, other Jewish leaders held to the centrality of Palestine even at the time of the First Zionist Congress (1897), a position which gradually shaped the modern Zionist movement. Here is where modern Zionism parted company with Messianism. Both recognized the land of Israel as the goal, but the Zionists looked not to God but to man to effect the transformation.

The return to Palestine, for the Zionists, could come about only by human will, human action and skill. The glorious promises of the Messianic age played no role in their program. The establishment of a state was sought as the only possible relief from a condition which could not otherwise be eliminated.

As Zionism spread, however, it began to appeal also to the sentiments of religious Jews who had been nurtured on the Messianic belief; inevitably some of its basic propositions were modified. What had begun as a secularist movement took on new overtones as religious Jewry affiliated and certain Orthodox rabbis, even before the rise of Zionism, encouraged settlement in Palestine and cultivation of its soil. Religious expectations were incorporated. In addition, the affiliation of Jewish workers and intellectuals with Socialist convictions brought prophetic ideals of social justice into Zionism.

As the movement reached the masses of European and American Jews, it became plain that though many subscribed to the principles of Zionism few saw Palestine as a homeland for themselves. In the mighty exodus of Jews from Eastern Europe between 1882 and 1914, only a fraction settled in Palestine; the majority emigrated to America or Western Europe. Yet these same immigrants continued to accept Zionism and contributed financially to its aid.

Thus, Zionism became a dream for most Jews—it was "Messianized" or transformed into the vision of a future state perfect in every detail, with social justice, religion and culture attaining the highest levels. It became synonymous with a Messianic age to be achieved by human effort. In this remarkable transformation, a plan of activity originally defined as human and understood as such by all who accepted it was reshaped to conform to the image of the future which divine intervention was to effect through the Messiah.

The Settlement of Palestine

In the early days of Zionism, in the 1880's, only small groups took seriously the Zionist thesis about settling in Palestine in order to lay the groundwork for the growth of a community in the Holy Land. Many Jews in Russia, Poland, Western Europe and America followed the resettlement of Palestine with interest and concern, and gave financial assistance.

Equally important, much political and educational activity was conducted by Zionist leaders and workers in order to realize the program adopted by the various Zionist Congresses. But the movement met with little success before World War I. Herzl, during the last years of his life, from 1896 to 1904, had gained access to government leaders in Britain, Germany and Russia, and twice received offers from England of territory other than Palestine, but neither had materialized.

With the outbreak of war in 1914, the World Zionist Organization renewed its efforts among both the Allies and Central Powers. The culmination was the issuance of the famed Balfour statement on November 2, 1917, expressing the British government's favorable disposition to "the establishment of a national Jewish home in Palestine." Although Arab leaders were hostile and the British administration in Palestine cool, the Balfour Declaration opened a new chapter. New settlers arrived in Palestine, mainly from Eastern Europe, which was ravaged by war and bloody pogroms in those early years of the Bolshevik revolution.

Under the League of Nations mandate assigned to Britain (1922), a Jewish community (generally called the *Yishuv*) began to develop, with many features which distinguished it from Jewish populations in other parts of the world. Its economic life was marked by the rise of an agricultural class, spearheaded by a large number of idealistic pioneers (*halutzim*), young men and women of generally high intellectual caliber who had come to Palestine to rebuild themselves as well as their homeland. They organized communes and built roads, drained swamps and raised crops. In the years between the two World Wars, the farming population of Palestine Jewry was close to 20 per cent of the whole, a remarkable development in view of the generally negligible number of Jews in agriculture in Western Europe and America. Similar developments in labor and heavy industry wrought a transformation of the Yishuv, which took on the character of an autonomous economic society.

Politically too, the developing Jewish community in Palestine assumed the characteristics of a national body. Along with English and Arabic, Hebrew became an officially recognized language. Jewish towns were governed by democratically elected mayors and city fathers. The Yishuv as a whole chose representatives to a national assembly which, in turn, elected a national Council (Vaad Leumi) to represent Jewish interests before the British mandatory administration. A Chief Rabbi was elected by the religious elements to act as their leader and spokesman. Unofficial self-defense units were created in the 1930's to provide protection against riots and other threats to life and property. This secret organization, the Haganah, gradually included almost all able-bodied men in a program of training, discipline and strategy, and later made it possible for the Jews to defend the independence granted Israel in 1948.

The cultural activity of the Yishuv was striking, the mixtures of immigrants from many diverse cultural backgrounds creating an exciting ferment. An educational system from nursery school to university was developed. A Hebrew press evolved, and Jewish literary figures from the Diaspora as well as publishing houses tended to concentrate in Palestine, where a favorable cultural milieu existed. The arts, drama and music were also cultivated, and enjoyed by highly literate ánd appreciative audiences.

Despite the cultural progress, the difficulties arising from the Balfour Declaration and the announced intention of the League of Nations to work for the establishment of a national Jewish home in Palestine proved to be serious obstacles and sources of grave tensions in the process of building the Yishuv. The complex and deteriorating world situation between the two World Wars augmented and intensified these birthpangs of a nation.

Arab leaders in Palestine and other lands maintained an unrelenting opposition to the assignment of Arab areas to Britain and France under mandate. Frustrated in their earlier hopes for the establishment of a united Arab empire, they balked at the presence of "foreigners" and foreign rulers on their soil, and rejected as unjustified and illegal England's initial action of issuing the Balfour Declaration and its recognition by the League of Nations. Never retreating from this position, the Arabs violently resisted every action taken to implement the mandate, foiled every attempt by the British to find a solution to the impasse, and snubbed every offer by Jews to come to terms. Four times Arab hostility erupted in riots—in 1920, 1921, 1929 and 1936—when the passions of the masses were inflamed to violence.

The British, troubled by the Arabs' refusal to accept the situation, were aware at all times of the implications of their policy and the inter-connection of events in the Middle East. In an attempt to placate the Arab leaders, they ruled in 1922 that Transjordan was excluded from the terms of the Palestine mandate, and proceeded to establish it as a kingdom under Abdullah, son of Husain. At the same time Palestine's economic absorptive capacity—as estimated by the British—was deemed a gauge by which to determine the number of certificates of entry to be issued to new Jewish immigrants. Following the riots of 1929, the 1930 White Paper announced that further immigration of Jews into Palestine and sale of land to them would be sharply curtailed if not altogether discontinued. Vehement protests by Jewish leaders resulted in a supplementary statement which was softer in tone but contained no significant concession. After further Arab riots in 1936, the Peel Commission reported that a conflict of two irreconcilable rights lay at the root of the disturbances. It proposed, as the most reasonable compromise, that the country be partitioned between the two parties, each enjoying a certain degree of autonomy and both governed by a British administration which would control foreign policy and other important matters.

This radical proposal reflected Britain's desperate situation. Not only were the conflicting claims of the Jews and Arabs proving impossible to settle amicably, but the general situation in Europe and the Middle East was also precarious. Relations between the mandatory powers of France and Britain and the Arab states, already strained, were aggravated by a barrage of propaganda issuing from Nazi Germany, Fascist Italy and Soviet Russia, each intent on embarrassing the Western powers by inciting unrest. All this only served to harden the intransigeance of the Arabs, and forced the British to search frantically for some way out of the dilemma. The Suez Canal and the oil of Iraq were much too vital.

The Jews showed willingness to take the partition plan under advisement. Outright rejection by the Arabs, however, led to the dispatch of another commission which recommended abandonment of the plan, and it was dropped. Britain undertook to arrange a round-table conference in London in February, 1939, but it came to nothing.

In May, 1939, less than four months before the start of World War II, Britain made up its mind to settle the Palestine issue once and for all: a new White Paper pledged Palestine independence within ten years. With this goal in mind, the mandatory would admit 75,000 Jewish immigrants during the next five years, with illegal immigrants (of whom considerable numbers were being brought in) to be deducted from the total granted for each year. At the end of those five years, the promise to build a national Jewish home in Palestine was to be considered fulfilled. In the interim, land transfers from Arabs to Jews were to be sharply restricted.

In this way the British government hoped to resolve the issue to the relative satisfaction of both parties. But neither side approved. The Arabs, pleased with the general aim of the White

Paper, objected to 75,000 additional immigrants. The Jewish world reacted with rage and bitterness, unwilling to acquiesce to a plan which would reduce the Yishuv to the status of a permanent minority, irrevocably deprived of any possibility of numerical change or development. They accused Britain of bad faith, hard-heartedness in the face of the plight of Jews, and miscalculation, contending that this act of submission to the Arabs would win neither their friendship nor their cooperation.

The Permanent Mandates Commission of the League also ruled that the British document could not be said to be "in conformity with the mandate."

But the White Paper soon yielded in importance to a much greater international crisis. The Nazi attack on Poland, precipitating World War II, made it necessary to shunt aside every issue not connected with the immediate task of achieving victory. The Jews of Palestine had no choice; they laid aside their grievances and joined in the struggle on the side of the allies.

In Palestine the White Paper took effect nonetheless, and the restrictive Land Transfer act was promulgated in 1940. The unflinching refusal of the authorities to admit fugitives from the Nazis resulted in three shipwrecks between 1940 and 1942, with the loss of some two thousand lives. Despite the fact that the British refused the request to organize a Palestine Jewish Brigade, some 40,000 Jews served in the armed forces and virtually the entire Yishuv geared itself to the war effort.

As the struggle continued and news spread of Nazi atrocities, Jewish leaders became increasingly anxious about the fate of their people. In May, 1942 a resolution was adopted, at the Biltmore Conference in New York, which pressed for the eventual creation of a Jewish commonwealth in Palestine and rejected bluntly the White Paper and its program.

With the end of the war, the situation in Palestine became increasingly critical. Those among European Jewry who survived the Nazi annihilation emerged from concentration camps or hiding-places in desperate need of a haven of refuge and rehabilitation. The leadership in the Yishuv, overwhelmed by the urgency, challenged British regulations and restraints against immigration, and strained every means to bring the survivors to Palestine. Ships slipped into harbors in the dark of night and their human cargo was secretly dispersed in various settlements.

The Royal Navy frequently intercepted the refugee barges and forced them to change their course to Cyprus, where a huge prison-camp awaited the displaced persons.

This clash between British intransigeance and Jewish defiance embittered both parties. A suggestion was made by President Harry S. Truman in August, 1945 that Britain admit 100,000 refugees without changing its general plan. Despite the support of this recommendation by a joint Anglo-American Commission of Inquiry in 1946, the British government did not retreat from its position. Its refusal to change the terms of the White Paper drove some Jews to fighting British administrative harshness with terrorism.

The British position in Palestine was deteriorating rapidly. All through the war Britain had striven to maintain close relations with the Arab states. In 1941 Anthony Eden, then Minister of Foreign Affairs, declared that his government would favor steps leading to Arab unification in the Middle East. In 1945 the League of Arab States was organized, the only common agreement being hostility to the Jewish community in Palestine. By 1947 Britain found itself caught between an angry, aggressive Jewish community in Palestine and an adamant, hostile and threatening Arab world. Unable to cope with this turbulence, the government turned the problem over to the United Nations, which appointed an eleven-nation commission of inquiry. After months of investigation, that body reached the conclusion, proposed earlier by the Peel Commission in 1936, that Palestine be partitioned between Jews and Arabs—a recommendation approved on November 29, 1947 by the General Assembly of the United Nations. Russia, France and the United States voted with the majority, while Britain and China abstained. The General Assembly also created a special Palestine Commission to oversee the peaceful transfer of authority to the prospective governments of the Jewish state and the projected Palestine Arab state.

The major objective of the Zionist movement, formulated at its first Congress in 1897, was now realized. The nations of the world, through the United Nations, gave legal and public status to a Jewish state. True, the area set aside for it was limited, but after years of waiting, after the vicissitudes and tragedies of the past half-century, it was a gratifying solution of a chronic problem and a welcome recognition of a basic principle.

Unfortunately, this radical solution did not bring peace to the land of Israel. The Arab states threatened to oppose partition with war. Britain refused to cooperate with the Special Palestine Commission. Even before the target date of May 14, 1948, the Arabs of Palestine, aided by volunteers from the outside, started hostilities against the Jews. The Yishuv was compelled to engage immediately in a struggle for its very existence. The community in Jerusalem underwent siege. By May 15, the entire question of partition was submitted to re-examination by the General Assembly of the United Nations on the recommendation of the Security Council. But the debate lost all cogency when news arrived that the Jewish leaders, gathered in Tel-Aviv on May 14, had solemnly proclaimed the birth of the Jewish state, to be known as the State of Israel. The United States granted *de facto* recognition instantly. On the same day, the Arab armies began an invasion. The Yishuv responded by driving the invaders out of and beyond the territory assigned to Israel. Armistice agreements were signed early in 1949, ending the hostilities but not the state of war. Israel emerged with a larger territory than originally assigned by the United Nations.

Since independence, Israel has absorbed over a million immigrants. Its law stipulates that every Jew, if not a convert to another faith, a criminal, or morally depraved, has the right to immigrate and become a citizen. It has developed many new settlements and urban centers, and has made great progress in agricultural self-sufficiency, industrial development and scientific research.

But the unabated hostility of Israel's Arab neighbors continues. Leaders of the surrounding Arab countries have refused to replace the armistice agreements with peace treaties, and they are continuing to threaten Israel with war and extermination. They maintain an economic boycott, seeking to blacklist American and European firms which maintain trade relations with Israel. They spread anti-Israel propaganda through press and radio, instilling hatred and fear in their nationals.

As a result, Israel must look vigilantly to its security. Funds that could better be used for growth and reconstruction must go for defense.

These strained relations are further aggravated by the "cold war," in which the Communists woo the Arab states and often support the hostile campaign against Israel. The Western countries, though generally friendly to Israel, also court the Arabs. The hope is that some day neighborliness will replace estrangement and bellicosity. Such a change could benefit both Israel and the Arab states economically, politically and culturally.

Israel and the American Jewish Community

Theodor Herzl believed that primacy in the Zionist program was to be given to political activity in behalf of "a home in Palestine secured by public law." This view differed markedly from the thinking of an earlier group, "the Lovers of Zion," which laid stress on resettlement and colonization. Herzl's frustrations and the Zionists' early political failures made it clear that the creation of a Yishuv in Palestine was of vital importance. As a result, Zionist work went forward on two levels. While that Jewish community was growing in Palestine, in Western Europe and America, leaders of the World Zionist Organization raised funds, circulated information and engaged in political activity.

Prior to 1948 the psychological position of Diaspora Jewry toward Palestine and the Yishuv's relations with Britain were relatively simple. Having absolved themselves of the duty of emigrating personally to the land, Jews acted in the role of deeply interested and vitally concerned friends of a cause which they deemed worthy. They dismissed any allegation of divided loyalty and dual allegiance. The defense of causes was in the best American tradition.

With the birth of Israel, however, the question assumed a more complicated character. The propriety of Diaspora Jewry's interest and concern raised questions as to the extent to which the latter can be maintained without meddling in Israel's internal affairs. And how far can American Jews see to Israel's interests without incurring the charge of being "foreign agents"?

There is little doubt that religious and cultural bonds which held world Jewry together through the centuries are becoming loosened. As Jews blend into society at large, there is danger of diversity and estrangement. In the United States, Jews practice a new form of Judaism, which is neither what Jews have always understood as religion nor a comprehensive way of life. It is rather a confession of Judaism with a minimal body of observance or performance. It requires no knowledge of Hebrew or of history. It needs no past and seeks no future: it is existential. And it cannot effectively promote contact with Israel.

While it is true that many organizations exist to keep the unity of the Jewish people alive, what is lacking today is a genuine rather than formal unity, a sense of belonging felt by the individual rather than proclamation at public demonstrations.

Groups and individuals in the Diaspora concerned about these dangers must devise more meaningful kinds of contact with the land and people of Israel. Tours which afford more than a glimpse of the land, and exchange visits, particularly by the younger generation, should be encouraged. Personalities in public life, especially in the arts and sciences, should appear in both Israel and the United States to provide information about the culture and life in each. American Jewish students should be persuaded to spend a year in Israel. The literature and press of both groups should be made available to each, in original or in translation.

The hope is that the difficulties faced by the young state, both international and economic, will eventually be removed and, with them, the emergencies, concern and anxiety which they provoke. But it must be borne in mind that the attainment of these goals will accentuate the threat of separation between American and Israeli Jews, since the bonds born of crisis will disappear. This makes the need for thoughtful reflection and planning of immediate urgency.

FOR FURTHER READING

AVINERI, Shlomo, *The Making of Modern Zionism* (New York: Basic Books, 1981). A helpful, lucid introduction to the main individual figures in the history of Zionism. Provides a clear over-view of the major participants and their philosophies.

DAVIES, W.D., *The Territorial Dimension of Judaism* (Berkeley: University of California Press, 1982). A rich, sympathetic study of the theological meaning of the Land of Israel within Judaism by a noted Christian scholar.

HALKIN, Hillel, *Letters to an American Friend* (Philadelphia: Jewish Publication Society, 1977). A direct challenge regarding the viability of one Jewish community outside the State of Israel. Raises profound and disquieting issues.

HESCHEL, Abraham Joshua, *Israel, An Echo of Eternity* (New York: Farrar, Straus & Giroux, 1969). A beautiful, moving, exposition of the deeper meaning of the State of Israel.

LAQUEUR, Walter, *A History of Zionism* (London: Weidenfeld & Nicolson, 1972). A distinguished history of Zionism by a distinguished scholar. Very good on the ideological components of the movement.

VITAL, David, *The Origins of Zionism* (New York: Oxford University Press, 1975). See next entry.

VITAL, David, *Zionism: The Formative Years* (New York: Oxford University Press, 1982). This, and the volume listed above by Vital, provide the most detailed, well-constructed, thoughtful history of early Zionism which exists in any language.

3 . The American Jewish Community

C. BEZALEL SHERMAN

T H E A M E R I C A N Jewish community[1] defies definition either on the basis of Jewish historical precedents or in terms of American experience with other ethnic groups. The community is here; it functions; its position in American life is significant. Constituting the largest aggregation of Jews in one land in history, its role in world Jewry is decisive. It is the home of a staggering number of organizations and movements, but as a totality it has no central authority, no firm framework, no delineated sphere of action. It constitutes neither a national minority nor a mere religious fellowship; nor is it a communal body with specified membership qualifications, duties or rights. And yet, in some loose way, it is all of these things and more. It is therefore easier to observe its development in the light of the activities of its component parts than by following its operation as a whole.

Foundations of the American Jewish Community

Jews came to America to stay. Other immigrants could, if they so chose, return to their old countries; for Jews there was generally no way back. When they left their native lands, they burned all their bridges behind them. They came with their families, determined to build permanent homes here. There were virtually no "birds of passage" [2] among them, as a comparison of the number of immigrants among the Jews and among others shows. From 1908 to 1937, general reverse migration from the United States was never less than one-quarter of the immigration; among Jews it was never greater than seven per cent. During the period from 1925 to 1937, which included the depression years, the general reverse migration was over 40 per cent of the immigration; the reverse Jewish migration was barely four per cent. As for the "old" immigration, that prior to the 1880's, figures show that there were one and one-half times as many returnees among non-Jewish immigrant groups as among Jews.[3] "The Jewish immigration," wrote Samuel Joseph, an authority on this subject, "must . . . be accorded the place of distinction in American immigration for permanence of settlement." [4]

Another distinction of Jewish immigration was its fragmentation. Jews did not come from one country or one territory but from a variety of lands far removed from each other not only geographically but also in regard to political, economic, social and cultural development. The three waves of Jewish immigration—the Spanish-Portuguese, the German, the East European—reflected the situation in the lands of emigration. Each major wave was actually made up of a number of smaller waves emanating from different countries.

Each Jewish wave was an independent stream that had practically no relation to other streams. They were also disparate in time. The Sephardis, coming mostly from Holland and partly from England, arrived during the colonial period; they belonged to the category of "settlers" and participated in the creation of the American republic. The German Jews arrived during the Civil War epoch and contributed to the unification of the American nation. The East European Jews came during the "Gilded Age" and took part in the expansion of the American industrial empire. These divisions marked the levels of prestige within the evolving Jewish community.

Jewish immigrants regarded America not only as their permanent individual home; they also sought to establish a flourishing Jewish community, each group having its own conception of how to build that community. They brought with them diverse backgrounds, mother tongues, cultural influences and communal experiences; and they all tried to transport their respective ways of life. They also imported some of the prejudices and divisions that had characterized relations among Jewish communities in the Old World. Sephardim had little in common with Ashkenazim, and German Jews considered themselves superior to the East Europeans. In view of the time lag that separated the arrival of one Jewish group from that of the other, the group coming earlier emerged as the dominant factor in Jewish life and retained its leadership even after succeeding waves of immigration had reduced it to a fraction of the total Jewish population. The five synagogues in existence at the time of the Declaration of Independence were all led by Sephardim and adhered to Sephardic ritual even though Ashkenazim came to constitute a majority of their membership. Later, the German Jews stood at the helm of Jewish communal life long after they had been numerically overwhelmed by East European Jews.

The Sephardim were not part of a large emigration from their former lands. Scanty in numbers, they early exchanged their Spanish-Portuguese mother tongue for English and were quick to adopt American patterns in their secular activities, maintaining the synagogue as the focus of their Jewish interests. They were firmly established socially and economically at the time the Ashkenazim were reaching American shores in substantial numbers. The Sephardim regarded themselves as an elite and behaved accordingly vis-a-vis the latter Jewish immigrants. Through their uncompromising insistence on full civic equality they made an important contribution to the history of American civil rights, but they left no lasting impression on the Jewish community structure.

The Jews from Germany came here at a time when a general mass immigration from that country was going on. Arriving during the period when the westward expansion of the frontiers was in full swing, great numbers of German Jewish immigrants shouldered packs and followed the routes of the covered wagons. Superb organizers and spread over wide areas, the German Jews laid the foundation for scores of new Jewish communities, while establishing temples, religious schools and philanthropic institutions in the old communities. At the same time they participated in activities aiming to strengthen German culture in this country. Religious services were conducted partly in German in practically all the early Reform congregations, and the rabbis all came from German-speaking lands. David Einhorn, the most important theoretician of American Reform Judaism in the mid-nineteenth century, insisted that Jewish Reform was impossible without the German language. With a religious trend of their own, and making rapid strides socially and economically, German Jews constituted a distinctive sub-community which occupied a commanding position in Jewish life.

Despite their exclusiveness, the German Jews erected their institutions on firm communal bases; and it was comparatively easy to convert those institutions into agencies serving the entire Jewish population when conditions demanded it. Such a demand was created by the mass influx of Jews from Eastern Europe during the last decades of the nineteenth century. Unable to check this influx, the German Jews offered substantial aid to their newly-arrived co-religionists, stopping short, however, of regarding the latter as their peers.

The East European immigration was much more diffused and fragmented than the German. While the German Jews, tasting the fruit of West European emancipation, brought with them a profound attachment to the culture of their former *homeland*, the East European Jews, emerging from lands of oppression and persecution, brought with them a loyalty to the Jewish communities of their native *towns* and *shtetlech*. Characteristically, the synagogues founded by Sephardim and German Jews bore communal names like Shearith Israel, Emanuel, Mikveh Israel, Beth El and Beth Elohim. On the other hand, a good many of the synagogues built by immigrants from Eastern Europe used the word *Anshe* (people from)—Anshe Minsk, Anshe Bialostok, Anshe Pinsk—in their names to denote the founders' town of origin. The East Europeans also organized thousands of *landsmanschaften* bearing the names of their hometowns.

The East Europeans also introduced a number of secular movements, of which only the Jewish labor movement was a real force prior to the outbreak of World War I. The founders of this movement, guided ideologically by rigid Marxian concepts which regarded any kind of collaboration with non-workers' groups as a betrayal of the class interests of the proletariat, shied away from general Jewish activities. Labor was thus prevented from producing leaders for Jewish community life. As for Zionism, its weakness during the early twentieth century is best illustrated by the fact that, though the movement was composed overwhelmingly of East European immigrants, it had to look for leadership to its few American-born or Western followers.

Jewish immigration from Eastern Europe coincided with

general mass immigration from that part of the world. But, unlike their German brethren, East European Jews did not gravi-
tate to the colonies of their non-Jewish compatriots in this country. They soon became the largest sub-community within American Jewry, with a spiritual and material complexion of its own
despite internal divisions. Yiddish was the center of its culture;
and its economy, largely based on the needle crafts, included
small industries, trade and the professions.

The Jewish population of the late nineteenth and early twentieth centuries thus divided itself into two sub-communities,
which came to be known symbolically as Uptown and Downtown—Uptown being the residential area of the wealthier Jews
of German origin, and Downtown representing the crowded
ghettos of the East European Jews.[5] Ambassadors of good will
tried to build bridges between the two sub-communities, but
with little success. However, what they could not accomplish
was in time achieved by Jewish accommodation to American
conditions, on the one hand, and the responsibilities placed upon
American Jews by the situation in world Jewry, on the other.
The contradictory processes of full acceptance of Jews by the
American *state* and of discrimination against Jews on the part of
American *society* combined to bring about a socio-economic
rapport among the various Jewish groups. The deterioration of
Jewish life in Europe crystallized this rapport into unified action.

The Synagogue

As long as the majority of the Jewish population consisted of
immigrants still under the influence of the Old World conceptions and ideologies they had transplanted, the synagogues served
as bases for the various groups and tended to keep them apart.
The Sephardic congregation with its rigid discipline was as
alien to German Jews as the latter's temples were to East Europeans. The divisions did not spring from geographic origin alone;
they also reflected the degree of acculturation each group had
achieved. As for the secularists, they were much closer, from a
socio-economic and cultural point of view, to the Orthodox
shulen than to the Uptown temples.

Until the end of the nineteenth century, religious conflicts were waged mainly between Orthodoxy and Reform. Because of its better organized and more affluent membership, the Reform group was able to set itself up as the spokesman of American Jewry to the outside world. In the late 1880's a third trend, Conservatism, appeared on the arena of organized Jewish religion. It became a serious factor after the turn of the century, drawing its following primarily from the new middle classes the East European sub-community was beginning to produce.

By that time groups were emerging within Reform which felt that their movement had gone too far in its anti-Zionism and in its discarding of traditional Jewish practices. Among the Orthodox, on the other hand, there were those who realized that some modifications were necessary in order to make Jewish religion more relevant to life in the United States. Conservatism proved attractive to the moderates of both camps. Its flexibility contributed toward bridging the gulf that had previously existed between the two sub-communities.

The synagogue ceased to be the divisive factor it had been during the immigration periods once it began responding to the requirements of an acculturated Jewish population. The divisions persisted, but the acerbity subsided and gave way to a cooperative spirit. The formation, in 1926, of the Synagogue Council made up of representatives of Orthodoxy, Reform and Conservatism signified the extension to religion of the trend toward greater unity in Jewish communal life generally.

What is noteworthy is that not one of the three religious trends lost ground as a result of cooperation.[6] On the contrary, all have registered tremendous growth since World War II—so much so that the synagogue has again become the center of Jewish identification in America both in a religious and communal sense. With 90 per cent of the Jewish schools congregationally supervised and operated, the synagogue has practically monopolized Jewish education in the United States, all but wiping out the unaffiliated community schools. The Jewish day schools or *yeshivot*, which have become an important factor in Jewish education since the Second World War, are an exception. They are almost exclusively Orthodox in their orientation and are primarily identified with groups within the Orthodox fold rather than with congregations.[7]

Philanthropy and Social Services

A second pivot in Jewish communal life is the network of philanthropic, social service, cultural, community relations, mutual aid and leisure-time institutions. Originally these institutions functioned as parochial bodies, with each sub-community primarily concerning itself with needs in its own environment. Until 1825, Jewish charity was under control of the Sephardic congregations. 1844 saw the founding of the German Hebrew Benevolent Society of New York, which was mainly devoted to aiding Jews from Germany and which not infrequently refused to assist immigrants from Eastern Europe. Small wonder that the latter built their own institutions, compounding the chaos that existed in Jewish welfare work.

This chaos was finally surmounted by the ancient tradition of *kol Yisrael arevim zeh lozeh* (all Jews are responsible for each other). Guided by this tradition, Jewish communities throughout the ages have taken care of their underprivileged members. American Jewry adhered to this tradition without the aid of the compulsory religious authority which the old *kehillot* enjoyed and which Jewish communities still enjoy in a number of lands. Precisely because of its voluntary character, it was possible for the Jewish community continually to broaden its concepts of *tz'dakah* to keep up with the shifting scene in American Jewish life.

Charity institutions which had started by offering assistance to the destitute gradually came to service the needs of the entire Jewish communiy. Out of institutions like the Jewish Educational Alliance of New York and the Jewish People's Institute of Chicago—established by Uptown philanthropists to "Americanize" their Downtown co-religionists—evolved the modern Jewish Community Center, perhaps the most all-embracing agency outside the synagogue in current American Jewish life.

The first step in the process of consolidation was coordination and merging of the various institutions maintained by the subcommunities. This gave rise to the Federation movement, which brought under one roof all local Jewish philanthropic institutions operating on a city basis. The Federation paved the way for the Welfare Fund, which took up where the former had left off by centralizing community fund-raising in behalf of institutions and agencies functioning on a national scale, and by providing for Jewish overseas needs. In recent years, the functions of the Federation and Welfare Fund have been amalgamated into a single agency in practically all Jewish communities outside New York City, where no Welfare Fund exists. The central agencies are, as a rule, governed by representative bodies which strive to extend the areas of community cooperation without impinging on the organizational and ideological integrity of the groups they represent.

The coordination achieved in philanthropy fanned out into other fields. In 1927, one year after the formation of the Synagogue Council, the National Appeals Information Service, forerunner of the Council of Jewish Federations and Welfare Funds,[8] came into being. The National Jewish Welfare Board had been organized about a decade earlier as the central body of the Jewish Community Centers and as the governmentally recognized agency charged with servicing the religious needs of Jews in the American armed forces. The Jewish Education Committee of New York, survivor of the abortive attempt to organize a *kehillah* in New York, stimulated the development of local boards and bureaus of Jewish education and of the national American Association for Jewish Education, composed of all trends in the Jewish educational system. In 1944, the National Community Relations Advisory Council (NCRAC) was formed. As of October, 1963, it was made up of 69 Jewish local and regional Community Relations Councils active in the struggles for civil liberties and civil rights plus all the national community relations agencies, with the exception of the American Jewish Committee and the Anti-Defamation League of B'nai B'rith.

Jewish institutional cooperation and centralization stand in direct proportion to the degree of acculturation a Jewish group or local Jewish community has achieved. The more native-born and homogeneous its constituency, the better and more comprehensive its organization. In other words, the farther a Jewish group moves away from the transplanted attitudes and the deeper its roots in American soil, the broader and more democratic is its base of operations.

It is no longer possible for small bodies of prominent individuals to wield the influence they once exercised. B'nai B'rith, founded in 1843 by German Jews and formerly discouraging Russian or Polish Jews from joining, has been transformed into a mass organization with a membership overwhelmingly of East European origin. The American Jewish Committee, originally a body of carefully selected notables, is today a membership organization with offspring of East European immigrants probably forming the majority in most chapters. The Council of Jewish Women has undergone a similar shift of membership.

Here we see the socio-economic progress the Jews have registered as individuals profoundly affecting the collective life of the group. This progress has not been unmarred by anti-Semitic manifestations which, as will be shown later, contributed to the solidification of the Jewish community. However, conditions in this country were not alone in bringing about this solidification; a third significant stamp of Jewish distinctiveness—the interdependence of world Jewry—played a major role in this process.

Solidarity with World Jewry

The status of a nation outside the United States has always affected the descendants of that nation in this country. The worse off that nation has been in its homeland, the more closely knit were the American ethnic groups springing from it. Since American Jews derive from the most oppressed of peoples, there was never a moment in the history of the American Jewish community when it has been free of concern for fellow Jews in other countries and for the status of the Jewish people on a global scale.

As the needs of the Jews abroad constantly increased, so too did the responsibilities of the Jewish community in the United States. Even Jews estranged from traditional values could not resist the pull of the ancient principle of helping brothers in distress. Indeed, activities on behalf of Jews in other lands have always proved to be the most effective way of uniting American Jewry. The first time the Jews appeared as a community in the United States was more than a century ago in connection with the Damascus affair.[9] The Mortara case in Italy[10] brought about the foundation, in 1859, of the Board of Delegates of American Israelites as a "national organization for the purpose of securing and maintaining like rights at home and abroad." The Kishinev pogrom[11] in 1903 led to the formation of the American Jewish Committee three years later.

By the second decade of the twentieth century, the American Jewish community was far enough advanced economically to undertake the heavy financial burden of reconstructing overseas Jewish communities ravished by World War I. Political help followed, including support for Jewish demands in Europe, intervention on behalf of Jewish interests in Palestine, and protests against violations of the rights of Jews in other lands. American Jewry entered the First World War as a conglomerate of fragmented Jewish bodies and emerged a community that had come of age.

The unity of the community was further strengthened by the steadily deteriorating position of European Jewry after World War I. The Hitler catastrophe literally placed the fate of millions of European Jews in the hands of American Jews. The struggle for a Jewish commonwealth in Palestine as the only effective answer to the holocaust cemented the Jewish community, bringing together all three factors making for Jewish group cohesiveness: religion, philanthropy, Jewish interdependence. The situation called for new forms of action and higher standards for fund-raising. That American Jewry largely met the challenge is a tribute to its maturity and to the democratic society in which it has evolved.

The Joint Distribution Committee, the United Jewish Appeal, the campaigns of Hadassah and Histadrut, the Welfare Funds— these and many other agencies and institutions owe their existence to the tasks American Jews were called upon to perform by events affecting the Jewish people as a whole. About a million Jews make financial contributions to Jewish causes, in amounts unmatched proportionately by any other group in American society.

The emergence of the State of Israel has lifted the involvement of American Jewry in world Jewish affairs to still greater heights. Though gaining of political independence by subjugated nations invariably has weakened ethnic ties among the descendants of these nations in the United States, the opposite has been true in the case of the Jews. The rise of Israel has prompted a more dynamic concern for Judaism. A number of surveys show that American Jews do not conceive of Israel merely as a haven of refuge for homeless and persecuted Jews. They recognize that the existence of Israel has enhanced the dignity of Jews everywhere and has added a new dimension to the status of the American Jewish community.[12] The rootedness of the Jew in American soil has been deepened by the consciousness that he is now a son of a people that is no longer nationally uprooted.[13]

Negative Factors

Contributing to Jewish cohesiveness and distinctiveness on the American scene are also a number of negative factors. Although anti-Semitism has never been the serious problem in the United States that it has been, and still is, elsewhere, American Jews have encountered discrimination in employment, in education and in the social sphere. To be sure, discriminatory practices have lessened considerably in recent years, but they still persist in certain areas, underscoring Jewish "otherness." Many anti-Semitic attitudes have been imported from abroad, but some may be traced to certain traits in the American mentality. There is the heritage of the frontiersman, admiring innovation and originality in material matters, but suspicious of unfamiliar ways in cultural processes. There is the strongly anti-immigrant and anti-urban influence of populism, lingering on long after the movement itself had disappeared from the political arena. And there is the tradition of isolationism, exposing the nationalistic mind to "anti-foreignism" propaganda in time of international crises. These factors added to religious bigotry have produced stereotyped views of the Jews. There is also a conspicuousness which bears little relation to the place they actually occupy in American political and economic life.

The Jewish community is frequently held responsible for the behavior of the individual Jew, but the individual Jew is not allowed to shed his Jewish group label even if he no longer cares to stay in the Jewish community. This creates a gap between him and his non-Jewish neighbors while introducing an element of compulsion into his association with fellow-Jews. In this sense, we may speak of membership in the Jewish community as not being altogether a matter of voluntary choice.

The Jewish Community Today

Immigrants from all parts of the world have contributed to the development of the American Jewish community—first as disparate groups and subsequently as a distinctive strand in the fabric of American society. Five and one-half million strong, it is a young community despite the fact that in 1954 it celebrated the three hundredth anniversary of its founding. Largely the product of the twentieth century, it is now composed of a membership that is about 80 per cent American-born. Its leadership is decisively in the hands of the second generation, and the third generation is forging ahead.[14]

It is largely a middle-class community, enjoying a high standard of living in terms of material accommodation and educational attainments. A pragmatic community, it has not been built according to plan, but has evolved under pressure of internal and external needs often assuming the urgency of crises. Overcoming former sectional conflicts, it is now guided by a spirit of give-and-take in its social activities. Philosophic clashes are frowned upon in collective undertakings, and ideological controversies, if not altogether eliminated, are held to a minimum. The Jewish community spends upward of 300 million dollars a year (exclusive of Bonds for Israel) on Jewish causes in addition to contributing heavily to all general civic and philanthropic causes. Functionally it is tri-dimensional: a community in relation to itself; an entity in the American social system; and a branch of the Jewish people.

The Jewish community has deviated in many respects from the course other ethnic groups have followed in this country. The greater the distance the latter have travelled on the road to integration, the farther they have moved away from their ethnic moorings. The Jews have proved to be an exception: the longer they live in the United States, the more consolidated their community life has become. Jews have accomplished through adjustment what others could only achieve by total assimilation and group dissolution. The Jews have at times made acculturation serve their group ends and have in some cases converted it into an instrument for cementing ethnic solidarity.

But as their acculturation deepens, Jews become more conformist in their patterns of living and scale of values. They no longer feel a strong need for spiritual reinforcement from Jews in other lands, regarding their own actual and potential cultural accomplishments as sufficient to satisfy their requirements as Jews and as Americans. Moreover, they are trying to turn their Jewishness into an aspect of their Americanism. Precisely because they feel so thoroughly at home, American Jews face the danger of drifting away from the rest of Jewry and of developing a paternalistic attitude toward Israel. Isolationist tendencies are already making themselves felt among them, and a growing number are convinced that Jews in the United States will bypass the laws which have governed Jewish history for millennia.

These are danger signals that cannot be ignored. Nevertheless, the disappearance of the Jews as a group in the United States is not in sight. They have no prospective status other than that of a religio-ethnic minority. What they will make of that status will be determined by their ability to fill with creative content their community structure in all of its dimensions.

FOR FURTHER READING

DAWIDOWICZ, Lucy S., *On Equal Terms: Jews in America 1881–1891* (New York: Holt, Rinehart & Winston, 1982). A concise, eminently readable, opinionated history of American Jewry by an able historian.

ELAZAR, Daniel J., *Community and Polity: The Organizational Dynamics of American Jewry* (Philadelphia: Jewish Publication Society, 1976). The now standard work on the structure of organized American Jewish life.

FORSTER, Arnold and Benjamin R. Epstein, *The New Anti-Semitism* (New York: McGraw Hill, 1974). A light but helpful update of a perennial, painful subject.

LIEBMAN, Charles, *The Ambivalent American Jew* (Philadelphia: Publication Society, 1973). An informed, critical study of the American Jewish community by a leading Jewish social scientist.

SKLARE, Marshall, a) *The Jew in American Society* and b) *The Jewish Community in America* (New York: Behrman House, 1974). A distinguished collection of essays on central themes edited by the foremost sociological student of American Jewry.

SKLARE, Marshall, editor, *Understanding American Jewry* New Brunswick [N.J.]: Transaction Books, 1982). A scholarly collection assessing the present state of the major issues in the study of the sociological character of American Jewry. Armed with it, and its bibliographies, a reader can gain an up-to-date picture of the size, shape, and projected future of the community.

WAXMAN, Chaim, *America's Jews in Transition* (Philadelphia: Temple University Press, 1983). An excellent study of the dynamics operative in the present American situation.

TORAH,
THE JEWISH WAY
OF LIFE

The Bible is admittedly a literary classic of the highest rank. "There is none that hath ever made an end of learning it, and there is none that will ever find out all its mysteries. For its wisdom is richer than any sea and its word deeper than any abyss" (*Acclesiasticus* 24:28, 29). It is repeatedly acclaimed as the noblest of religious, ethical and literary possessions of mankind. Thus T. H. Huxley exclaims: "By the study of what other book could children be so much humanized and made to feel that each figure in that vast historical procession fills, like themselves, but a momentary space in the interval between the Eternities; and earns the blessings or the curses of all time, according to its effort to do good and hate evil?"

But how can the Bible be both the source of highest religious and ethical teachings and of such crude barbarisms as are represented by the off-quoted injunction: "An eye for an eye, a tooth for a tooth"? To one who is not a student of the Bible this is confusing.

Added to this confusion are the revelations of modern scholarship. Biblical criticism, based on studies in comparative religion, cognate languages and archeological discoveries, has challenged some of the accepted traditional views regarding the Bible as the word of God revealed to Israel at Mount Sinai and later through the prophets. While some have found in these scholarly studies added light on the profound religious teachings of the Bible, there have been others for whom the very foundations of Biblical teaching have been shaken. Still others have concluded that the Bible is merely another ancient literary classic, the Jewish saga of their God. The uninitiated layman is perplexed and asks some relevant questions. Is the Bible the word of God or is it just another human document? If it is the latter, what becomes of Judaism and, for that matter, of Christianity and of Western civilization, all of which rest fully or partially on Biblical foundations?

More perplexing are the echoes that occasionally reach the ears of the non-specialist regarding the other areas of learning that are encompassed by the concept of Torah. For example, Jewish traditional sources speak of the "Sea of the Talmud," for the Talmud is as deep as the ocean and as vast. It is concerning this vast literature that one hears challenges, emanating mostly from Christian sources. They denounce the Talmud as a dry, legalistic, hair-splitting work. Is not the Talmud the handiwork of the Pharisees, who have been labelled as legalists and hypocrites? Thus condemned, the Talmud has repeatedly been attacked as superstitious, heretical and subversive. It has been censored and condemned to extinction. It was burned at auto-de-fe's over and over again. But like the people whom it has served so faithfully, it has shown remarkable vitality and has survived the many verbal and fiery persecutions.

Jewish scholars who have spent their lives studying Torah—the Bible, the Talmud and other rabbinic writings included in its broad definition—have found that vast literature an inexhaustible source of intellectual, ethical and religious sustenance. They have consistently derived instruction, solace and inspiration. To those who have studied and lived by its teachings, the Torah has provided both religious and ethical guidance. The accepted principle has been "search in it, for everything is to be found therein." Oblivious to Christian criticism and firm in his faith girded by millennia of experience, the Jew daily affirmed that the Torah was and is the source of Israel's life everlasting.

While some Jews in the twentieth century still find the Bible and the rabbinic literature that grew out of it applicable to modern life, others question the authenticity of some of its teachings. It is the purpose of the second section of this book, containing five essays on different aspects of Torah, to stress the essence of the Torah and its relevance to modern life.

Chapter Seven by the late Professor Isaacs, the only chapter in this volume not written especially for this work, has been included because it deals with Torah as worship, a subject not fully treated elsewhere.

4 . *Torah as God's Revelation to Israel*

BERNARD J. BAMBERGER

T H E B I B L E deals largely with communication between God and man, especially God's communication to man of His will and His commandments. God is represented as speaking to Adam, Noah and the patriarchs, occasionally through an angel—that is, a messenger—more often directly. He summons Moses to be the liberator of His people, and directs his actions. Even before the people come to Sinai, Moses begins to receive God's instructions for their conduct.

At Mount Sinai, the Bible further relates, the entire people of Israel heard a divine voice proclaim the Ten Commandments. Thereafter, a large body of legislation was given to Moses for the people. It includes what we now call civil, criminal and domestic law, as well as ethical injunctions and extensive cere- monial prescriptions.

The general name in Hebrew for revelation of the divine will is *Torah*. "Law" is not an incorrect translation, but it is inade- quate. Torah includes law, but its basic meaning is guidance, direction, instruction. Torah is divine guidance for human living. The Five Books of Moses, or Pentateuch, are referred to as *the* Torah; the scroll containing these books and used for public reading in the synagogue is called *Sefer Torah*. But it is not only in the Five Books that Torah is to be found.

Men desire not only general rules of conduct, but specific guidance in particular situations. Ancient peoples were accus- tomed to consult a divine oracle in time of personal or national crisis. To this end, many techniques of divination were devised. Their usual purpose was to divine the future rather than to determine what the god wanted of his followers. These techniques were condemned and forbidden by the religion of Israel, which recognized three legitimate means of discovering God's purposes: by dreams, by *Urim* and by prophets (*N'vi'im*) (I Samuel 28:6). But dreams are rarely mentioned in the Bible except in two books—Genesis and Daniel. The *Urim* seems to have been a kind of lot by which yes-or-no answers were obtained. It fell into disuse at an early date, and we have only vague fragments of information about it. The prophets remained as a unique and distinctive feature of the history and religion of Israel.

Prophets

The Hebrew word *Navi* means spokesman. The prophets were regarded, and regarded themselves, as spokesmen of God. They sometimes predicted the future, but as often dealt with the challenge of the present.

Moses is called a *Navi*. He is the first Biblical figure to be so called aside from a single reference to Abraham. The Torah declares that no prophet equal to Moses has ever appeared in Israel. Yet in one of his addresses to the people, he promises that God will raise up other prophets after him: their directions are to be followed as long as they are compatible with the fundamental teachings of the Torah. This passage (Deuteronomy 18:15 ff.) touches on a problem that was to trouble later generations: how can one distinguish a true from a false prophet?

The historical books of the Bible which follow the Torah have much to relate about seers and prophets. The Books of Joshua, Judges, Samuel and Kings are known in Jewish tradition as the Earlier Prophets. The Later Prophets consist chiefly of addresses by various *N'vi'im*, beginning with the eighth century B.C.E. —four to five hundred years after Moses. These messages are marked by tremendous religious and ethical intensity, and by sublime poetic expression. The prophets state in the bluntest terms that their message is the word of God; they refer to visionary experiences in which they beheld God's presence and heard His voice. One prophet reports that the message he was told to transmit was so unpopular that he tried for his own protection to keep silence; but the divine word burned within him, and he could not suppress it (Jeremiah 20:7-9). Despite the frequent vehemence of the prophetic utterances, they are usually clear and orderly in thought, and marked by penetrating insights into the economic and political realities of the ancient world.

In Jewish tradition, the prophets have been regarded chiefly as eloquent champions of the Torah already revealed through Moses. Had the people been faithful to their heritage, more prophets would not have been needed. A different view on this subject will be presented later.

The Oral Torah

The third section of the Hebrew Bible (Writings) does not deal with revelation to any great extent. Some books in this section, notably the Psalms, depict man addressing God rather than the reverse. Jews have often referred to the entire Bible as Torah; but during the period of the Second Jewish Commonwealth— the five centuries preceding the Christian era—a new concept of Torah was developed. This period was marked by the decline of prophecy, the editing of the sacred books and an ever widening concern with the study and practice of the Mosaic law.

Every legal document requires interpretation. In our own legal system, the courts are constantly attempting to redefine older laws in their application to new cases and circumstances. Such interpretations often become precedents by which future cases are decided. The pattern was similar in ancient Israel regarding the provisions of the Torah. In addition, there were many widely accepted legal and religious procedures which the Bible does not mention. These popular traditions, together with the continuing interpretations of the Written Torah, grew into a body of teaching which in time came to be known as the Oral Torah.

The notion of an oral law was not adopted without challenge. The Sadducees—a group of prosperous conservatives, chiefly members of the hereditary priesthood—insisted that the divinely revealed law is to be found only in the Five Books of Moses. The written commandments must be followed strictly and to the letter. Should problems arise for which Scripture provides no solution, the priestly leaders are authorized to give direction. As for the unwritten popular customs, the Sadducees rejected them altogether.

But their views did not prevail. The Pharisees, who taught and defended the Oral Torah, had the confidence and support of the Jewish masses. They legitimized many customs dear to the people; and their interpretations of the Written Torah were flexible and imaginative, so that the provisions of the Torah were kept applicable to changing needs and circumstances. In the hands of the Pharisees, the Torah was dynamic—a living force in the daily affairs of men.

Eventually, the theory was advanced that the Oral Torah, too, had been given to Moses at Sinai. Along with the written text, God had revealed its correct interpretation and application. Transmitted by word of mouth from generation to generation, the oral teachings now set forth by the Pharisees and their successors, the Rabbis, were no less divine in origin than the Written Torah. In effect, the Oral Torah had a higher degree of authority, since the meaning of the written commandments was fixed by the oral tradition.

The oral material discussed in the rabbinic schools at the beginning of the Christian era grew rapidly in bulk and complexity. Eventually it was organized and then reduced to writing. The Mishnah, Talmud, *Midrashim* and the later codes based on these classic works—the *Shulḥan Arukh* is the best known—are compilations of the Oral Torah.

The End of Direct Revelation

Implicit in this development was the consciousness that the old prophetic type of spontaneous revelation was a thing of the past. When the *N'vi'im* first disappeared from Jewish life, their absence was felt as a tragic loss.[1] Later, however, this situation was not only accepted but accepted comfortably. The painful problem of distinguishing the genuine prophet from the false was eliminated. How, indeed, can one be sure whether a prophet is inspired, deranged or lying? But the qualifications of a Torah-scholar can be examined with some objectivity. Direct prophetic inspiration, the Talmud declares, ceased after the days of Haggai, Zechariah and Malachi. The Torah is no longer in heaven; no new revelation is needed. It is sufficient that the sages study, interpret and apply what has already been revealed to us.

This attitude doubtless was conditioned in part by opposition to the rising Christian movement, which claimed to possess a new and more perfect revelation replacing the Torah of Sinai. The Rabbis were therefore impelled to stress that the revelation at Sinai was complete, final and perfect: nothing new was needed or admissible. Even the novel insights which might be advanced in the future by some brilliant student were already implicit in the teaching given to Moses. (The Church later took a similar stand, and outlawed sects which claimed prophetic inspiration.)

Orthodox Jews of today hold that the Torah is divine in origin and content. It is so in both the written text and the oral exposition, as embodied in Talmudic literature and the codes. Being of divine origin, the Torah possesses divine authority.

Revelation and Reason

Though men have sought certainty by recourse to supernatural guidance, they still have had to direct their lives largely by relying on human resources—on intelligence developed and disciplined by experience. Man's reason, of course, may be regarded as a gift from God; but there is a difference between what man learns by utilizing that gift and what God communicates to him through an act of grace that involves no human effort.

Scripture and tradition not only take note of human intelligence, but often appeal to it. Sometimes dogmatic statements are made without explanation or justification, but frequently the Biblical writers defend their position by appeals to logic, experience or the common conscience of mankind. Several books of the Bible are devoted to "wisdom" (*Hokhmah*)—a concept that included a smattering of natural science, much practical advice for daily conduct and some speculation on the universe and its Ruler, without reference to prophetic inspiration or divine revelation. Judaism, for the most part, did not set up a contrast or opposition between this kind of wisdom and Torah; rather it tended to see in wisdom another name for Torah or a special aspect of it.

The post-Biblical teachers, too, recognized the claims of reason. They expounded Scripture and debated legal questions by logical methods which they formulated with considerable precision. The Rabbis, moreover, noted that the commandments of the Torah are of two sorts: moral laws of obvious social utility, and ritual laws for which no rational explanation can be found and which must be obeyed simply because they are "decrees of the King." (The dietary laws are mentioned as an example of the second category.)

Neither Bible nor Talmud, however, attempts a thoroughgoing examination of the problem: how are reason and revelation related? They assume that the Torah is fundamentally reasonable. Can one regard idolatry as anything but ridiculous? Can one fail to perceive the humanitarian value of the Sabbath and of many other prescriptions of the Law? Yet there are commandments whose intent we are unable to fathom. If revelation appears to conflict with reason, we follow the Torah. And there are occasional warnings against speculating on ultimate questions that are beyond our competence. What existed before the creation of the world is such a question.

Philosophy and Faith

The Greek philosophers gave men a view of the world based not on theology but on scientific or quasi-scientific principles. Their science was very different from ours, yet it started from the same basic assumption: that the universe is governed by fixed, impersonal principles which can be discovered through observation and reasoning and stated (more or less adequately) in mathematical terms. Such an outlook does not preclude belief in a God who is First Cause, Source, Cosmic Principle. But it does not seem compatible with the Biblical doctrine of a God who enters into relationships with man, who cares about man, who gives man laws and responds to man's prayers. As Jewish and Christian and, later, Moslem thinkers became aware of the Greek philosophic contribution, they found themselves faced by a disturbing challenge: how to reconcile philosophy and revelation, reason and faith?

The first Jew known to wrestle with this problem was Philo, who lived in Alexandria during the first Christian century.[2] Widely read in Greek philosophy, Philo was also a devout and loyal Jew. His writings are an attempt to harmonize the two elements of his background. He was convinced that whatever is true and sound in Greek thought is no more than an expansion and elaboration of Moses' teachings. (There are, in fact, passages in Plato and the Stoics that are akin in spirit to Biblical monotheism.) On the other hand, he sees in the Torah an embodiment of what he calls the "unwritten law," that is, those universal religious and ethical truths which all men can discover by philosophical inquiry.[3]

But what are we to say of those rituals whose rational intent is not evident? Or of fanciful tales that depict a talking serpent and a tree whose fruit makes the eater immortal? Such difficulties are met by Philo through allegorical explanations. The serpent is a symbol of the love of pleasure, the tree of life stands for piety. Similarly, symbolic meanings are given to various legal provisions. For Philo, every verse of the Torah has such a "higher," "intellectual" meaning in addition to its plain sense. The discerning eye finds profound philosophic conceptions in all of Scripture.

But Philo did not make his religious faith abjectly subordinate to philosophy. Though he speaks of God—after the manner of the philosophers—as eternal, changeless and impassive, he succeeds in connecting God with the changing world of human affairs through concepts of intermediaries and emanations. The changeless God did choose Israel and give them the Torah. The laws of nature are no doubt fixed and regular except when God suspends them. Thus Philo saw no need to reject Biblical miracles. Though he allegorized the stories of the patriarchs and of the Exodus, he made it plain that these stories are also to be understood literally. And he repeatedly declared that understanding the symbolic, inner meaning of a commandment does not release us from the obligation of performing the outward ritual.

Philo's works, written in Greek and preserved by Christian scribes, were for centuries unknown to Jewish teachers. Yet when, after a long interval, there was a philosophic revival in Judaism, later thinkers adopted an approach not unlike Philo's.

The first of these medieval Jewish philosophers—who learned of Greek thought through Arabic translations and expositions—was Saadia Gaon,[4] who lived most of his life in Babylonia (892-942). His philosophic position was more extreme in some respects than that of his successors. The Torah, he declared, is completely rational. God, the Source of truth and wisdom, could not have taught anything contrary to the laws of truth and reason. Theoretically, at least, we could have learned by rational inquiry alone all the principles contained in the Torah. But the processes of reason are slow and difficult. A logical structure is cumulative. An error of fact or logic at any point will invalidate all subsequent inferences; and the whole reasoning process is in vain unless it is pursued to its final conclusion. Thus if God had left us to find out His truth and His will by our own resources, even the small elite possessing sufficient ability, training and leisure to attempt this task would have arrived at uncertain and inaccurate results at best. The vast multitude would have been left in spiritual darkness. Therefore God revealed His truth and His law so that everyone might know the right way with certainty. The simple believer has the guidance that he needs; and the philosopher has the "correct answers" against which he can check his reasoning.

Saadia is convinced that where reason and revelation appear to conflict, careful analysis will reveal some mistake in the reasoning process. He is prepared to interpret figuratively some Scriptural passages which reason tells us could not have been meant literally. Unlike Philo, the constant allegorist, Saadia would limit this method to cases where the plain sense is obviously not admissible.

As against the Greeks, who taught that the physical universe is eternal, Saadia argues vigorously that the world came about by God's creative fiat. This stress was adopted by later Jewish thinkers, including some whose outlook and methods were different from Saadia's. For if the world were eternal, we should have to conclude that the laws of nature are likewise eternal and changeless. But if God created the world by an act of will, the natural laws he established might—so to speak—be provisional; there is room for the possibility of suspending these laws by miracle, above all by the supreme miracle of revelation.

Thus Saadia was radical only in his primary assumption: the complete agreement of reason and revelation. In his theological and practical conclusions he was not extreme. Other Jewish philosophers went further than he in developing the implications of rational thought, but were more cautious about the general principle. Moses Maimonides (1135-1204)[5] attempted to give a rational explanation of all the commandments. He also attempted to describe what we might call the "mechanics" of revelation.

But he was constrained to confess that God's purposes can be comprehended only in part.

Thus Maimonides states that a man can attain to the prophetic level only if he has perfected himself in the moral and intellectual disciplines, and if he also possesses a powerful imaginative faculty. But all these qualities in combination do not suffice to make a man a prophet unless divine grace so wills it. The greatest of the Jewish rationalists is compelled to admit (no doubt reluctantly) the limitations of reason.

Other thinkers, of a more conservative stamp, were far more outspoken concerning their distrust of reason. Judah Halevi (about 1080-1145)[6] had challenged the tendency to make reason the decisive factor in religious thought. Speculative philosophy is always uncertain. Besides, we do not need it, being in posses- sion of a Torah whose authenticity was attested by six hundred thousand persons who stood at Sinai, beheld the marvels and heard the divine voice—and by an unbroken chain of tradition from that time to the present. Rational philosophy is useful chiefly as an instrument for criticism, helping us to avoid illogi- cal inferences from Scripture, and also to deal with such prob- lems as freedom of the will, about which the revealed documents are not entirely clear. Halevi himself employed philosophy for such purposes; yet in one of his poems he warns the reader that the Greek wisdom bears flowers but not fruit!

The last of this series of philosophers, Hasdai Crescas (died 1412), employed his brilliant intellect to attack "reason"—that is, Aristotelian philosophy—by pointing out its logical inadequa- cies. This criticism prepared the way for a reaffirmation of faith guided by revealed Scripture and tradition.

Meantime, a sect had appeared which reverted to the old view- point of the Sadducees, rejecting the Oral Torah and demanding a strict literalist approach to the written revelation. This sect was known as the Karaites (Scripturalists). It arose in Babylonia and Persia in the eighth century. It repudiated the Talmud and the authority of the Rabbis, and called for a return to the uncor- rupted truth of the Bible. Though the movement stimulated Biblical studies, stirred up piety and even developed some philo- sophic expositors, Karaism was essentially reactionary. The Talmudic development had enormously complicated the simple provisions of Biblical law, and the Talmudic teachers sometimes departed from the plain sense of the Bible text. But this process had resulted in many humanitarian and socially useful regulations. Moreover, the Talmudic method made it possible to adapt the principles of the Torah to changing circumstances. All this progress was repudiated by the Karaites, at least in theory. Actually, they never succeeded in wholly "liberating" themselves from rabbinic tradition. Scripture must be interpreted, and the Karaites often adopted rabbinic interpretations, perhaps without realizing it.[7] The Karaite sect, committed to a static outlook, soon lost its original energy and survives only in small vestigial groups.

Crescas, the last of the philosophers mentioned above, lived in an age of steadily increasing persecution. Spain, long a leading center of Jewish life, had become the scene of oppression and massacre. By the end of the fifteenth century the Jews were expelled from the Iberian Peninsula. Disasters turned the mood of the Jewish people and its intellectuals away from cool, abstract rationalism. The establishment of ghettos tended to reinforce ethnic and religious loyalties and to inculcate submission to authority. The dominant spiritual force in these countries was the mystical doctrine (or doctrines) known as the *Kabbalah*. The Kabbalists read novel and fantastic notions into the words—even into the letters—of the Bible. But such fanciful and imaginative development was predicated on the divine origin and authority of the sacred text.

The Modern Revolt

The concepts of revelation we have described were paralleled in Christianity and Islam. Both possessed systems of tradition comparable in many respects to the Oral Torah. But though the subject matter of revelation varied from faith to faith, similar notions about revelation were widely held. Then a revolt began in the Christian world against the idea of revealed religion and the authority of religious documents and functionaries. The Jews, shut up in their own segregated communities and denied participation in the cultural life of the world about them, were long insulated from these new tendencies. One of the few exceptions was Baruch Spinoza, but he had been estranged from his Jewish background long before he was formally expelled from the Jewish community of Amsterdam.

The new trend was stimulated in large measure by the development of natural science in the sixteenth and seventeenth centuries. Once again stress was laid on the notion of a world order operating impersonally according to law that can be formulated in mathematical terms. Again men felt the contrast between this view and the belief in the Biblical God who has wondrously revealed His commandments and has singled out certain individuals and peoples for His service.

Progress in the natural sciences was only one factor. The rule of law had been the basic assumption of ancient science, too; but men like Philo and Maimonides had been able to harmonize scientific doctrine with the documents of revelation, interpreting the latter rather freely. Statements in Scripture, if they appeared to conflict with reason, were given a symbolic or allegorical meaning. Such passages—it was held—were intended to convey philosophic truth in unphilosophic terms suitable to the minds of simple folk.

This method of solving difficulties was now blocked by advances in linguistic science, literary and historical criticism, and comparative religion. The methods already employed in editing and explaining Greek and Latin classics were now applied to the sacred texts. As a result it became increasingly harder to explain or allegorize away those passages whose plain sense was not acceptable. Men learned more about the great Oriental religions. The rediscovery of the ancient Near East, with its advanced civilizations and rich culture, began at the end of the eighteenth century. It was found that many of the teachings of Jewish and Christian Scriptures are paralleled in other literatures, and that some Biblical doctrines had their origins in earlier pagan sources. Moreover, scholars encountered ritual laws strikingly similar to certain provisions of the Torah which had long been explained as "decrees of the King." Thus the Judeo-Christian heritage required extensive re-evaluation.

The critical analysis of the Bible led to some startling conclusions. In this area Spinoza was a noteworthy pioneer. He took his cue, not from the literary and historical critics of the Renaissance, but from certain medieval Hebrew Bible commentators, especially Abraham Ibn Ezra, who had made some rather daring suggestions. Developing these hints, Spinoza argued that the Pentateuch in its present form could not have been completed in the time of Moses, and ventured the guess that it was edited in the days of Ezra—some eight hundred years later. Spinoza's Biblical inquiries were incidental to his central purpose: to assert the right of philosophers and scientists to freedom of thought and expression. In his independent approach to the Bible he was followed by a number of lesser men, some of them animated by skeptical and anti-clerical intent. But not much solid, objective scholarship resulted until the nineteenth century.

Modern Biblical Science

In the last century and a half, textual study, historical criticism and archeological research have revolutionized our understanding of the Bible. Once we approach the text without the prior assumption that the manuscripts are absolutely accurate and the documents divinely authoritative, entirely new results emerge. Most students are now convinced that the Hebrew text contains many mistakes due to careless copying and other accidents; some passages have been so badly damaged that we cannot hope to recover their original meaning. The Torah is a composite; much of it was written down long after Moses' day. Traditions regarding the authorship of certain other Biblical writings are not invariably reliable. Some stories—those of the Creation and the Flood, for example—are adaptations of myths known to other ancient peoples of the Near East. Parallels to a number of laws and ritual prescriptions of the Bible appear in other early codes.

The men who made these findings were not anti-religious propagandists. Most of them were committed Christians and Jews. Nor were the results of their investigations only negative. Though certain passages of the Bible are regarded as mythical, and others (especially miracle tales) as legendary, scholars have been able to show that most of the Biblical records and histories are highly reliable and accurate. While the Biblical writers borrowed much from their environment, the monotheism they proclaimed is unique and the ethical standards they upheld unequaled elsewhere. Indeed, the very materials that were borrowed from the common stock of Near Eastern lore have been refashioned and transformed into something far nobler and loftier than the older versions. Most modern scholars recognize that certain primitive notions have survived in the Bible. They cannot be dismissed as allegory. But those survivals provide us with a means of measuring the enormous ethical and spiritual advance within the Bible itself.

In the view of many modern scholars, the prophets represent the highest level of Biblical thought and piety, and the appearance of these seers marked one of the loftiest peaks in the spiritual history of mankind. Whereas tradition considered the prophets to be simply eloquent champions of the Torah, they are now held to have played a far more creative role.

It is sometimes stated that recent archeological discoveries have discredited nineteenth-century Bible criticism, especially in the synthesis of Julius Wellhausen. This famous German scholar published his chief works about eighty years ago; obviously, Biblical studies have made much progress since. Present-day views are in some respects more conservative, especially regarding the age and authenticity of many Biblical reports. This is not to say that modern scientific studies have confirmed the claims of Orthodoxy. Chemistry text books published far more recently than 1885 are already out of date; but the older chemists have not been "discredited." All scientific findings are subject to revision.

Contemporary Approaches

Some who are well versed in the Bible and related studies regard the Torah as divinely revealed to Moses, as a single unified document without errors or inner discrepancies, as completely accurate in the narration of events and as eternally authoritative in its commandments. They start out with this belief and with the will to believe. They accept the findings of modern science insofar as these findings are compatible with their own theological assumptions. Where science and religious tradition come into conflict, the Orthodox challenge the correctness or the conclusiveness of the scientific arguments.

But those who cannot in good conscience set limits to free inquiry, who are not prepared to start with the assumption that the Biblical documents are supernatural in origin and who regard the methods of historical criticism as valid, have been forced to revise their concept of revelation.

No serious student of the Bible today regards the claims which it contains as fraudulent, even as pious fraud. (Such a notion was widespread in the eighteenth century.) The Biblical writers wrote in good faith. The various documents of the Torah embody old traditions, even though not all traditions go back as far as Moses, and even though historical memories were sometimes adorned by legendary decorations. Likewise, when legal sections were modified for humanitarian reasons the assumption was that God had so intended and Moses had thus originally taught. (Books such as Jonah and Job were not intended as official works of revelation; they were meant to be taken seriously but not literally, like all great works of the creative imagination.)

The Biblical lawgivers and prophets sincerely believed themselves agents of divine revelation. The modern unbeliever properly cannot accuse them of fraud. But he may regard them as mistaken. Indeed he may consider all religious belief, including belief in revelation, to be a survival of culture patterns from an earlier age, possessing no more than historical interest.

But there are many who accept all the findings of Biblical research, and still regard the Bible as the great document of revelation. How is this possible?

During the nineteenth century, the teachers of Reform Judaism proclaimed the doctrine of "progressive revelation"—a viewpoint also implicit in the thought of the leaders of Conservative Judaism. This doctrine holds that the continuing education of mankind is the result of divine illumination and guidance. God reveals Himself, His truth and His will, not in a few times and places, not only in certain sacred documents, but in the gradual discovery by all men of what is true and good. Man is not merely the passive recipient of revelation: his intellectual and moral effort are necessary to this process, as well as the grace of God. Nor is revelation mediated only by the prophets and teachers of religion: philosophers and scientists, poets and other creative artists, moralists and social reformers all contribute their share. But since men are involved in the process of revelation, no truth we obtain can claim absolute purity, perfection and finality. The divine radiance is always mingled with earthly elements. Ideas are conditioned by the limitations of the human mind, by the intellectual and cultural patterns of the specific time and place. If revelation is an ongoing process, our knowledge can never be complete. We cannot relax in the comfortable assurance that God has already taught us all we need to know. The need to keep on learning is unending.

According to this doctrine, all nations and peoples have (at least theoretically) some share in the unveiling of divine truth. Yet the facts of history seem to support the claim that Israel has been a chosen people and that the Bible is the book of revelation par excellence. Let us judge the Hebrew Scriptures not in terms of their alleged supernatural origin, but simply on the basis of their ethical and religious grandeur and of the relevance to modern life of so much that they contain. Let us consider further that Judaism and its holy books have exerted an incalculable influence on the world through Christianity and Islam, which are deeply rooted in the Hebraic sources; further, that many humanistic philosophies claiming to be secular are largely inspired by the teachings of the prophets. In the light of these realities, the Bible appears pre-eminently as the word of God. The exponents of progressive revelation are not unduly troubled because the Bible contains—in addition to much that is sublime and perennially valid—some historical and scientific errors, mythological and legendary passages, sacrificial ritualism and even elements that are morally indefensible to us. They do not need either to justify such elements or to explain them away. Indeed, the presence of these primitive survivals enables us to trace the process of spiritual advance and ascent within the Bible itself.

The doctrine of progressive revelation is held, implicitly or consciously, by most Jews who are religious believers but who are not Orthodox. Despite many merits, this doctrine has certain weaknesses.

It seems to reduce, or even to negate, the specifically religious character of revelation. If God reveals Himself in the discoveries of the laboratory and the reasonings of the philosopher, if the experience of the prophet is comparable to the "inspiration" of the poet or composer, what is the distinctive character of religious experience and religious truth? If, moreover, we decide what *we* consider to be the word of God in the Bible and what we discard as all too human adulterations—that is to say, if we measure the sacred text against our present-day notions of science, history and morality—are we not depriving religion of authority?

These difficulties are serious; perhaps they cannot be over-come. But an attempt to reckon with them has led to a somewhat different approach, exemplified by such thinkers as Franz Rosen-zweig and Martin Buber,[8] and by others associated with "existen-tialist" trends. These thinkers do not challenge the methods or the results of Biblical criticism. Though they take issue with the spokesmen of liberalism, it is not in the name of Orthodoxy. Studying the documents of revelation, this newer school finds testimony to only one fact: that God revealed Himself, that man encountered the divine.

That is the only certain truth of Scripture. As soon as those who experienced the divine presence tried to express what they had experienced, they could only struggle to convey something that is essentially beyond communication. In all honesty, they interpreted the overwhelming event that had befallen them in terms of ethical or ritual content. These ideas, moral exhortations, legal provisions are human explanations of the encounter with God. These explanations are subject to all the relativities and ambiguities we have previously noted. All we are sure of is that these men did find God.

Such essentially subjective assertions can hardly admit of rational criticism. But one fact is worth pointing out. In modern speech, personal experience of the Divine Presence may be called "revelation," but in Hebrew the term Torah is never applied to it.[9] This experience is most often called *Gilluy Sh'khinah*, "mani-festation of the Divine Presence." For a person to have such an experience has been deemed a high privilege, a testimony to the spiritual level he has attained. But it conferred no authority on the fortunate visionary, still less upon his doctrine. And the cen-tral objective of Jewish existence has not been to attain *Gilluy Sh'khinah*. It has been to learn, understand and practice the Torah. Judaism has been preoccupied with the content far more than with the experience of revelation.

To Sum Up

Three possibilities present themselves to the Jew of today:
1. He may cling to the traditional belief that the Written and

Oral Torah as expounded by Orthodox authorities is literally the divine revelation. He will then adjust this affirmation as well as he can to any facts that appear to contradict it.

2. He may abandon the concept of revelation altogether and attempt to explain Jewish experience in purely human terms. For such a person, Torah is simply an old-fashioned name for the national culture of the Jewish people.

3. He may adopt some version (liberal, existential or other) of the view that God's revelation has occurred and still occurs, and that Jewish Scripture and tradition are notable, perhaps unique, instances of that revelation. This view requires the acknowledgment that we know only part of God's truth and must struggle to learn and discover more. Such an approach leaves many uncertainties unresolved; but uncertainty is the inevitable concomitant and price of freedom.

FOR FURTHER READING

BAMBERGER, Bernard and Gunther Plaut, *The Torah: A Modern Commentary* (Cincinnati: Union of American Hebrew Congregations, 1982). A clear, judicious presentation of the Reform view of Torah in context.

BLEICH, David, *Contemporary Halakhic Problems*—in two volumes (Hoboken, NJ: Ktav Publishing, 1983). A thoughtful introduction to Orthodox Jewish views on Torah and related concepts by one of the leading Orthodox thinkers of the present generation.

FACKENHEIM, Emil, *God's Presence in History: Jewish Affirmations and Philosophical Reflections* (New York: New York University Press, 1970). A leading Jewish philosopher's attempt to explicate the meaning of revelation in the context of the Holocaust and reborn State of Israel.

JACOBS, Louis, *We Have Reason to Believe* (London: Valentine and Mitchell, 1963). A learned as well as passionate defense of a modern, non-literal, non-orthodox, historical conceptualization of the meaning of Torah.

KAUFMANN, Yehezkel, *The Religion of Israel* (New York: Schocken Books, 1972). A one-volume English abridgement of Kaufmann's brilliant, if in places arguable, reconstruction of Biblical history and its inner theological meaning. A classic work of Jewish sensibility.

MARTIN, Bernard, Editor, *Contemporary Reform Jewish Thought* (Chicago: Quadrangle Books, 1968). An articulate contemporary expression of Reform Judaism's theological attitudes to Torah and Revelation, among other matters, by its leading theologians.

5 . Torah and the Personal Life

LOUIS JACOBS

THE KEY terms in Jewish life—*Torah* and *mitzvah*—are inextricably linked. In English translations of the Bible, Torah is rendered as "Law." The idea of a God-given law was foremost in the minds of Jews when they spoke of Torah. But its actual meaning is far more embracing.

In classical Jewish sources Torah was used in three senses: as the Pentateuch; as the Bible as a whole (including the Prophets and the Writings); and as the sum total of Jewish religious teaching. In the latter sense, Torah is synonymous with religious Judaism. Torah is regarded as the word of God: it suggests worship of the Most High and demands that the Jew recognize his Creator in all that he does.

If Torah is divine doctrine, *mitzvah* (from a root meaning "to command" and signifying a "good deed") is the concrete expression given to that doctrine in human action. Thus to keep the Sabbath is to express Torah in the form of *mitzvah*. Torah as a way of life involves knowledge of and performance of Jewish practice, joy in teaching and practice as divinely ordained means of bringing man nearer to God.

In the Jewish evening service the following prayer is found:

> With everlasting love Thou hast loved the house of Israel, Thy people; Torah and commandments, statutes and judgments hast Thou taught us. Therefore, O Lord our God, when we lie down and when we rise up we will meditate on Thy statutes. Yea, we will rejoice in the words of Thy Torah and in Thy commandments for ever; for they are our life and the length of our days, and we will meditate on them day and night.

When the composer of this prayer (of uncertain date but of undoubtedly early origin) and the millions of Jews who have recited it spoke of Torah as "life" they had two ideas in mind: that Torah has something significant to say in every one of life's situations, and that only when Jewish life is shaped by Torah does it possess true spiritual vitality.

The emphasis on particular forms of behavior, on rules and regulations in Judaism, has long been a stumbling block. Some argue that a religion which pays so much attention to correct patterns of conduct risks the evils of formalism and loss of spontaneity. But Jewish religious experience demonstrates that the psalmist who sang of Torah and *mitzvah* as "more to be desired than fine gold and sweeter than honey" (Psalms 19:11) was a better judge of vital religion than the critic who sees it only from the outside. The dangers of a mere mechanical, soulless routine are obvious: Jewish masters of the spiritual life warn of the perils of dull conformity.

Yet those who practice the *mitzvot* obtain constant glimpses of eternity. The Jew who takes a cup of wine in his hand on Sabbath eve to praise God as the Creator of all, the Jew who observes the Sabbath in recognition of God's sovereignty does find that, in the words of the Jewish mystics, "the Sabbath sweetens the world." A new dimension is added to his life. However banal and trivial his daily round, on this day he gains insight into ultimate reality. As Abraham Isaac Kuk, the late Chief Rabbi of Palestine, said, "just as there are laws of poetry there is poetry in laws."

Man needs a system of observances to give concrete expression to his religious ideals and strivings. The Jew accepts a system evolved by his people in the course of its long history, through the prophets and lawgivers, the saints and sages of Israel. He keeps the *mitzvot* not as folkways but as God's demands on him.

In the Middle Ages, Jews believed that almost every detail of their observance was divinely inspired. It is true that the most distinguished medieval thinkers sought to discover reasons for the *mitzvot*. Their conviction was that God was no arbitrary tyrant imposing meaningless rules on His subjects. But they kept the commandments whether or not the reasons advanced were satisfying.

The modern Jew, however, sometimes finds it impossible to accept this view of Torah and *mitzvah*. He is unwilling to sacrifice his intellectual integrity. The social sciences lead him to appreciate how human institutions develop; they inform him that even religious practices have a history. They prevent him from accepting a static picture of how Judaism came to be. Yet for all this awareness of the interaction of the divine and the human in the emergence of the *mitzvot* some modern Jews can still look upon them as divine command. In this matter there are basically three approaches.

Three Approaches to the Validity of Mitzvot

First is the approach that the *mitzvot* were dictated by God to Moses at Sinai in all their details (except for some of the rabbinic precepts such as the kindling of the *Hanukkah* lights). Many traditional Jews accept this as the only authentic view. But there are others who cannot disregard the human element in the emergence of Jewish practice.

The second approach states that though *mitzvot* are purely human, having evolved from primitive forms, they ought to be kept for the values to which they give expression. Some sincere thinkers favor this view, but it does not commend itself to those who see the real power of the *mitzvot* in the expression they give to the divine will.

The third view holds that the *mitzvot* evolved gradually through normal historical processes, but this evolution is the means God has used to teach His will to His people. This combines a dynamic conception of Judaism and the need for divine sanction.

An illustration of the three approaches can be seen in the laws governing the separation of meat and milk. Observant Jews do not eat meat and milk dishes at the same meal, a prohibition based in rabbinic literature on the Biblical verses prohibiting the seething of a kid in its mother's milk.[1] The Rabbis derived from those verses the prohibition against the cooking together of any meat and milk, and then extended the ban to include eating the two at the same meal.

Maimonides, in his *Guide for the Perplexed*, suggested long ago that the original prohibition was a protest against idolatrous practices. There seems much in the idea that Scripture rejects the seething of a kid in its mother's milk (as a kind of sympathetic magic) as part of its general struggle against idolatry. Among the clay tablets found at Ras Shamra in Syria between 1929 and 1939, instructions to Canaanite priests dating from the second half of the second millennium B.C.E. were discovered. Although the reading is disputed by some scholars, it does seem as if the priests were ordered to seethe a kid in its mother's milk and scatter the mixture over the fields to make them fruitful.

Advocates of the traditional approach will maintain that God dictated the prohibition of cooking milk and meat together and that this was the original meaning of the text. For some reason the text speaks of a "kid" and the "milk of its mother" but, in reality, any meat and any milk are meant. If it be objected that this does violence to the plain meaning of the text, advocates of the traditional view can only say that we cannot know why God should have chosen this roundabout method of declaring the more comprehensive prohibition.

Advocates of the second approach feel that to say this is to abandon reason and they will point to the Ras Shamra texts in corroboration. The full prohibition, they will argue, can only have come into Jewish life at a later stage as a human cultural development.

Advocates of the third approach will take full account of these implications, but they will see the hand of God in the whole evolutionary process. They will dwell on the religious value of the separation of meat and milk both as a reminder of Israel's fight against base worship and as a powerful practical lesson of the need for moral discernment in life. But over and above the other values in the practice they will find in it a means of submission to the will of God.

Either one sees the glory of such submission or one does not. But if one does, this in itself is the most powerful reason for Jewish observance. It is not argued that everything which has come down from the past is of equal value. The problem of establishing proper and convincing criteria is indeed a heavy one for the advocates of the third view. But the argument is sound, nonetheless: for a sound religious outlook it is necessary to recognize that Jewish institutions which are accepted by Jews have their value increased a thousandfold through seeing them under the aspect of eternity, as God's way of guiding His people.

A more telling example can be quoted. The Sabbath and the festivals begin, Jewish tradition has it, on the previous evening at nightfall and they come to an end at nightfall. This is based in rabbinic literature on the verse: "And there was evening and there was morning, one day" (Genesis 1:5). In the Middle Ages, however, some commentators argued that the real meaning of the verse was not that evening precedes morning but that once night had fallen ("and there was evening") and then day had dawned ("and it was morning"), one day had passed. It is not without significance in this connection that with regard to the Day of Atonement Scripture says: "from even unto even, shall ye keep your Sabbath" (Leviticus 23:32), which appears to suggest that other festivals and the Sabbath begin in the morning and end the next morning. Furthermore, some scholars argue that in Bible times the Sabbaths and festivals were observed from morning to morning, and they call attention to the fact that some ancient sects did keep their Sabbaths and festivals in this way.

Now advocates of the first view are obliged to turn a blind eye to all the evidence and hold fast to the opinion that our present practice was the Biblical one. Followers of the second approach, while they may or may not be convinced by the evidence, refuse to close their minds to the possibility, at least, that Jewish traditional practice has here departed from the Biblical. But, they will argue, the Jew does not go to the Bible for his present-day observance but to Jewish tradition, and his present practice is valid because this is how the method of Sabbath and festival observance has evolved. Advocates of the third approach will similarly keep an open mind on the subject but they will not only see their observance as validated by tradition but go on to see tradition itself in terms of God's guidance and God's will.

The Mitzvah of Prayer[2]

Whatever their approach, many modern Jews understand that the *mitzvot* have come to be the way through which the people of Israel draw near to God. Torah teaches prayer, which for most people means asking God to grant requests. Some thinkers throughout the ages have looked askance upon petitionary prayer as selfish, futile, arrogant. They have argued that inexorable laws of nature cannot be altered by man's wishes, nor does God need to be told what He should do. Yet this common form of religious expression belongs to Torah as a way of life.

Even if we assume that the laws of nature are not commutable and that God needs no reminders, cannot the very act of turning to Him in prayer add an important factor to the circumstances surrounding any request? Petitionary prayer need not be selfish. Where it is offered on behalf of others, it is an expression of man's benevolent instincts. Concern for another's physical needs, said a famous Jewish moralist, is a spiritual concern. Even when prayer is offered for oneself it can be an act of devotion: a man may pray to God to grant him a livelihood to provide for his family. Prayers for health may be motivated by the desire to serve God and man in full bodily and mental vigor.

The Jewish prayer book also contains many prayers that are not petitionary. Many celebrate God's sovereignty. But here another difficulty presents itself. What need has God of praise? The religious person explains the idea behind praising God, the yearning for worship, as the divine spark in the human soul reaching out for its source in God. When man has a sense of wonder, when he marvels at the amazing universe in which he lives, he feels the urge to shout aloud in joy that the Great Power behind all things really exists, that beauty, truth and goodness cannot have emerged by mere blind force, that we are not the playthings of chance but children of a benevolent Creator. The Midrash comments on the verse: "And they believed in the Lord and in His servant Moses. Then sang Moses and the children of Israel" (Exodus 14:31-15:1), by saying: "When Israel believes, Israel sings."

Jewish tradition sets great store by communal worship. The special function of the synagogue lies in the opportunity it affords like-minded people to congregate and help each other in furthering their common faith. Alfred Whitehead's definition of religion as "what a man does with his solitariness" is not the whole truth. From the earliest times men saw the need to meet together to find inspiration from their common links with the past and their hopes for the future. The idea of congregational prayer is the gift of Judaism to higher religion. The synagogue is the mother of church and mosque. Historically it is a center of Jewish life far beyond the "house of prayer." It has always had a special role in fostering Jewish consciousness, in keeping the spark of Jewish faith alive and in educating young and old in Jewish values and ideas.

Torah and the Jewish Home

The Torah also contains patterns of conduct and lofty ideals for application in the home. Externally the Jewish home is distinguished by the *m'zuzah*, containing the words of the *Shema*. Fixed to the doorposts of the house, it is no talisman but serves as a permanent reminder of the beliefs, ideals and practices inherent in Judaism. "Hear, O Israel, the Lord is one." The Rabbis of the Talmud make specific reference to the *m'zuzah* and speak of the Jew in his home as "surrounded by the *mitzvot*."

The *m'zuzah* sets the tone for the Jewish home by attaching a distinguishing mark of recognition that God is in the background. Husband and wife express their love for each other through the physical side of marriage without prudishness. But Judaism also demands self-control, mutual respect and complete faithfulness.

Marriage as Judaism sees it is a religious duty. The Babylonian teacher, Rabbi Hisda, said that the verse "in want of all things" (Deuteronomy 28:48) refers to the man who has no wife. The Palestinian teacher, Rabbi Eliezer, said that a man without a wife is no proper man. Scripture says: "Male and female created He them and called their name Adam" (Genesis 5:2). The importance attached to marriage can be seen from the old rabbinic ruling that one may sell a scroll of the Torah in order to obtain the means to marry. As described in an oft-quoted rabbinic saying, when husband and wife live in harmony the *Sh'khinah*, the divine presence, dwells with them in their home.

Children are looked upon as God's blessing. Two Scriptural verses were quoted frequently by the Rabbis to support their contention that procreation is a religious duty: "Be fruitful and multiply" (Genesis 1:28) and "He formed it (the world) to be inhabited" (Isaiah 45:18). The School of Shammai ruled that a couple should have at least two sons. The School of Hillel, whose opinion is generally followed, ruled that they should have at least one son and one daughter.

The relationship between parents and children is also the subject of the Torah's teachings. The Fifth Commandment is treated seriously in the Jewish tradition. Indeed, tradition itself derives its authority chiefly from the respect due to those who have gone before, though this is not allowed to become a form of ancestor worship. With its emphasis on the practical, Jewish teaching gives concrete examples of the behavior involved in obeying the abstract commandment of honoring parents. Specifically, children should not contradict their parents or sit in the place set aside for them in home or synagogue. Honoring parents also includes taking care of their physical needs. With delicacy of feeling the medieval *Book of the Pious* advises a son who has done something at his mother's request, which he senses might anger his father, to take the blame on himself rather than to cause strife between his parents.

Parents likewise are given precise commandments. It is forbidden, say the Rabbis, for a father to strike his grown son or to be excessively strict with his children. The devotion of Jewish parents to their children is proverbial, but the tradition recognizes the dangers of excessive love. Rigid parental control is also frowned upon: for example, a son is not obligated to give up the girl of his choice in obedience to his parents' wishes. In fact, it is far from certain that Judaism enjoins obedience to parents as distinct from honor and respect. During the early days of *Ḥasidism*, some young men defied their parents by embracing the fresh religious ideas and customs of that movement. A number of *Ḥasidic* teachers held that one must work out one's own future even if that involved a measure of disobedience to parents and teachers. Respect and honor are due, teach the Rabbis, not only to parents but to older brothers and sisters, in-laws, step-parents and other members of the family.

The ideal Jewish home is noted for the readiness with which it offers hospitality to guests and strangers in need. It all began with Abraham, whose house, says the Midrash, had a door facing each direction so that the hungry wayfarer could enter immediately. Jewish mystics wax eloquent on the virtue of having the poor—"God's representatives"—at table, particularly on Sabbaths and festivals. A Sabbath whose joys are confined to the immediate family circle is called "*your* Sabbath" and is not always pleasing to the Lord, while a Sabbath whose pleasures are shared with the unfortunate and friendless is "the *Lord's* Sabbath." Only a religion which sees hospitality as a high virtue can teach that to welcome guests to the home is greater than to welcome the *Sh'khinah!*

The Centrality of Ethics

A man's religious commitment makes ethical as well as religious demands. "And thou shalt love thy neighbor as thyself" (Leviticus 19:18) is the version in which the Golden Rule appears in Scripture, complimented by Hillel's negative formulation. "That which is hateful unto thee do not unto thy neighbor." That great teacher's intention—which is the whole point of the story in the relevant Talmudic passage—was to inform a prospective convert to Judaism that "love thy neighbor" is the vital precept and "the rest is commentary."

Judaism provided for brotherly love in the most positive of forms—in the practice of benevolence, in visiting the sick, burying the dead, clothing the naked, feeding the hungry. Societies for these purposes were organized in every Jewish community. Poor relief was the norm in Jewry centuries before welfare measures were enacted in Europe. It goes without saying that in the world of today the traditional Jewish ideal embraces such things as cancer research, social welfare, care for the aged and infirm, and alleviating the sufferings of hungry children in the desperate plight they find themselves in many countries. Working for peace on earth and combating racial prejudice and discrimination are obviously included.

Hillel also said: "If I am not for myself, who will be for me? And being for myself only, what am I?" (*Ethics of the Fathers* 1:14). Maxim Gorky used this piece of rabbinic wisdom as a strong staff on his earthly pilgrimage.[3] A man must care for himself, must further his own interests, is entitled to his hopes and ambitions for the future. He must not impose his care on other people. But if his sole regard is for his personal life, if his altruism never comes into play, if he refuses obligations as a member of society, then his life will be useless, ugly, meaningless. Judaism is

sufficiently realistic to appreciate man's egotistic claims. At the
Synod in Usha, in ancient Palestine, it was decreed, and this became the norm in Judaism, that a man should not give more
than a fifth of his wealth to charity. And yet nothing could be
further from the Jewish ideal than a coldly calculating approach
to virtue. The Jew who wishes to make the Torah his way of life
must be conscious that everyone is a child of God and that God
is concerned for all His creatures.

The Rabbis extend the prohibition of "wronging another"
(Leviticus 25:14) to embrace what they call "wronging with
words." This includes looking at goods one has no intention of
buying, giving someone bad advice, taunting a repentant sinner
with his former deeds or a convert to Judaism with the misdeeds
of his ancestors.

Judaism demands the loftiest standards in man's dealings with
his fellows. The Rabbis comment on the Scriptural injunction
against "taking vengeance" and "bearing a grudge" (Leviticus
19:18). They explain that the first prohibition refers to a man
who refuses to do his neighbor a good turn because his neighbor previously had refused to help him. The second prohibition
refers to the man who repays evil with good but gloats over his
superiority and magnanimity. To insult one's neighbor and put
him to shame in public is, in the eyes of the Rabbis, a heinous
offense. One of the Rabbis went so far as to declare that the
man who shames his neighbor in public has no share in the world-
to-come. Slander and tale-bearing were as rife in rabbinic times
as they are today. "Everyone is guilty of a modicum of slander"
is a rabbinic dictum. Jewish teachings frown on malicious gossip
of any kind, even if true. It is even forbidden to praise a man in
the presence of his enemies for this will certainly lead them to
speak ill of him.

Imitation of God: Torah's Ultimate Purpose

The ideal of the Torah as a way of life involves more than
patterns of behavior. There is a saying attributed to the Baal
Shem, founder of *Ḥasidism*, that the purpose of the Torah is
that man should himself become a Torah. The great Babylonian
teacher Rav said: "The *mitzvot* were given to refine God's
creatures." This calls attention to the significance of the Torah

as a means of character education. The ideal is imitation of God. "As God is merciful, be thou merciful; as He is compassionate, be thou compassionate" is the Jewish goal. To be God-like is to emulate the attributes by which God is praised in Scripture.

But we cannot all be saints. The Jewish emphasis is therefore on the good society, an ideal which implies that the group is constituted of many imperfect individuals all pooling their resources and working together for a common aim. However, the lofty teachings in classical Jewish sources on the moral life of man are powerful reminders that there does exist a Jewish call to the devout life in which man strives to be holy as God is holy.

Maimonides' praise of the golden mean has had a great influence on the Jewish character. A student of both Greek philosophy and rabbinic ethics, Maimonides seeks to create a synthesis between the two. He advises the Jew to choose the middle way and reject extremes of character. Thus, for Maimonides, a man should be neither too niggardly nor too generous. He should not lead a life of indulgence nor should he lead too ascetic a life. He should avoid the extremes of frivolity and solemnity, reticence and bravado, sentimentality and cruelty. The Maimonidean ideal is that of a sagacious harmony of character. S. D. Luzzatto, a severe critic of Maimonides' affinity for Greek sources, dubbed this Atticism. According to Luzzatto, Judaism does not see ethics as an offshoot of esthetics. The harmonious, well-balanced character may have been sufficient for the Greeks, says Luzzatto, but Judaism tends to applaud the unusually generous nature as the ideal. Disciples of Abraham should choose the extreme of compassion.

The debate continues. Even Maimonides admits that one should go to extremes in rejecting pride and vanity. Moses is described as humble in the extreme: "Now the man Moses was very meek, above all the men that were upon the face of the earth" (Numbers 12:3). Another great medieval Jewish teacher, Nahmanides, advises his son to cultivate the trait of humility:

Let all thy words be softly spoken. Let thine eyes gaze downwards and thy heart upwards. Let every man be thy superior in thine eyes. If he is a greater scholar or wealthier than thou art, surely he is thy superior in these respects. But if he is inferior to thee in both learning and riches, consider that he is thy superior in righteousness, for if he sins he does so out of ignorance, whereas thy sins are committed with full knowledge of their enormity. If thou wilt thus reflect continually, pride will be impossible for thee and it will be well with thee.[4]

Anger, too, is, for the Rabbis, a trait of character one should go to extremes in avoiding. Whoever breaks things in temper, according to a typical rabbinic saying, is like an idolator. Another saying is that the life of a person prone to flying into severe rages is a living hell. The righteous, said one of the Rabbis, do not retaliate even when they are the victims of abuse. They serve God in love and rejoice in their suffering. Of them Scripture says: "But they that love Him are as the sun when he goeth forth in his might" (Judges 5:31). Special care should be taken to treat widows, orphans and others in distress with the greatest tenderness and compassion. No wounding words should ever be directed toward them. The Jewish mystic Moses Cordovero (1522-1570) taught that man should be God-like in extending his compassion to all creatures, neither destroying nor despising any of them. It is said that he refused to kill even mosquitoes which plagued him since they, too, had been placed on earth by the wisdom of the Creator. The ideal Jew, observes this teacher, finds good in all men, ignoring their defects. On beholding one who suffers, he should say to himself: "Behold, in God's eyes this man is superior to me for he is plagued with suffering and poverty and cleansed from sin. How, then, can I hate one whom the Holy One, blessed be He, loves?"[5]

The Ideals of Study and Practice

The complementary ideals of study and practice, of Torah and *mitzvah*, are the ingredients of the Torah way. They are ideals which can never be fully realized. No matter how much Torah a Jew has studied there is always more to be studied. When a young man was asked by a distinguished rabbi whether he knew Torah he replied: "A little." "That is all any of us can hope to know," the sage observed. No matter how many *mitzvot* a Jew has carried out there are always further claims on his piety and devotion; always, in the poetic imagery of the Rabbis, there are new angels waiting to be created through man's deeds.

A Jew who takes his religion seriously must lead a student's life, at least in part. The wisdom of the Bible, the Talmud and the other classical sources of Judaism demand unremitting attention. Of equal if not greater significance is the task of "creating Torah," as the Rabbis put it. For the Torah is not something given once and for all. Its message is for each generation. Relating the eternal truths of Judaism to the challenges of the twentieth century and the fresh insights of contemporary thought is a worthy task for the true follower of Torah. That there are problems of both theory and practice for the modern Jew no one can deny. That all of these will be solved in our generation no one can affirm. A way of life need not be mapped out in all its details before one embarks on it. A good map is essential, and this the Jew has in the teachings of Jewish tradition.

FOR FURTHER READING

BOROWITZ, Eugene, *Choosing A Sex Ethic* (New York: Schocken, 1969). An introductory guide for teenagers to sexuality from a Jewish perspective. Borowitz is very much a man of modern sensibilities and thus speaks directly to contemporary young people.

FELDMAN, David, *Marriage, Birth Control and Abortion In Jewish Law,* (New York: Schocken, 1974). An outstanding detailed and nuanced discussion of fundamental issues by a distinguished conservative Rabbi.

JACOBOVITZ, Immanuel, *Jewish Medical Ethics* (New York: Bloch Publishing, 1975). A now classic exploration of basic issues raised by modern medicine. Though much has been written since its publication, it is a wonderful place to begin one's exploration of the complex issues at hand.

KAPLAN, Aryeh, *Meditation and Kabbalah,* (York Beach, ME: Weiser, 1981). In an age of the rediscovery of spirituality, this volume introduces the forms and content of Jewish meditation. Though an elementary work, it is perhaps the most reliable guide to these matters available to the beginner.

KIMELMAN, Reuven, *Tsedakah & US* (New York: National Jewish Resource Center, 1983). Philanthropy has become for many, if not most American Jews, the key form of their expression of their Jewishness. In this introductory pamphlet Kimelman explains in contemporary and available terms the religious and communal significance of this *Mitzvot.*

6 . *Torah and Society*

MORRIS ADLER

I T would be fallacious and futile to seek in Judaism a ready and adequate answer to all the social problems by which our age is perplexed. To stretch classical texts to yield solutions for complex circumstances that the propounder of those texts could not have foreseen is to misuse the wisdom of the past. Reading into those venerated words our particular partisan views is in the last analysis an attempt to sanctify our opinion with an authority beyond our own. The study of the past may in some or many instances offer guidelines, suggest directions or goals; it can never yield a blueprint for the resolution of our present dilemmas. The intricacies of contemporary social and political conditions require a knowledge of facts which in many instances can be ascertained only by specialized and highly technical study. Policies for our times that are not based on such knowledge will not be relevant to modern problems and must in the long run prove ineffective if not mischievous in arriving at their solution.

Nor is there to be found in Jewish thought, teaching or literature a rubric "social doctrine," or "social views" or "the Jew's social gospel." The views about man's social life that may be distilled out of an examination of the Jewish tradition are integral to a larger context, and their validation and rationale are to be found in the totality from which they are abstracted. Judaism is neither a sociology nor a theology in the conventional sense. It is a living, developing and responding outlook vitalized by its experience and interacting with its environment. Solomon Schechter elaborated a famous classic figure of speech applied to the great compilation of rabbinic law and lore, the Talmud:

> The Jews of olden times were wont to speak of the Talmud as *Yam Ha-Talmud*, the "sea of the Talmud." And the figure has much force. To one who has grasped its meaning and felt its spirit there is the ocean-like sense of immensity and movement. Its great broad surface is at times smooth and calm, at other times disturbed by breakers of discussion, stormy with question and answer, assertion and refutation. Its waves of argument, as they follow and tumble over one another, all give a constant sense of largeness and of motion. And to continue the figure, we find the sea fed by innumerable brooks and mighty rivers of traditional lore: we remember that these sources ran not through unbroken country, but through bad spaces and good, so that it is little wonder if, on the one hand, some of them lost volume on the way and, on the other, some of their streams were defiled and corrupted by foreign elements gathered in their course and borne into this great sea.[1]

Schechter's description of the surging sea of the Talmud is no less apt when applied to Judaism as a whole. It is a tradition that has not hardened into a dogmatic formulation; has not congealed into a structured philosophic system; has not remained imprisoned within the bound confines of its many volumes.

Woven of Many Strands

Judaism is at once a response to life in all of its cosmic expansiveness marked by intensity, passionate earnestness and moral fervor; a collective experience of a group in constant and active relations with other peoples, yet preserving a zealous belief in its unique destiny; the ecstasy of a galaxy of prophetic spirits whose words have burned themselves deep into the group-consciousness; the song of God-intoxicated psalmists who lifted their hearts to a divine Father whose presence they felt with unequalled immediacy; the legislation of wise counsellors seeking to turn the great ideals and values into the habits of daily living; the sadness of a people buffeted by hostility and oppression and uplifted by a Messianic hope which the darkness of reality could never extinguish. These and many other strands Judaism has woven together into a patterned fabric which has a consistency of design in the midst of its variety of components.

The social teachings of Judaism are thus interwoven with the whole intricate texture. They are correlated with Judaism's belief in God and its concept of man and man's relation to God. They are conditioned by the historic experiences through which Israel has passed. They are informed with the vision of great masters who taught, interpreted and applied its laws. They are affected by the depressed status which it endured as a minority. (Thorstein Veblen related the Jew's passion for social justice to the marginal position which society forced upon him.) The Jew's outlook on society is compounded of doctrine, feeling, experience, faith and historic memory.

An example may suggest the difficulty, even the impossibility, of extricating from the total synthesis the single aspect of social attitude. The greatest figure of the rabbinic epoch and very likely the greatest of all post-Biblical figures, Rabbi Akiba, found the cardinal principle of the Torah in the verse "Thou shalt love thy neighbor as thyself" (Leviticus 19:18). Incomparable legalist that he was, he saw in the Golden Rule the heart and center of Jewish teaching. Who can estimate the impact upon the minds of unnumbered generations of an emphasis given authority by one of Israel's most venerated masters? Yet there was etched into the collective spirit of the Jew the memory of his people's experience as slaves in Egypt. "Ye shall love the stranger, for ye were strangers in the land of Egypt" (Deuteronomy 10:19) is a sentiment expressed many times in the Bible. At the Passover *Seder* the Jew annually re-enacts that experience by means of vivid symbols, relives the bitterness of bondage, the alienation of the rejected as well as the exhilaration of liberation. By what measures of judgment can we determine which predisposed the Jew more decisively to a humane attitude to others: the teaching of the great masters or the memory which tradition directed him to preserve in all vigor and freshness? Experience and doctrine, tradition and history united to inspire an alert and sensitive Jewish consciousness. The further fact that the religion of Israel grew out of the life of a community which believed itself to be covenanted to God and in which its members were linked one to another by intense bonds of mutuality allowed the

Jew to carry over to his universal vision of human kinship an emotional intensity that gave it body and reality.

Doctrine and Experience

We have said that the term "theology," in the sense that it is understood in the Western world, is not present either in the Bible or the Talmud. Indeed, to this day the Hebrew language does not possess a term for this concept. For the Hebrew the belief in God was not the end of an intellectual examination and analysis; it was the great affirmation, the intense conviction with which he began. As Lou Silberman points out, the *Shema* as understood by the Rabbis "was not an abstract philosophical statement about the metaphysical being of God. It was a passionate proclamation of His providential activity in the world." [2] The God who was recognized as a result of the emotional and moral experience of Israel was a God of justice, love and righteousness. He was omnipotent and omniscient, but these attributes were secondary to His ethical nature. In a sense His power was the collateral for His justice and love. The Rabbis point out that wherever Scripture refers to God's power it also refers to His humility. The proof texts cited are "He doth execute justice for the fatherless and widow and loveth the stranger" (Deuteronomy 10:18), "With Him also that is of a contrite and humble spirit" (Isaiah 51:15), and "a father of the fatherless and a judge of the widows" (Psalm 68:6). The verses chosen indicate that the Rabbis were suggesting that God's power is always allied with His righteousness and compassion. [3] God is celebrated in the Jewish tradition more often as the Father of all men and the Sovereign of human history than as the Creator of the universe and its galaxies. Judaism is a God-centered faith whose chief concern is man. God has stamped His divine image upon man and has thus endowed him with the capacity to fulfill his destiny, which is to live in accordance with His law.

The concept *imitatio dei*, emulation by man of God's qualities, represents the highest aspiration toward which man can strive. God is not only the King who commands but the Father whose example is to be lovingly followed. The Bible says, "Ye shall walk after the Lord your God" (Deuteronomy 13:4). The

Rabbis ask how could man walk after God, who is described as a devouring fire (Deuteronomy 4:24)? The meaning, they explain, is to emulate His attributes. He clothes the naked (Genesis 3:21); He visits the sick (Genesis 18:1); He comforts the bereaved (Genesis 25:11); He buries the dead (Deuteronomy 34:6). Man should similarly perform these benevolent acts.[4]

Alfred N. Whitehead makes a perceptive distinction: "In a communal religion you study the will of God in order that He may preserve you; in a purified religion rationalized under the influence of the world concept, you study His goodness in order to be like Him. It is the difference between an enemy you conciliate and the companion whom you imitate."[5] Man has the freedom to accept this destiny or to rebel against it. Here is the arena of man's greatest dilemma and decision. Man's freedom, while exposing him to incitements to evil, also offers him the latitude to emulate on the human level the attributes which God manifests on the divine.

The above was no mere mental image of the nature of the world which Israel had fashioned. These ideas took for the Jew the form of deeply-felt convictions, which burgeoned forth into commitments and immediate consequences for his behavior and attitudes. Since man was invested at creation with a cosmic dignity, he must bear himself in an appropriate manner. Secondly, he should accord to his neighbor the honor due one as royally born as himself. One profanes God when one dishonors the divine image with which His children are instinct. Man was created singly at the beginning to dramatize the unduplicated distinctiveness and uniqueness of each individual on the one hand, and the common ancestry of all men on the other. The tension between man's individuality and his inseparableness from mankind finds its resolution in his life in a community as a free and participating member. The good society will not alone affirm and protect the individuality of each of its citizens but will also confer upon each a social dignity commensurate with his cosmic dignity.

The Deed Resides in the Thought

A whole family of principles or "value-concepts" (to use the term which Max Kadushin has so illuminatingly applied to what he terms the "organic" thinking of the Rabbis in contradistinction to philosophical thought) issues from this groundwork of conviction. As Dr. Kadushin points out, "organic thinking" does not begin with preliminary definitions and end with the structured organization of the conclusions that flow from the assumptions. Rather the value-concept springs from a particular experience and is then transposed to a conceptual term. The concept, however, is never so completely severed from the experience as to achieve sovereign intellectual detachment. Therefore, it is not given to definition, since it never becomes purely reflection or generalization; and the impact of experience continues to persist within it. Such value-concepts are motored by an inner drive to concretion. Characteristic, therefore, of Jewish classic thought is its integration of both reason and an emotional power impelling its fulfillment. The concrete is generalized, but the generalization never becomes abstract.

The social ethic of Judaism, which is an integral part of the total outlook, partakes of this general character. Every "independent" statement or law has as its frame of reference the centrality of God's rule, the nature of man and his duty to God, and man's inseparable linkage with his fellow men. The immediate teaching or decision or admonition is organically related to the Jewish view of the ultimate reality. This is what gives coherence and consistency to Judaism, despite its lack of a systematic formulation of beliefs. The ethical teaching of the sage of the first century abides in the same universe of discourse as that of the teacher of the fifth or sixth century. The total view no less than the individual judgment goes beyond the intellectual and is apprehended emotionally as a felt experience.

In order not to impose upon Jewish social teaching a structure which is inherently alien to it, we shall not proceed with a systematic delineation of its principles. We shall attempt rather, by a series of quotations, to convey something of the quality of its sensitivity and the comprehensiveness of its concern. More than to marshal a compilation of Biblical verses or rabbinic dicta, the intent is to choose such texts as suggest and represent the larger context from which they are drawn. Only thus can one capture the passion, the religious fervor and power with which the content is inspirited, and glimpse the background of belief, aspiration, piety, experience and a will to achieve what one scholar has described as a non-ecstatic experience of the holy from which it sprang. Far from exhaustive, the selections offered here seek only to intimate the spirit of the whole.

Illustrative Selections

We start with the Five Books of Moses, replete with social teachings which in turn stimulated their further extension in all of Biblical and rabbinic literature.

Abraham, pleading to God to spare Sodom if there are righteous men in the city's midst, asks the question that Israel Zangwill has described as epochal, "Shall not the Judge of all the earth do justly" (Genesis 18:25)?

The fourth of the Ten Commandments unites the social with the religious motif.

> Remember the Sabbath day to keep it holy. Six days shalt thou labor and do all thy work. But the seventh day is a Sabbath unto the Lord thy God, in it thou shalt not do any manner of work, thou, nor thy son, nor thy daughter, nor thy man-servant, nor they maid-servant nor thy cattle, nor thy stranger that is within thy gates. For in six days the Lord made heaven and earth, the sea, and all that in them is, and rested on the seventh day, wherefore the Lord blessed the Sabbath day and hallowed it.
>
> (Exodus 20:8-11)

The nineteenth chapter of Leviticus opens with an address that Moses is commanded by God to speak to the children of Israel. The prelude to the address is "Ye shall be holy; for I the Lord your God am holy." No definition of holiness is offered. The chapter, however, contains the following verses:

> And when ye reap the harvest of your land, thou shalt not wholly reap the corner of thy field, neither shalt thou gather the gleaning of thy harvest. And thou shalt not glean thy vineyard, neither shalt thou gather the fallen fruit of thy vineyard; thou shall leave them for the poor and for the stranger: I am the Lord your God . . .
>
> Thou shalt not oppress thy neighbor nor rob him; the wages of a hired servant shall not abide with thee all night until the morning . . .

Ye shall do no unrighteousness in judgment; thou shalt not respect the person of the poor, nor favor the person of the mighty, but in righteousness shalt thou judge thy neighbor . . .

Thou shalt not take vengeance, nor bear any grudge against the children of thy people, but thou shalt love thy neighbor as thyself. I am the Lord . . .

And if a stranger sojourn with thee in your land, ye shall not do him wrong. The stranger that sojourneth with you shall be unto you as the home-born among you, and thou shalt love him as thyself; for ye were strangers in the land of Egypt; I am the Lord your God. Ye shall do no unrighteousness in judgment, in meteyard, in weight or in measure. Just balances, just weights, a just ephah and a just hin, shall ye have: I am the Lord your God who brought you out of the land of Egypt.

In the Jubilee year all the land that had been sold during the 49 years was to return to the original owners so that the land would not remain the possession of the few. "And the land shall not be sold in perpetuity; for the land is Mine; for ye are strangers and settlers with Me. And in all the land of your possession ye shall grant a redemption for the land" (Leviticus 25: 23-24).

The insistence on impartial justice in the courts which stressed that the judge was to be moved neither by fear of the mighty litigant nor by sympathy for the poor man was summed up in the phrase so often cited in later literature, "Justice, justice shalt thou pursue" (Deuteronomy 16:20).

Even though slavery was a legally recognized institution under Biblical law, as it was throughout the ancient world, Scripture hedged it about with a number of humane restrictions. "Thou shalt not deliver unto his master a bondman that is escaped from his master unto thee; he shall dwell with thee, in the midst of thee, in the place which he shall choose within one of thy gates where it liketh him best; but thou shalt not wrong him" (Deuteronomy 23:16-17).[6]

The dignity and human needs and rights of the debtor or pauper were always to be safeguarded.

When thou dost lend thy neighbor any manner of loan, thou shalt not go into his house to fetch thy pledge. Thou shalt stand without, and the man to whom thou dost lend shall bring forth the pledge without unto thee. And if he be a poor man, thou shalt not sleep with his pledge. Thou shalt surely restore to him the pledge when the sun goeth down, that he may sleep in his garment and bless thee; and it shall be righteousness unto thee before the Lord thy God. Thou shalt not oppress a hired servant that is poor and needy, whether he be of thy brethren, or of thy strangers that are in thy land within thy gates. In the same day thou shalt give him his hire, neither shall the sun go down upon it; for he is poor and setteth his heart upon it; lest he cry against thee unto the Lord and it be sin in thee.

(Deuteronomy 24:10-15)

The Prophetic View

The prophets of Israel have been described as "tribunes of righteousness" and "spokesmen of God." Their God-centered, moral view of history led them to condemn with inspired fury the social evils and inequities of their own time. Their passion for righteousness and their lofty vision of the "end of days" imparted a deeper note of awareness and feeling to the entire tradition.[7]

But they shall sit every man under his vine and under his fig-tree;
And none shall make them afraid,
For the mouth of the Lord of hosts hath spoken.

(Micah 4:1-4)

Morality for the prophets—individual and social—becomes the absolute and indispensable value in the religious life. As Yehezkel Kaufmann writes,

Moral attributes are of the essence of God Himself . . . Paganism aspired to apotheosis, seeking by means of mysterious cultic rites to deify man. Israelite religion had no room for such a notion. Man cannot become God in life or afterward. But man can and must become Godlike in moral attributes.[8]

The Lord standeth up to plead
  And standeth to judge the peoples
The Lord will enter into judgment
  With the elders of His people and the princes thereof:
    "It is ye that have eaten up the vineyard;
      The spoil of the poor is in your houses;
    What mean ye that ye crush My people,
      And grind the face of the poor."
Saith the Lord, the God of hosts.

(Isaiah 3:13-15)

The anger of the prophet is especially enkindled by the oppressor of those who have no protector, namely, the orphan and widow.

Woe unto them that decree unrighteous decrees,
    And to writers that write inequity;
To turn aside the needy from judgment
    And to take away the right of the poor of My people,
That widows may be their spoil,
    And that they may make the fatherless their prey!
And what will ye do in the day of visitation,
    And in the ruin which shall come from far?
To whom will ye flee for help?
    And where will ye leave your glory?
They can do nought except crouch under the captives,
    And fall under the slain.
For all this His anger is not turned away
    But His hand is stretched out still.

(Isaiah 10:1-4)

Perhaps the most eloquent expression of the futility of ritual unaccompanied by virtue and moral behavior occurs in Isaiah. That these verses were chosen by the Rabbis to be read publicly on *Yom Kippur* is ample evidence that the entire tradition is pervaded by this prophetic idea.

Is such the fast that I have chosen?
    The day for a man to afflict his soul?
Is it to bow down his head as a bulrush,
    And to spread sackcloth and ashes under him?
Wilt thou call this a fast,
    And an acceptable day to the Lord?
Is not this the fast that I have chosen?
    To loose the fetters of wickedness,
To undo the bands of the yoke,
    And to let the oppressed go free,
And that ye break every yoke?
    It is not to deal thy bread to the hungry,
And that thou bring the poor that are cast out to thy house?
    When thou seest the naked, that thou cover him,
And that thou hide not thyself from thine own flesh?
    Then shall thy light break forth as the morning,
And thy healing shall spring forth speedily;
    And thy righteousness shall go before thee,
The glory of the Lord shall be thy reward.

(Isaiah 58:5-8)

Jeremiah, perhaps the most tragic figure among the prophets, whose name has given the English language the noun "jeremiad," saw impending catastrophe with an immediacy that gave added dimension to his sorrow. The catastrophe did come in his day, and it came upon the people he loved deeply. His plea and forewarning went unheeded. He spoke in grief-saturated syllables of his frustration and pain. The prophet in his own life represents the obligation to speak out for social justice even when to do so subjects him to defamation and persecution.

O Lord, Thou hast enticed me, and I was enticed,
   Thou hast overcome me, and hast prevailed;
I am become a laughing-stock all the day,
   Every one mocketh me.
For as often as I speak, I cry out,
   I cry, "Violence and spoil";
Because the word of the Lord is made
   A reproach unto me, and a derision, all the day.

And if I say: "I will not make mention of Him,
   Nor speak any more in His name,"
Then there is in my heart as it were a burning fire
   Shut up in my bones,
And I weary myself to hold it in,
   But cannot.

For I have heard the whispering of many,
   Terror on every side:
"Denounce, and we will denounce him";
   Even of all my familiar friends,
Them that watch for my halting:
   "Peradventure he will be enticed, and we shall prevail against
      him,
And we shall take our revenge on him."

But the Lord is with me as a mighty warrior;
   Therefore my persecutors shall stumble, and they shall not
      prevail;
They shall be greatly ashamed, because they have not prospered,
   Even with an everlasting confusion which shall never be for-
      gotten.

(Jeremiah 20:7-11)

Yet, like all the prophets, Jeremiah speaks also in accents of tenderness and immovable faith. He buys a home from a kinsman at the very moment that the Babylonian army was besieging Jerusalem and Jeremiah himself was a prisoner.[9]

The prophet is troubled by the fact that the people have become so calloused as not to recognize the evil of their wrongdoing.

> How trimmest thou thy way
>   To seek love!
> Therefore—even the wicked women
>   Hast thou taught thy ways;
>
> Also in thy skirts is found the blood
>   Of the souls of the innocent poor;
> Thou didst not find them breaking in;
>   Yet for all these things
>
> Thou saidst: "I am innocent;
>   Surely His anger is turned away from me"—
> Behold, I will enter into judgment with thee,
>   Because thou sayest: "I have not sinned."
>
>   (Jeremiah 2:33-35)

Their moral obtuseness is further augmented by an affluence that blinds them to the presence of need, oppression and injustice in many parts of their society.

> They are waxen fat, they are become sleek;
>   Yea, they overpass in deeds of wickedness;
> They plead not the cause, the cause of the fatherless,
>   That they might make it to prosper;
> And the right of the needy do they not judge.
>
> Shall I not punish for these things?
>   Saith the Lord;
> Shall not My soul be avenged
>   On such a nation as this?
>
> An appalling and horrible thing
>   Is come to pass in the land:
> The prophets prophesy in the service of falsehood,
>   And the priests bear rule at their beck;
> And My people love to have it so;
>   What then will ye do in the end thereof?
>
>   (Jeremiah 5:28-31)

Perhaps those who merit the greatest condemnation are the misleaders—the false prophets who exploit their people's weaknesses and cater to their desire for approval.

Therefore thus saith the Lord of hosts concerning the prophets:
Behold, I will feed them with wormwood,
And make them drink the water of gall;
For from the prophets of Jerusalem
Is ungodliness gone forth into all the land.

Thus saith the Lord of hosts:
Hearken not unto the words of the prophets that prophesy
unto you,
They lead you unto vanity;
They speak a vision of their own heart,
And not out of the mouth of the Lord.
They say continually unto them that despise Me:
"The Lord hath said: Ye shall have peace";
And unto every one that walketh in the stubbornness of his own
heart they say:
"No evil shall come upon you";
For who hath stood in the council of the Lord,
That he should perceive and hear His word?
Who hath attended to His word, and heard it?

Behold, a storm of the Lord is gone forth in fury,
Yea, a whirling storm;
It shall whirl upon the head of the wicked.
The anger of the Lord shall not return,
Until He have executed, and till He have performed the pur-
poses of His heart;
In the end of days ye shall consider it perfectly.
I have not sent these prophets, yet they ran;
I have not spoken to them, yet they prophesied.
But if they have stood in My council,
Then let them cause My people to hear My words,
And turn them from their evil way,
And from the evil of their doings.

(Jeremiah 23:15-22) [10]

The failure of individual character is a social calamity.

The heart is deceitful above all things,
And it is exceeding weak—who can know it?
I the Lord search the heart,
I try the reins,
Even to give every man according to his ways,
According to the fruit of his doings.

As the partridge that broodeth over young which she hath not
  brought forth,

So is he that getteth riches, and not by right;
In the midst of his days he shall leave them,
And at his end he shall be a fool.

(Jeremiah 17:9-11)

Melancholy, frustration and bitterness are frequently the lot
of the prophet whose spirit is aglow with divine fire. Despair,
however, is entirely alien to him, for it would represent a
blasphemy against the Eternal, as grievous as that which he was
condemning in his people.

Behold, the days come, saith the Lord, that I will make a new
covenant with the house of Israel, and with the house of Judah;
not according to the covenant that I made with their fathers in
the day that I took them by the hand to bring them out of the
land of Egypt; forasmuch as they broke My covenant, although
I was a lord over them, saith the Lord. But this is the covenant
that I will make with the house of Israel after those days, saith
the Lord, I will put My law in their inward parts, and in their
heart will I write it; and I will be their God and they shall be
My people; and they shall teach no more every man his neighbour,
and every man his brother, saying: "Know the Lord"; for they
shall all know Me, from the least of them unto the greatest of
them, saith the Lord; for I will forgive their iniquity, and their
sun will I remember no more.

(Jeremiah 31:31-34)

Unlike paganism and its ritual, shrines, priesthood, festivals
and mysteries, the Torah relegates the cult to a secondary place
as a means of expressing reverence for God and as an instrument
for His worship. The Ten Commandments are preponderantly
moral and social in character. Ritual is no longer the automatic
guarantee of winning the favor of the deity. As Yehezkel Kaufmann points out, the prophets "did not unconditionally repudiate
the cult or utterly deny its value." They gave such unquestioned
primacy to morality as to make the cult valueless without it.
Thus morality, individual and social, was placed at the very heart
of the Jewish religion. This view recurs in many of the prophets.

For I desire mercy, and not sacrifice,
And the knowledge of God rather than burnt-offerings.

(Hosea 6:6)

I hate, I despise your feasts,
And I will take no delight in your solemn assemblies.
Yea, though ye offer Me burnt-offerings and your meal-offerings,
I will not accept them;
Neither will I regard the peace-offerings of your fat beasts . . .
But let justice well up as waters,
And righteousness as a mighty stream.

(Amos 5:21-24) [11]

And when ye spread forth your hands,
I will hide Mine eyes from you;
Yea, when ye make many prayers,
I will not hear;
Your hands are full of blood.
Wash you, make you clean,
Put away the evil of your doings
From before Mine eyes,
Cease to do evil;
Learn to do well;
Seek justice, relieve the oppressed,
Judge the fatherless, plead for the widow.

(Isaiah 1:15-17)

With morality as the core and a universal God as the source, the Jewish religion is expanded into a universalism that encompasses all mankind. The Book of Amos opens with prophecies concerning other nations: "The prophet moves around as in the swing of a scythe of destiny from Damascus to Gaza to Tyre, to Edom and Ammon and Moab before coming at length to his own people." [12] The condemnation that is levied against these nations is based on a moral judgment. They are guilty of ethical and moral crimes which are an offense against the God of Israel, who is the God of righteousness. Israel remains at the center but is not the exclusive concern of God.

Are ye not as the children of the Ethiopians unto Me,
O children of Israel? saith the Lord.
Have not I brought up Israel out of the land of Egypt,
And the Philistines from Caphtor,
And Arm from Kir?

(Amos 9:7)

In that day shall Israel be the third with Egypt and with Assyria, a blessing in the midst of the earth; for that the Lord of hosts hath blessed him, saying: "Blessed be Egypt My People and Assyria the work of My hands, and Israel Mine inheritance.

(Isaiah 19:24-25)

The finest summary of religion is offered by the prophet Micah.

> It hath been told thee, O man, what is good,
> And what the Lord doth require of thee:
> Only to do justly, and to love mercy, and to walk humbly with
>   thy God.
>
> (Micah 6:8)

Ethical Act Is Will of God

The Book of Psalms has been called the hymnbook of mankind. The most personal of all Biblical books, it too stresses the ethical act as the will of God.

> Lord, who shall sojourn in Thy tabernacle?
> Who shall dwell upon Thy holy mountain?
> He that walketh uprightly, and worketh righteousness,
> And speaketh truth in his heart;
> That hath no slander upon his tongue,
> Nor doeth evil to his fellow,
> Nor taketh up a reproach against his neighbour;
> In whose eyes a vile person is despised,
> But he honoureth them that fear the Lord;
> He that sweareth to his own hurt, and changeth not;
> He that putteth not out his money on interest,
> Nor taketh a bribe against the innocent.
> He that doeth these things shall never be moved.
>
> (Psalm 15)

Job, in rejecting the idea advanced by his comforters that his suffering is the consequence of his sins, points to his ethical life rather than ritual observances as proof of his righteousness.

> If I did despise the cause of my man-servant,
> Or of my maid-servant, when they contended with me—
> What then shall I do when God riseth up?
> And when He remembereth, what shall I answer Him?
> Did not He that made me in the womb make him?
> And did not One fashion us in the womb?
>
> If I have withheld aught that the poor desired,
> Or have caused the eyes of the widow to fail . . .
>
> If I have seen any wanderer in want of clothing,
> Or that the needy had no covering . . .

If I have lifted up my hand against the fatherless,
Because I saw my help in the gate;
Then let my shoulder fall from the shoulder-blade,
And mine arm be broken from the bone.
For calamity from God was a terror to me,
And by reason of His majesty I could do nothing.
If I have made gold my hope . . .
If I rejoiced because my wealth was great,
And because my hand had gotten much;
If I beheld the sun when it shined,
Or the moon walking in brightness;
And my heart hath been secretly enticed,
And my mouth had kissed my hand;
This also were an iniquity to be punished by the judges;
For I should have lied to God that is above.

If I rejoiced at the destruction of him that hated me,
Or exulted when evil found him . . .
If the men of my tent said not:
"Who can find one that hath not been satisfied with his meat?"
The stranger did not lodge in the street;
My doors I opened to the roadside.
If after the manner of men I covered my transgressions,
By hiding mine iniquity in my bosom—
Because I feared the great multitude,
And the most contemptible among families terrified me,
So that I kept silence, and went not out of the door.

Oh that I had one to hear me!—
Lo, here is my signature, let the Almighty answer me—
And that I had the indictment which mine adversary hath written!
Surely I would carry it upon my shoulder;
I would bind it unto me as a crown.
I would declare unto him the number of my steps;
As a prince would I go near unto him.

If my land cry out against me,
And the furrows thereof weep together;
If I have eaten the fruits thereof without money,
Or have caused the tillers thereof to be disappointed—
Let thistles grow instead of wheat,
And noisome weeks instead of barley.

(Job 31:13-40)

The Rabbinic Approach

In rabbinic law there is a fusion of the legal and the prophetic.
As heirs of the tradition of the prophets, the Rabbis sought to

transpose the great ideals and the passion for righteousness of the seers of Israel into the key of social legislation and statute. They attempted to incorporate in their enactments not only laws governing behavior and outlining relationships, but also the faith and principle with which Biblical law is instinct. The interweaving of spirit and statute, ethical ideal and practical need are characteristic of the rabbinic approach.

Travers Herford, a Christian student of rabbinic teaching, has pointed out the kinship between the prophet and the sage.

> Between the prophets and the Pharisees there was no breach whatever. There was a change of method but not of principle. The Pharisees and the Rabbis took note of the fact that the line of the prophets had come to an end, and that they had been followed by the wise and they claimed that they were not merely *de facto* but *de jure* the successors and heirs of the prophets. "Prophecy was taken from the prophets and given to the wise; and it has not been taken from these" (*Bava Batra* 12a). The Pharisees never dreamed of repudiating the prophetic teaching. On the contrary, they desired to make it effective, to bring out, in the lives of those whom they could influence, the fruits of "godly, righteous and sober life" which the prophets would have brought out if they could. Pharisaism is applied prophecy . . .[18]

The tradition which the Rabbis espoused and interpreted was rooted in a community. A people rather than an ecclesiastical class was to be its bearer. The arena for the fulfillment of the Torah was the life of the Jewish people and beyond it—humanity. The Rabbis habitually thought in terms of community rather than of church. The individual was seen in the context of the group, for Judaism was not meant for isolation and monastic withdrawal. "Separate not thyself from the community" was an oft-repeated teaching of the saintly Hillel which was re-echoed by other teachers. The concept "worldly" with the specific connotation it received in Christianity was absent from the thought pattern of the Rabbis. The physical, economic and social were proper provinces of religious legislation. The Talmud recounts that Rabbi Huna once asked of his son Rabbah why he did not attend the lectures of Rabbi Hisda, who was noted for his wit. The son replied, "When I go to him he speaks of mundane matters; he tells about certain natural functions of the digestive organs and how one should behave with regard to them." His father rebuked him, saying, "He occupies himself with the life of God's creatures and you call that a mundane matter. All the more reason you should go to him" (*Shabbat* 82a).

The stress on social obligation was not a denial of the rightful and primary place the individual occupies in Jewish teaching. The dignity and welfare of the individual and indeed his inner development and fulfillment (to borrow modern terms) are fostered by a society in which men are responsive to their duty to one another and to God. A few selections from rabbinic teaching indicate this trend.

Man was created a single individual to teach us that whoever destroys one life, Scripture ascribes it to him as though he had laid waste to the entire world, and whoever rescues one life, Scripture accounts it to him as though he had saved the whole world.
(*Sanhedrin* 4:5)

He who publicly humiliates his neighbor is, as it were, guilty of murder.
(*Bava M'tzia* 58b)

Rabbi Akiba was wont to say, "Beloved is man in that he was created in the divine image. Special love was extended to him in that he was created in the image of God as it is said (Genesis 9:6) —in the image of God made He man."
(*Ethics of the Fathers* 3)

Whoever hateth any man hateth Him who spoke and the world came into existence.
(*Sifre Zuta* 18)

The verse states "Happy is he that considereth the poor" (Psalms 41:2). Note, said Rabbi Jonah, it is not written "happy is he that giveth to the poor" but "that considereth the poor." Consider well how to help him without offending his dignity.
(*Leviticus Rabbah* 34)

He who gives alms to the poor is rewarded with six blessings; he who speaks kindly to him is rewarded with eleven blessings.
(*Bava Batra* 9b)

When a needy person stands at your door God Himself stands at his side.
(*Leviticus Rabbah* 34:9)

The act of charity is measured by the lovingkindness with which it is administered.
(*Sukkah* 49b)

If a man inflicted a wound on his fellow, he becomes liable on five counts: for injury, for pain, for healing, for loss of time and for indignity inflicted. "For injury"—thus if he blinded his fellow's eye, cut off his hand or broke his foot, his victim is looked upon as if he were a slave to be sold and the diminution in his worth is assessed. "For pain"—if he burnt his fellow with a spit or a nail— it is estimated how much money one would be willing to take to suffer so. "For healing"—he must assume the cost of healing which was occasioned by the hurt he did to his fellow. "For loss of time"—he is looked upon as watchman since having been paid for the injury to hand or foot, he is now capable only of acting in the capacity of watchman of a field. "For indignity inflicted"— in accordance with the station in life of him who inflicted it and of him who suffered it.

(Mishnah Bava Kama 8:1)

Even though a man pays him who suffers the indignity, he is not forgiven until he seeks forgiveness from the victim.

(Ibid., 7)

The slave and the thief are not beyond the purview of the law's concern and interest. For law that is bound up with morality and religion goes beyond the preservation of order and the maintenance of justice. The violator and the submerged are objects of its interest and compassion.

If a man was half bondman and half freedman (having been jointly owned by two partners, only one of whom gave him his freedom), he should labor one day for his master and one day for himself. This was the view of the School of Hillel. The School of Shammai dissented, "You have arranged it well for his master, but not for the slave. Seeing that he is half free, he may not marry a bondwoman; being half slave he may not marry a free woman. Is he then never to marry? Was not the world created for fruition and increase, as it is written? He created it not a waste, but formed it to be inhabited" (Isaiah 45:18). In the interest of human welfare, the master is instructed to set him free and the bondman writes him a note of indebtedness for half his value. The School of Hillel was persuaded and changed its view to conform to that of the School of Shammai.

(Mishnah Gittin 4:5)

If a man stole a beam and built it into a structure, he need only repay its value, although from a strictly legal point of view the original owner has the right to demand that he tear down the structure and restore the original beam to him. This amendment was enacted in order not to discourage the thief from penitence by imposing the full severity of the law upon him.

(Mishnah Gittin 5:5)

Property rights are never absolute. The community through the court has the right to subordinate an individual's property to public welfare. A well found in a field privately owned was to be made available to the people of the nearby town. Profits are subject to limitations set by the community. Necessities in particular were not to be sold at inordinate profit. In rabbinic times overseers were appointed to prevent overcharges by unscrupulous merchants. There were communal inspectors to watch that the scales and measures were honest.

Intent is particularly significant in a legal system that functions in the context of a religious ethic.

Even as the law prohibits fraud in buying and selling, it forbids fraud that is perpetrated solely by the spoken word. A man may not say (to a merchant) "how much does this article cost?" if he has no real intention of making a purchase (the fraud is found in the fact that he raises the merchant's hopes falsely). To a sinner who has repented one may not speak of his former deeds. One is forbidden to say to a man descended from proselytes, "remember the deeds of thy father," for it is written (Exodus 22:20) "a stranger shalt thou not wrong, nor shalt thou oppress him."

(Mishnah Bava M'tzia 4:10)

What Is Required of Man

The Rabbis said that *G'milut Hasadim*—the performance of deeds of lovingkindness—is superior in three respects to charity. Charity can be done only with one's money, while *G'milut Hasadim* can be done with one's person as well as with one's money. Charity can be given only to the poor, while *G'milut Hasadim* can be extended both to the rich and poor. Charity can be given to the living alone. *G'milut Hasadim* can be done both to the living and to the dead. But charity is not a substitute for justice, for the Talmud recognized that it is easier to be generous than just.

The Talmud considers it unworthy to give charity when one does not pay his debts or give his employees a proper wage.[14]

The giving of alms does not condone unjust practices, and one should not make charity a means for personal advantage.[15]

The rights of labor were recognized and the dignity of labor upheld. A parent was obligated to teach his son a trade. The Rabbis of Talmudic times engaged in worldly occupations for their own support. We hear of sages who were woodchoppers, blacksmiths, bakers, cobblers, scribes, gravediggers and merchants. There was a limit set upon the hours that hired help were permitted to work. Workers were permitted to join together and set a wage scale. Employers were forbidden to pay their labor in kind, since this exposed the worker to the risk of receiving inferior goods appraised at inflated prices. Where meals were included in the stipulated compensation, the employer was obliged to provide the highest quality of food. A laborer's wages were not to be reduced during a period of absence caused by illness.[16] The worker was forbidden to work in his field by night and hire himself out for the day, since he would not bring to his work the full measure of his energy.

In rabbinic times a hostel was attached to each synagogue so that no wayfarer would remain without shelter. Honored and trusted collectors went forth weekly to solicit contributions for the support of the needy. A fund called *Tamhui* was used to distribute food and victuals, and a fund called *Kuppah* disbursed money to the needy. The poor of each municipality received every Friday assistance sufficient for a full week for themselves and their families. Orphans were supported out of community funds and dowries were provided for poor or orphaned brides. Free burial of the indigent was part of each community's responsibility. The fund that stirred the deepest sentiment, and which existed till late in the Middle Ages, was *Pidyon Sh'vuyim* —the fund for redemption of captives held for ransom.

But helping a man was not exhausted by providing him recurringly with the elementary necessities. The responsibility of the community was to raise him out of the condition of dependence to the status of a self-supporting individual.

The Bible says, "If thy brother be waxen poor and his hand fail with thee, then thou shalt uphold him, yea, though he be a stranger or a sojourner that he may live with thee" (Leviticus 25:35). This means, says the Talmud, that you are obligated to provide him with means whereby he can live.[17] In another part of the Talmud the idea is stressed that he who lends money to the poor earns greater merit than he who gives alms. Best of all is he who invests money with a poor man in partnership.[18] It is in conformity with this rabbinic concept that Maimonides, in enumerating eight degrees of charity, places on the topmost rung of benevolence the giving of a loan to a poor man or finding him employment or setting him up as partner.[19] Hence in every tradition-governed Jewish community there was a *G'milut Ḥesed* society for the purpose of granting to those in need loans without security or interest.

The goals of both collective and individual striving are suggested by the rabbinic comment, "The world exists by reason of three things, truth, justice and peace. As it is written (Zechariah 8:16) 'Truth and judgment of truth and peace judge ye in your gates' " (*Ethics of the Fathers* 1:18). A further comment adds, "The three are in reality one, for when justice is done, truth prevails and peace is established" (Jerusalem Talmud *Ta'anit* 4:2). The government is a means to these ends. When it sees itself as absolute and makes its power or aggrandizement the be-all and end-all of its effort, it blasphemes against God. The concept for so long honored that "the king can do no wrong" was rejected by Judaism, which believed God to be the Source of law and justice its goal. The "right of sovereignty" should be subordinate to the "sovereignty of right." The nemesis that haunts human history arises from the pathetic fallacy that turns means into ends and instrumentalities into purposes. Government exists not only because men are evil and must be restrained, but also because men are good and should be aided. When government, however, moves beyond its proper domain as a suppressor of the evil and a promoter of the good in men and invades the domain of the God-given "inalienable rights" of its citizens (rights which it did not confer and which it has no authority to revoke), it becomes a *malkhut har'sha'ah*) or *memshelet zadon*, an evil and wicked empire.

It becomes the responsibility of each alert and high-minded individual to resist the encroachments upon justice, truth and peace which constitute the foundations of freedom. No man may stand aside and remain neutral in the ongoing struggle to achieve in human life a fuller approximation of virtue and righteousness. To abdicate such an obligation is to abet the forces of evil and to become an accomplice in the perpetuation of wrong. "Whoever is able to protest against the transgression of his household and fails to do so, will suffer the penalty of their sins; whoever is able to protest against the transgressions of his city or indeed the misdeeds of all mankind and fails to do so, becomes accountable for their sins" (*Shabbat* 54b). Apathy becomes a sin of commission, increasing the decadence that prevails.

Erich Fromm has indicated that religion, which has won such eminent respectability and wide acceptance in terms of its doctrines and values, meets defeat on the field of the daily practices, norms and mores which men habitually follow. The Rabbis read a man's theology not in his professions and creedal affirmations but in his customary actions. The faith in God which does not culminate in service to man is a mockery. One of the Rabbis was asked by a philosopher: "Who is the most hateful man in the world?" The sage replied, "The man who denies his Creator." Pressed to explain, the Rabbi elaborated, "Honor thy father and mother; thou shalt not murder; thou shalt not commit adultery; thou shalt not steal; thou shalt not bear false witness against thy neighbor; thou shalt not covet—behold, a person does not repudiate any of these laws before he has repudiated the Root from which they sprang (namely, God who ordained them). One does not commit a sinful act without first denying Him who prohibited it" (*Tosefta Sh'vuot* 3:6).

What then does it mean to believe in God? "How does a man find his Father who is in heaven? He finds Him by good deeds and the study of Torah. The Holy One blessed be He finds man through love, brotherhood, truth, peace, humility, study; through a good heart; through a NO that is a firm NO and a YES that is a firm YES" (*Seder Eliahu Rabbah* 23).

FOR FURTHER READING

LANDES, Daniel, editor, *Omnicide: Jewish Responses To The Nuclear Peril* (Los Angeles: Simon Wiesenthal Center, 1985) The key issue of our time discussed from many differing Jewish perspectives. An important volume and the place to begin one's study of the Jewish view of nuclear destruction.

KONVITZ, Milton, *Judaism & Human Rights* (New York: W.W. Norton, 1972). A valuable collection of essays on one of the critical issues of our time.

KONVITZ, Milton, *Judaism & The American Idea* (Ithaca, N.Y.: Cornell University Press, 1978). A significant meditation on the meaning of America from the Jewish perspective.

TWERSKY, Isadore, "Judaism & The Welfare State", In Norman Lamm and Walter S. Wurtzburger, Editors, *Treasury of Tradition* (New York: Hebrew Publishing Co., 1967). A master Jewish scholar reflects on one of the central issues of contemporary socio-political life.

7 . *Study as a Mode of Worship* *

NATHAN ISAACS

T H E   A N C I E N T world knew many ways of expressing man's devotion to his God or his idol: fasting and feasting, abstinence and orgies, caressing and pelting with stones, magic divination. Small wonder that Israel had to be warned not only against the worship of strange gods, but against strange worship of the true God: "Thou shalt not do so unto the Lord, thy God; for every abomination to the Lord, which He hateth, have they done unto their gods; for even their sons and their daughters do they burn in the fire to their gods" (Deuteronomy 12:31).

Among the carefully selected methods of worshipping God that were open to Jews, perhaps the most important one, and one unknown among the gentiles, was the *mitzvah* of *Talmud Torah*. The study of Torah is not merely a means to an end; it is in itself a highly meritorious act and a mode of worship. This notion had its origin in Judaism and has served the needs of Jews and Judaism peculiarly well. It was the non-Jewish scholar George Foot Moore who recognized in the rabbinic zeal for learning a true religious enthusiasm: "This conception of individual and collective study as a form of divine service has persisted in Judaism through all ages, and has made not only the learned by profession but men of humble callings in life assiduous students of the Talmud as the pursuit of the highest branch of religious learning and the most meritorious of good works." [1]

There are three senses in which Torah study may be referred

* Adapted and reprinted with permission from *The Jewish Library*, first series, edited by Leo Jung (Macmillan, N. Y., 1928).

to as a method of worship among the Jews. First, it is reckoned as a *mitzvah,* and one of such importance that its regular performance is to be assured by incorporation into the daily ritual. Second, Torah study ranks as worship even in the narrowest sense because it takes the place, according to Jewish doctrine, of the altar service of old. Finally, in a much more significant sense, Torah study is worship because it brings the Jew and his God into closer contact. It is the direct course leading to *Da'at Elohim,* "knowledge of God," which is the nearest Hebrew equivalent of "religion."

Torah as Mitzvah Incorporated in the Liturgy

The Biblical commands are found chiefly in Deuteronomy:

Make them known unto thy children and thy children's children (4:9): "And the words which I command thee this day shall be upon thy heart . . ." (6:6).[2]

When thy son asketh thee in time to come saying: "What mean the testimonies and the statutes and the ordinances which the Lord, our God, hath commanded you?" then shalt thou say unto thy son: "We were bondsmen . . . and the Lord commanded us to do all these statutes" (6:20-24).

And Moses commanded them [the priests and elders] saying: "At the end of every seven years, in the set time of the year of release, in the feast of tabernacles, when all Israel is come to appear before the Lord thy God, in the place which He shall choose, thou shalt read this law before all Israel in their hearing. Assemble the people, the men and the women and the little ones, and the stranger that is within thy gates, that they may hear, and that they may learn, and fear the Lord your God, and observe to do all the words of this law; and that their children, who have not known, may hear and learn to fear the Lord your God, as long as ye live in the land whither ye go over the Jordan to possess it" (31:10-13).

Closely related to the idea of learning and teaching are those sentences which prescribe the publication of the laws, the writing of them and the use of devices calculated to keep the people reminded of them, to keep them, so to speak, constantly at hand and before the eyes.[3]

In order to understand the role of Torah as *mitzvah* as part of the liturgy, it is necessary to understand the way in which the Book of Deuteronomy is organized. It consists of four orations, a song, and the blessing of Moses, with a code of laws inserted between the second and the third oration. The code is the thing talked about or sung about in all of the other parts of the book. It is the document referred to when the other parts speak of "these words which I command thee this day" or "the statutes and the ordinances which I command thee this day."

The first oration (1:6-4:40) is an historical introduction that warms up to an admonition "lest thou forget the things which thine eyes saw." It is also an appeal to the Israelites in the name of history to appreciate their Torah, which is destined to constitute their wisdom and their understanding in the sight of the peoples: "Ask now of the days past, which were before thee, since the day that God created man upon the earth and from the one end of heaven unto the other, whether there hath been any such thing as this great thing is, or hath been heard like it. Did ever a people hear the voice of God speaking out of the midst of the fire, as thou hast heard, and live?"

The second oration (5:8-9:32) calls attention to underlying principles. It contains the Ten Commandments, the *Shema* and the grand summary: "And now, Israel, what doth the Lord thy God require of thee, but to fear the Lord thy God, to walk in all His ways, and to love Him, and to serve the Lord thy God with all thy heart, and with all thy soul; to keep for thy good the commandments of the Lord, and His statutes, which I command thee this day?"

The code, including a group of laws cast into the impressive form of a curse, occupies sixteen chapters (12-27). The third oration is a plea on social and political grounds (28) in which obedience to the Law is pointed out as the road to public welfare and disobedience as the road to national ruin. It contains the great *tokhaḥah* or admonition.

The fourth oration (29:1-31:8) represents an approach to Torah through individual ethics. It is the beginning of individual religion: "Ye are standing this day all of you before the Lord your God, your heads, your tribes, your elders and your little ones, your wives, and the stranger that is in the midst of thy camp, from the hewer of thy wood unto the drawer of thy water." All that stood here that day and also they that were not there are included.

From this outline it is clear that the passages on *Talmud Torah* are not a part of the code; they are its frame. They are not ordinary precepts, but stand out against the whole of the Law, coordinate with all the rest of it put together. When the lawgiver says, "these words, I command thee this day" and "my commandments which I command you this day," in two passages known to every Jew, he is not referring to any formula. It is the whole code, the *mishneh ha-torah*, that "shall be upon thine heart," that "thou shalt teach diligently unto thy children," that "thou shalt talk of when thou sittest in thine house, and when thou walkest by the way." In fact, the sense of the text is not satisfied unless the whole code is represented in the sign upon the hand, the frontlets between the eyes, on the doorposts of the homes and at the city gates. The Jewish practice of posting an ordinance, with its command to teach and to teach again, to talk of and to publish and to keep before the mind and ready at hand the whole of the Law, embodies the commandment of *Talmud Torah*, which is the equivalent of all the other commandments put together.

Laws Governing the Learning and Teaching of Torah

Throughout Jewish history the ordinances as to learning and teaching Torah have been taken to heart. Study and teaching have been put into the ritual as an element of worship. The laws governing this fall into two groups: those dealing with the reading of the Torah on stated occasions (such as holidays, New Moons, Sabbaths, Mondays and Thursdays) so that three successive days could never pass without some public reading from the Torah; and those concerned with insuring a minimum of Torah study daily and nightly by each Jew.

The synagogue reading is subject to elaborate regulation. Though the cycle for the completion of the Five Books differed in Palestine and Babylonia, there were traditional principles as to the types of passages with which to begin and end, as to what breaks were proper, and numerous other details that have been embodied in the annual cycle that now predominates in most parts of Jewry. Strict rules were also laid down as to the accuracy of the handwritten scroll from which the reading was to take place, as to who could and who must be called up to read from the scroll or stand by during the reading and pronounce the prescribed blessings. Special portions for special Sabbaths, the selection of appropriate companion pieces from the prophets for *haftarot*, the study by the individual to supplement the reading, twice in the original and once in the *Targum* (the Aramaic translation)—these are topics on which thought has been concentrated throughout the history of the synagogue.

The second branch of study appearing in the liturgy sheds light on Jewish services. I speak of services rather than of prayer because the word "prayer" in its original and ordinary sense is misleading when used in connection with Judaism. Praying or asking for what we selfishly desire, that is, the use of *t'hinot* (for matters other than forgiveness), forms a remarkably small part of Jewish liturgy. It is practically excluded from the Sabbath and festival services. Even the week-day Eighteen Benedictions must be changed on those days because they contain too many allusions to our daily cares.

What, then, are the contents of Jewish services? They are words of praise and thanksgiving to the Lord, confessions of our imperfections and words of high resolve, declarations of faith and of love for God and His Torah and recitations of historical narratives constituting a kind of philosophy of history. All of these elements ask for nothing; they are merely wholesome meditation. Then there is the intenser meditation—study.

Torah in the Prayer Book

The early portion of the morning service is devoted largely to the commandment of Torah study. It includes the opening words of the *Mishnah Pe'ah* in which Torah study is glorified among the commandments for which no maximum is set and among those whose fruits are enjoyed in this world while the stock remains for the world to come. It is equal to all the rest of these commandments put together. Among the first benedictions in the service is that which is intended to precede the Torah study of the day:

Blessed art Thou, O Lord our God, King of the Universe, who hast sanctified us by Thy commandments, and commanded us to occupy ourselves with the words of the Law. Make pleasant, therefore, we beseech Thee, O Lord our God, the words of Thy Law in our mouth and in the mouth of Thy people, the house of Israel, so that we with our offspring and the offspring of Thy people, the house of Israel, may all know Thy name and learn Thy Law; Blessed art Thou, O Lord, who teachest the Law to Thy people Israel. Blessed art Thou, O Lord, our God, King of the Universe, who hast chosen us from all nations and given us Thy Law. Blessed art Thou, O Lord, who givest the Law.

(*B'rakhot* 11)

The last part will be recognized as the very words of the first blessing pronounced by one who is honored by an *aliyah*, an invitation to officiate at the reading of the Torah. In the service it is immediately followed by three Biblical verses, the minimum number constituting a connected passage requiring the recitation of the blessing. The three verses chosen here are those of the priestly blessing.

Then to complete the threefold cord of learning that the Rabbis have prescribed, we read passages from the Mishnah and the *G'mara*. Also included as an element of learning are the thirteen principles of interpretation of Rabbi Ishmael. We pass then through the meditative "verses of praise" and come upon Torah study again in the *Shema* paragraphs and the blessings that surround them. These take up the subject matter of the first books of the Bible with the Torah represented by the *Shema* in its historical setting. The first blessing has to do with creation, the second with Israel's selection, and the third with its redemption.[4]

In the evening service the *Shema* is placed in a similar setting. The Rabbis looked upon the reading of the *Shema* as a satisfactory minimum of Bible study, yet they were cautious not to mislead the ignorant by giving undue publicity to this view (*M'nahot* 99). Naturally they devoted much attention to the time and place and conditions of the recitation of the *Shema* (e.g., at the beginning of *B'rakhot*) and not once did it occur to them to think any the less of it as a service because they saw in it a fulfillment of the obligation to study. The one idea embraced the other.

Study as a Substitute for Specific Temple Service

To understand the second phase of the identification of study
with worship we revert to the peculiar choice of Mishnah and
G'mara passages in the services to complete, with the Bible
passages, the threefold cord. The Mishnah passage deals with
details of the sacrifices in the Temple, and the *G'mara* passage
with the burning of incense there. With these are recited Biblical
references to the regular daily sacrifice and other details of the
Temple cult.

In the light of a Jewish doctrine that the study of these passages is the equivalent of the performance of the commandments
therein, this part of the service is a substitute for the Temple
service and thus constitutes an unbroken tradition of *avodah* in
the strictest sense of the word. A passage printed in some of the
larger prayer books gives voice to this theory:

> Sovereign of the Universe, Thou didst command us to offer the
> daily sacrifice at its appointed time; and that the priests be at their
> service, and the Levites on their platform and the Israelites at their
> station. But now, because of our sins, the Temple is laid waste and
> the daily sacrifice is discontinued. We have no priest at his service,
> no Levite on the platform, no Israelite at his station. But Thou
> hast said of us, "We shall render for bullocks the offering of our
> lips (Hosea 14:3)." Therefore may it please Thee, O Lord our
> God, and the God of our Fathers, that the words of our lips be
> accounted, accepted and esteemed before Thee as the equivalent
> of having offered the daily sacrifice at its appointed time and
> having stood at our station.

Study as Religious Activity Outside of the Liturgy

It would be misleading, however, to argue, as is sometimes
done, that Jewish devotion to learning has come about as a result
of the loss of everything else that seemed of significance in
Jewish life—national independence, homeland, the sanctuary,
the priesthood. In this connection the story of Johanan ben
Zakkai is sometimes repeated: at the fall of Jerusalem he saved
Judaism by establishing a place where the study of the Torah
could go on.

But it is idle to seek the beginning of the importance attributed to Torah study so late in Jewish history. The Bible is full of it. Psalm One declares that man happy whose "delight is in the Law of the Lord; and in his Law does he meditate day and night." The Nineteenth Psalm begins: "The Law of the Lord is perfect, restoring the soul." And the longest of all psalms, the Hundred and Nineteenth, is an eightfold acrostic poem in every verse of which there is a synonym for the Torah. Isaiah (2:3) and Micah (4:2) look forward to the time when Torah will go forth from Zion and the word of the Lord from Jerusalem. Jeremiah even while rebuking Israel bears witness to their pride and confidence that the Law of the Lord is with them (Jeremiah 8:7). The last of the prophets calls on Israel to remember the Law of Moses (Malachi 3:22).

There is hardly a break between this Biblical commendation of the study of the Law and the Midrashic and Talmudic elaboration of it. One need only turn to the sixth chapter of *Ethics of the Fathers*, every line of which sets learning above the priesthood and kingship. In fact the *talmid ḥakham* of illegitimate birth outranks an illiterate high priest in the estimation of the Rabbis.

In all these discussions the Rabbis are too practical to overlook the tremendous importance of the study of Torah as a means to an end. Sometimes they stress the relative importance of the works to which it leads a little more than at others. But they never forget that it is also an end in itself. It is best to study for the purpose of mastering and teaching, of keeping and performing the Law; but it is also worth while to study without reference to putting the teachings into practice. Nay, we are advised to study regardless of our motive, for, beginning *lo' lishmah* (not for its own sake), one comes naturally to a point where he studies *lishmah* (for its own sake), that is, with the proper intent (*P'saḥin* 50). It is important to bear in mind this Jewish feeling that Torah study is a good act in itself if we are to estimate its meaning in Judaism as a form of worship.

There have, of course, been several reactions in Jewish history against the exaltation of learning as an end in itself. Something akin to this prevailed in the troublous times that gave birth to Christianity, and was taken advantage of by those trying to sway the masses. Something of the sort has also cropped out occasionally among Jewish mystics, medieval and modern. But at

no time in Jewish history has Jewish respect for learning fallen
so low that it could not serve the body of Israel as a means of
communion with God.[5]

Torah in Jewish Tradition

There is a traditional Jewish attitude behind this feeling
toward learning. It is the attitude that mothers pour into cradle
songs that foretell careers for their children as men of learning.
I can find no other cradle songs that dream of intellectual
achievement. The same trait is reflected in Jewish hero-tales. The
heroes are intellectual giants who have wrestled with difficult
Torah questions. We need only remember how the Anglo-
Saxons found even the partly illiterate founders of Christianity
too intellectual for their poetic needs and converted them into a
chieftain with twelve warriors bold who went forth to battle
with shining helmets.

In like manner but in a different spirit the *Haggadists* could
imagine Father Jacob spending his youth in no more appropriate
way than in study in the tents of Shem and Eber. No question is
entertained about the familiarity of the outstanding figures of
Israel, even the crude Jephthah, to say nothing of David and
Solomon, with the *Halakhah*. A villain to assume heroic propor-
tions must be as learned as Doeg and Ahithophel. The readiness
to see beauty, heroism and joy as well as duty, piety and intrinsic
worth in Torah study is the quality that has made the Jew fit to
use the Torah as an instrument of worship. But the ritual is only
a beginning.

The Duty of Daily Study

Daily study is a duty for every Jew. The synagogues have
never ceased reverberating with the hum of Bible groups, Mishnah and *G'mara* groups, and even groups for the study of mystic
literature. In connection with the public reading of the Torah,
the practice of interpreting and explaining at great length led to
the development of the sermon. True, this custom fell into decay
in the Middle Ages but it has recently been revived not only as
a substitute for something else in the service, as among the early

Reformers, but as a supplement to the prescribed amount of Torah study as it was in former times.

We can imagine the confusion of the ancient Greeks and Romans who peered into the Jewish synagogues and failed to see anything that reminded them of their temples. There were no images, no sacrifices, no ceremonies—nothing but a school so far as they could see. The early Christians, of course, copied the services of the synagogue. Soon, however, it was found difficult to keep the gentiles interested in the long excerpts from the wanderings of the ancestors of the Jews in the wilderness and from their "obsolete" laws. Gradually the intellectual element of the Christian liturgy, which had come from the Jews, was submerged in the sacramental part, which came from the pagans. All that was left of the teaching in the synagogue, so often spoken of in the Christian Bible, was the sermon, which had become an inspirational talk loosely connected with a brief text often wrested from its context.

A revival of interest in study has marked the liturgy of several Protestant sects in their beginnings, but the intellectual element has almost invariably been suppressed in the end or relegated to the Sunday-school class. Study is not ranked among the Christian methods of worship. It is missing, for example, in William James' well-known *Varieties of Religious Experience*.

Rabbi Halaphta ben Dosa said: "When ten people sit together and occupy themselves with the Torah, the divine presence abides among them." And the same is applied to five, or three, or two, and finally even to one. The inner satisfaction of hours spent in such nearness to the *Sh'khinah* illumines the popular Jewish picture of the world-to-come, a place where the righteous sit crowned, enjoying the splendor of the *Sh'khinah* (*B'rakhot* 17a). The exalted feeling of having well done a task divinely appointed, a task in which man proves himself most God-like, that comes from having mastered a particularly difficult bit of Torah, explains much of the devotion to learning for which Jews have long been remarkable. But then the capacity for experiencing that exaltation in learning is indispensable for keeping Torah study effective as a means of worship. This capacity is to a remarkable degree the peculiar inheritance of Israel. "He hath not dealt so with any nation; And as for His ordinances, they have not known them" (Psalm 147:20).

FOR FURTHER READING

BERNSTEIN, Marver, H., "Learning as Worship" A Jewish Perspective on Higher Education", in Raphael Jospe & Samuel Z. Fishman editors, *Go & Study Essays and Studies in Honor of Alfred Jospe* (B'nai B'rith Hillel Foundation, Washington, D.C.: 1980). An introduction to one of the building blocks of the Jewish tradition.

HEILMAN, Samuel C., *The People of the Book*, (Chicago: University of Chicago Press, 1983). A wonderful evocation of the spiritual significance of study within the context of modern Judaism.

HELMREICH, William, *The World of the Yeshiva* (New York: Free Press, 1982) introduces the too often misunderstood, closed world of high Jewish scholarship to outsiders.

HOLTZ, Barry, Editor, *Back to the Sources: Reading the Classic Jewish Texts* (New York: Summit Books, 1984). An extremely well conceived anthology of essays introducing most of the major areas of classical Jewish scholarship.

SOLOVEITCHIK, Joseph, *Halachic Man*, (Philadelphia: Jewish Publication Society, 1984). A masterful English translation by Lawrence Kaplan of Soloveitchik's classic reflections on the profound inner meaning of Talmudic study and behavior.

ZBOROWSKI, Mark, "The place of Book-Learning in Traditional Jewish Culture" in Margaret Mead and Martha Wolfenstein editors, *Childhood in Contemporary Cultures*. (Chicago: University of Chicago Press, 1965). The reflections of a distinguished anthropologist on the role study plays in Jewish education and culture.

8 . "Thou Shalt Teach"

SAMUEL M. BLUMENFIELD

THE TERM Torah has been used in a variety of ways. In the broad sense it connotes the sum of the Jewish spiritual and cultural heritage. But in its literal meaning, Torah is instruction, derived from the Hebrew root *yaroh*—"to cast," "to direct," "to teach."

Although Jewish tradition speaks of 613 precepts, in the course of the ages the precept of studying Torah has been accorded pre-eminence over all the others. Some two thousand years ago the Rabbis declared: "These are the things for which a man enjoys the fruits in this world, while the principal remains for him in the world-to-come: honoring father and mother, the practice of charity, and making peace between man and his fellow man; but the study of Torah outweighs them all" (*Pe'ah* 1:1). Another rabbinic source maintains: "The world stands on three things: on Torah, on worship and on acts of lovingkindness" (*Ethics of the Fathers* 1:2). Torah is first in the sequence.

Torah Study in Biblical Literature

The Bible contains numerous references to the duty, value, glory and exaltation that come with study and observance. There is hardly an endearing term in the Hebrew language that is not associated with the idea of Torah. The psalmist supplicates: "Open mine eyes that I may behold wondrous things out of Thy Torah" (Psalms 119:18). Its virtues and praises are sung in a variety of ways: "The Torah of the Lord is perfect, restoring the soul"; "Great peace have they that love Thy Torah"; "Thy Torah is in my inmost parts" (Psalms 19:8; 119:165; 40:9).

The objective of Torah study, as stressed in Biblical writings, is to inspire the fear of the Lord and to cultivate the love of man. A frequent synonym for education is *Hokhmah*, or quest for wisdom, and *Da'at Elohim*, knowledge of God, indicating that Torah enables man to choose good over evil.

Unlike the Western tradition which has associated education primarily with instruction of children, Judaism makes the study of Torah mandatory upon adults: "The book of the Torah shall not depart out of thy mouth, but thou shalt meditate thereon day and night" (Joshua 1:8). In turn they are bidden to impart it to their children (Deuteronomy 6:7).

Nor was the study of Torah limited to the priesthood or nobility, as in the ancient and medieval world. It was to become "an inheritance of the congregation of Jacob" (Deuteronomy 33:4), hence the concern of the entire community. The prophet Isaiah (Eighth Century B.C.E.) even aspired to the age when "all thy children shall be taught of the Lord" (Isaiah 54:13). The ideal of universal education inspired later generations to provide schooling for all children.

There is hardly any mention in the Bible of a school or institution devoted to education. Teaching in ancient Israel, as among other ancient peoples, was relegated to the family, particularly to the father, who was to train his sons in necessary skills as well as in religious precepts and observances.

> For He established a testimony in Jacob
> And appointed a law in Israel,
> Which He commanded our fathers,
> That they should make them known to their children;
> That the generation to come might know them, even the children
>   that should be born;
> Who should arise and tell them to their children.
>
>   (Psalms 78:5-7)

There are also Biblical references to instruction by Levites, priests, prophets and sages on the Sabbath, festivals and special assemblies.[1] These were in the nature of narratives, sermons, poems, proverbs and parables. In addition, special mentors and instructors taught the children of priests and nobility and leaders or "sons of prophets." [2]

Torah in Rabbinic Tradition

Rabbinic literature, like the Bible, abounds in praise for Torah and for its students and teachers. "The world was created only for the sake of the Torah" (*Genesis Rabbah* 1:4): "The more Torah the more life," "Torah is above priesthood and royalty," "Only he is free who is engaged in the study of Torah" (*Ethics of the Fathers* 2:8; 6:6; 6:2). Indeed, the Almighty Himself is engaged in the study and teaching of Torah and He proclaims, "Would they had forsaken Me but kept My Torah" (*Hagiga* 1:7).

Unlike the days of the Bible when teaching was essentially a family responsibility, education in post-Biblical Palestine became increasingly the concern of the community. The rise of Pharisaism marks a milestone in Jewish culture as instruction ceased to be the inherited prerogative of the priesthood and became the responsibility of every Israelite. In the rabbinic tradition, Torah implies both studying and teaching, learning and doing, contemplating and following precepts, authority yet not finality.

The Rabbis paid special attention to the obligation of teaching children: "The world exists because of school children," "A community which does not provide schooling for children is to be demolished," "The teaching of children should not be interrupted even for the building of the Holy Temple" (*Shabbat* 119b). "He who teaches a friend's son Torah is as though he gave him birth" (*Sanhedrin* 19b, 99b).

Two Talmudic statements present specific information about the establishment of elementary schools. One is associated with a leading Pharisee, Rabbi Simon, the son of Shetaḥ (first century B.C.E.), about whom it is recorded that he "arranged that children should go to school." The other refers to Joshua ben Gamala (first century C.E.), of whom it is said, "But for him the Torah would have been forgotten among Israel. Formerly he who had a father was taught the Torah by him, but he who had no father did not learn it . . . until Joshua ben Gamala came and arranged that teachers should be placed in every province and in every city, and that pupils should be admitted at the age of six or seven" (*Bava Batra* 21a).

In a discussion between two scholars of the fourth century,

one asked, "Is it possible to find any Jew without an elementary education?" He was answered, "Yes, it is possible—a child taken captive by non-Jews" (*Sh'vuot* 5a).

Other sources point to the spread of schooling as a community enterprise. The historian Josephus (37-95 C.E.) wrote, "We take most pains of all with the instruction of children, and esteem the observation of the laws and the piety corresponding with them." [3] The philosopher Philo, of about the same period, maintained, "Since the Jews esteem their laws as divine revelations and are instructed in the knowledge of them from their earliest youth, they bear the image of the law in their souls." [4]

On the basis of these and other rabbinic writings dating from the early centuries of the Common Era and before, some historians maintain that ancient Israel practiced universal compulsory education. What is abundantly clear is that the organized education of the young commanded the attention of religious leaders and scholars early in Jewish history.

The Synagogue School

During the Babylonian exile (sixth century B.C.E.), some scholars assert, significant changes in the cultural and spiritual life of Israel led to the creation of the synagogue. Removed from the central shrine in Jerusalem and deprived of the administrations of the priests, Jews gathered on the Sabbath in the synagogues where the more learned would read and explain portions from Scripture. The synagogue might therefore be considered as the first school of adult education. "A man upon returning home from the field in the evening should go to the synagogue. If he is accustomed to reading the Bible, let him read the Bible, and if he is accustomed to repeating the Mishnah, let him repeat the Mishnah . . ." (*B'rakhot* 4b).

It was also in the synagogue that the children were initiated into the teachings of Torah as they accompanied their parents on Sabbaths and holidays. At a later period the synagogue was used as a school for children. "Said Rav to Rabbi Hiya, how do women gain merit? By bringing their children to the synagogue to learn the Scriptures" (*B'rakhot* 17a).

There are indications that children entered school at the age of five, although some rabbis urged that they start at six for reasons of health. The terminal age is not known (some sources suggest thirteen). As for the size of the class, it was recommended that there be "twenty-five to a classroom; for fifty there should be two teachers, for forty a teacher and an assistant" (*Bava Batra* 21a).

The Biblical dictum, "He that spareth his rod hateth his son; but he that loveth him chasteneth him betimes" (Proverbs 13:24) seems to have guided the Rabbis and many pedagogues up to modern times. To be sure, there were urgent appeals against harsh punishment (*Bava Batra* 21a) and against threats that could lead to tragic results. One maxim offered the following counsel: "Let the right hand befriend when the left pushes aside" (*Sotah* 47a).

Although rabbinic sources make reference to such secular subjects as mathematics, astronomy, physiology and foreign languages, their study was limited primarily to children of the ruling classes. For the masses of children the curriculum of the Jewish school, from the days of the Talmud to the nineteenth century, revolved around Bible and Talmud and their commentaries. The Rabbis suggested that one should divide his studies, "one third for Scriptures, one third for Mishnah, and one third for Talmud" (*Kiddushin* 30a). It was also advised: "At five years of age, the study of Scriptures; at ten, the study of Mishnah; at thirteen, for the fulfillment of commandments; at fifteen, the study of the Talmud" (*Ethics of the Fathers* 5:24).

Rabbinic writings reveal interesting insights about the differing abilities of students. "Just as people differ in appearance, so do they in capacities," says the Midrash *Rabbah Pinḥas*. *Ethics of the Fathers* (5:18) refers to four kinds of students, "the sponge, the funnel, the strainer, and the sieve. The sponge soaks up everything; the funnel takes in at one ear and lets out at the other; the strainer lets the wine pass and retains the yeast; the sieve lets out the bran and retains the fine flour."

There is considerable discussion among the Rabbis regarding the best method of teaching. While some favored the inductive method of instruction, others preferred the deductive. Some stressed thoroughness in a limited area, while others called for the survey approach.[5] All found value in drill[6] and favored the aural-oral method of study, stressing the importance of cantillations.[7]

Above all, they encouraged lively disputations and free give-and-take of views on major as well as minor points of law, tradition and folklore. This method of inquiring into every statement or dictum and the ensuing clash of opinions led to the "pilpulistic" (dialectic) way of study that became widespread in Talmudic academies. Students of the history of education trace this method to the influence of the dialectic procedures of ancient Greece. William Boyd, author of *The History of Western Education*, points out the "curious irony" of the fact that "the Jews, in seeking to save themselves from being overborne by the Greek culture, should have adopted the Hellenic institution of the school for their children and the Hellenic practice of disputation for their young men." The ability to adapt techniques of other civilizations for the advancement of Judaism has become the hallmark of the Jewish genius. It played no small part in the survival of Jewry and its culture.[8]

What stands out in the pedagogy of the Talmud is the recognition accorded to the personality of the child and how to motivate him to learn. The Rabbis must have sensed that the process of learning can best be achieved if it starts on the level of the learner and his interests. Hence the saying, "A man can learn well only that part of the Torah which is his heart's desire" (*Avodah Zarah* 19a). "One does not put aside something that he likes for something he does not" (*Kiddushin* 64b). They also taught, "If you see a student who finds his studies as hard as iron, it is because his teacher does not show him a cheerful countenance" (*Ta'anit* 8a).

The Education of Adults

The concept of adult education in Judaism is rooted in the religious obligation to study Torah. Rabbinic lore is filled with exhortations and admonitions about adult learning, with the greatest stress placed by this in the Talmudic tractate *Ethics of the Fathers*:

"Be eager to learn Torah" (2:19).

"He who acquired Torah has earned the world-to-come" (2:8).

"The more you study Torah, the greater the reward" (2:21).

"Where there is no Torah, there are no manners" (3:21).

"Turn (the Torah) and turn it again, for everything is in it" (5:25).

While the readiness of a majority of adults to abide by the exacting demands of the Rabbis may be doubtful, it has been established that many did so regularly. Adult studies originally centered around the synagogue, and in later generations about the *yeshivot* (Talmudic academies) intended for scholars but also available to "lay" adults.

One of the earliest institutes of adult education (perhaps the first in the history of education) was the *Kallah*,[9] which developed in the Babylonian *yeshivot* about the second century C.E. and took place during the months preceding Passover and the High Holidays. These intensive sessions devoted themselves to a review of the studies by the adults during the preceding five months and to future assignments.

The *Kallah* months were of particular value to residents of distant communities who were thus given an opportunity for concentrated study and exchange of ideas under the guidance of great rabbinic personalities. So widespread was the participation in these institutes that Jews were exempted from court summons during the *Kallah* periods. Rabbinic literature offers interesting details on the proceedings and quotes one of the Rabbis as being amazed that the gentiles failed to become proselytes en masse after witnessing the ardor of the *Kallah* students at these vast assemblies.

These *Kallot* were of course for men. Indeed, there is little mention, either in the Bible or Talmud, of the education of daughters or the educational role of mothers. In Oriental as well as in Western culture, there was no provision until modern times for systematic schooling for girls. Only one of the Rabbis, Ben Azzai (first century C.E.), advocated "the duty to teach a daughter Torah" (*Sotah* 20a). This does not necessarily mean that women received no training in the precepts of Judaism and other skills. They learned mainly at home, in the temple or synagogue and in the "market place." Great women like Miriam and Deborah figured in the Bible, and Bruriah, a woman of wisdom and learning, in the Talmud. The feminine virtues that seemed to count most were those mentioned in the Book of

Proverbs—a mother and wife who is faithful, industrious, kind-hearted, dignified, and who "openeth her mouth with wisdom" (Proverbs 31).

Torah in Diaspora Culture

By the end of the tenth century, Jewry and Judaism had veered from their Oriental environment toward predominantly Western Christian civilization, first on the Iberian Peninsula, then in France, Germany and Eastern Europe. In Europe, as well as in the Islamic communities of Asia and Africa, the Jews, in the words of Heinrich Heine, carried with them their "portable homeland," the Torah.

For the next thousand years the Jews were buffeted from one land to another, from one civilization to another, at times welcome or tolerated, but more often abused and persecuted. Yet throughout these vicissitudes they managed to preserve their tradition of learning and teaching, and to produce a spiritual and literary legacy which in some ways matched if not surpassed that of preceding generations in Palestine and Babylonia. The poetry, philosophy and liturgy of Spanish Jewry have been described as the "Golden Age" in Jewish creativity. The scholarly works, legal discussions and pietistic writings of other European Jewries still remain a sustaining spiritual influence to this day.

The shift from an Oriental to a Western culture called for a certain degree of adjustment and acculturation. The Jews of Spain and other southern European communities shared actively in the study of the languages and cultures of their new homelands. Even in France and Germany, where contacts with non-Jews were more limited, the Jews of necessity learned the language and ways of their neighbors.[10]

But despite the impact of non-Jewish influences and acculturation to the new environment, the dominant factor in molding the character of Jewry and Judaism in the Diaspora remained the Jewish faith and the tradition of Torah. In the midst of the sea of illiteracy prevalent in Central and Western Europe up to the days of the Renaissance, Jews feverishly engaged in promulgating the study of Torah in elementary schools, *yeshivot* and study circles within and outside the synagogue. What Biblical literature had envisaged and the Talmud legislated about the obligations of Torah study, European Jewry carried out from the eleventh century until the rise of modernism, through a well-organized system of schooling both for young and old. The medieval commentator Rashi[11] maintained that "there is no 'empty one' in Israel, who does not have some knowledge of the Torah" (*Shabbat* 105b). His grandson, Rabbenu Tam, took it for granted that "those who do not know Talmud know Bible or Midrash." [12] That these were not biased views is attested by a Christian pupil of Peter Abelard (1079-1142), who makes the following comparison between Jewish and non-Jewish educational practices of his time: "A Jew, however poor, if he had ten sons would put them all to letters, not for gain, as the Christians do, but for the understanding of God's law." [13]

A deep concern for education is inherent in the conception of Torah as an integral part of Judaism. Another reason for the widespread, dynamic activity among Diaspora Jewry on behalf of Torah was the peculiar status of Jewry until the days of modern emancipation. In the Diaspora, Torah and Jewish education served as protective armor which sheltered the bruised and humiliated spirit of the people; without it Jewry would have collapsed or become demoralized. The authors of *Ḥukkay Hatorah* (The Laws of the Torah), who lived during the twelfth and thirteenth centuries, understood the psychological burdens of an underprivileged and abused minority as is evidenced by the following injunction:

> No teacher should teach more than ten children in one particular subject. Although the Rabbis of the Talmud say that the number should be twenty-five, this applies only to Palestine, where the atmosphere was enlightening at the time the Jews lived on their own land and felt self-reliant. For only a free, strong and self-confident spirit can receive knowledge and understanding. A soul that is sick, humble and subservient becomes dried up and is not capable of absorbing wisdom and understanding, particularly when such a spirit is subjected to arrogant and cruel masters who cast fear and dread upon their subservients; for wrath is the enemy of wisdom. Therefore, teachers must be careful not to accept more than ten children.[14]

Maimonides on the Study of Torah

Among the many architects and builders of the "Palace of the Torah," one of the greatest was Moses Maimonides. In his prolific writings on philosophy and Jewish law, he concerned himself with students, teachers and schools. But his major work on Jewish education is his treatise *Laws on Learning Torah*, which is part of the larger *Mishneh Torah*. This unique document is the only full, systematic and lucid treatment of the laws and regulations pertaining to Jewish education, and has played a decisive role in that field up to the present. His views have influenced pietists and rationalists, traditionalists and modernists, young and old, in keeping with his avowed purpose to reach "the whole house of Israel."

To be sure, Maimonides did not deviate from the teachings of the authorities who preceded him. He claimed that his primary purpose in writing *Mishneh Torah* was to record the views and decisions of his predecessors "in accordance with the conclusions drawn from the compilations and commentaries that appeared from the time of Moses to the present." [15]

However, Maimonides' version is marked by a fresh clarity and decisiveness. For example, the injunction to study the Torah at all times is a recurring motif in Biblical and post-Biblical literature, where its sources are fragmentary and mainly exhortative. But Maimonides' version is all-inclusive and mandatory: "Every Israelite is under the obligation to study Torah, whether he is poor or rich, healthy or sick, young or old and feeble. Even one who is supported by charity or burdened with family responsibilities must set aside time for the study of Torah." [16]

Another illustration is Maimonides' injunction on the obligation of a father to instruct his son. The precept to teach one's children occurs in both the Bible and Talmud, but there is no outright commandment or law which provides that "a father is obligated to hire a teacher for his son" as is recorded in Maimonides' *Laws on Learning Torah*.[17]

The subject of "study" versus "practice" is the theme of heated debate in the Talmud, with a majority decision in favor of "study." [18] Maimonides further clarifies this: "Thus you will find that study in *all* cases takes precedence over practice (observance and rituals) since it leads to practice, but practice does not lead to study." [19] In the *Guide for the Perplexed*, he asserts that "rituals and observances are essentially pedagogic devices for the cultivation and disciplining of the masses, the true end being knowledge of the divine through the study of Torah." [20]

Customs and Folkways of Torah

For a full appreciation of the role of Torah in the life of Jewry during the last millennium one must turn to its customs and folkways, the actual practices of people in their daily conduct.

School children and their teachers would visit newborn male children to chant the *Shema*, thus exposing them, as soon as they came into the world, to the teachings of Torah. Mothers lulled their children to sleep with songs glorifying Torah as the best *S'horah*, the most precious commodity in the world. Hardly had a child learned to speak when he was taken to the synagogue to kiss the Torah and to repeat or respond to benedictions. He was particularly encouraged to recite the *Shema* and the verse, "Moses commanded us the Torah, an inheritance of the congregation of Jacob" (Deuteronomy 33:4).

The day on which a boy began school was celebrated in different parts of the Jewish world with a variety of rituals. In some communities the first day of schooling would be on *Shavuot*, the festival commemorating the giving of the Torah. The teacher would hand the child a slate on which was written the Hebrew alphabet and a Biblical inscription related to Torah; after repeating the quotations, the child tasted some honey which had been spread on the slate to suggest that the words of Torah are sweet.

In Eastern Europe the father, accompanied by the mother, carried the child to the *heder* (religious school) wrapped in a prayer shawl. After pronouncing appropriate blessings, the family and friends celebrated with wine, cakes and other delicacies. The child was also welcomed the first time into the classroom by having a penny dropped on him from above, symbolizing a reward "from the angels." Another family celebration was held when the child was about to start the study of *Humash*, the Pentateuch, where a kind of ritualistic dialogue took place between teacher and child, the purpose of which was to emphasize the value and joy of Torah study.

Upon reaching the Bar Mitzvah age of thirteen, the boy was introduced as a full-fledged member of the religious community by being called up in the synagogue to recite the blessings over the Torah, and in some instances to read a portion from the Torah scroll. On the wedding day, the bridegroom was expected to deliver a Torah discourse at the nuptial feast.

Mastery of Torah bestowed status on both the family and community. While wealth and material possessions loomed large, they were not sufficient to win full recognition in the community. Affluent families sought to achieve status by marrying their daughters to scholars, no matter how indigent.

Although hardly a day passed without a ritual or reference to Torah, the special festival of *Simḥat Torah*, or "rejoicing in Torah," was dedicated exclusively to its glorification. Observed at the end of *Sukkot*, the holiday celebrates the conclusion of the reading of the Five Books of Moses and is given over to song, dance and unrestrained merriment. The Torah scrolls are taken out of the Ark and paraded in the synagogue and sometimes in the streets. Despite the joviality, the scrolls are treated as sacred objects. When age or damage renders them unusable, they are buried as though they were human. There are on record actual cases of pious Jews who gave their lives to rescue a Torah scroll from fire or desecration.

Jewish Education in Modern Times

With the French Revolution, significant changes have come about in the nature and scope of Torah study, first in Western and later in Eastern Europe. Hebrew schools, *ḥedarim* and *yeshivot* have continued to promote the study of Bible, Talmud and related subjects, but these no longer hold the central position they enjoyed in the past. For the overwhelming majority of contemporary Jews in the Diaspora, Judaic studies are supplementary to general studies. Even the extreme Orthodox *yeshivot* which oppose secular studies find it necessary to provide general studies in their curriculum. Thus, after some eighteen hundred years of a reasonably uniform philosophy of Jewish education, followed by a century of experimentation and adjustment between the requirements of general education and Jewish schools, three major trends have evolved in the theory and practice of Jewish education. These are the extreme Orthodox, the religio-nationalist and the assimilationist.[21]

The extreme Orthodox Jews, whose ranks were tragically decimated during the Nazi holocaust, seek to maintain islands of Torah in concentrated Jewish communities, in the spirit, if not altogether in the practice, of the traditional *ḥedarim* and *yeshivot.* Study of secular subjects, to the extent that they are included, is viewed as a concession to government regulations or to the exigencies of a technological age. Major emphasis is still placed on sacred literature and religious observances. This type of school, though limited to a small number, performs the function of holding the fort against the waves of secularism and assimilation which threaten to engulf Diaspora Jewry.

At the other extreme are the advocates of full cultural assimilation as enunciated by spokesmen of the Napoleonic Sanhedrin (1807): "Jews are Frenchmen of the Jewish faith," and "France is our *Eretz Yisrael,* her mountains our Zion, her rivers our Jordan; let us drink from her living waters."

In this conception of Judaism, Jewish education is limited to the acquisition of the basic articles of the Jewish faith. It eschews such aspects of the Jewish tradition as the brotherhood of Israel, the Hebrew language, the love of Zion or other manifestations of ethnic and cultural ties among the different Jewries. The adherents of this theory of Jewish education are few, but their influence is potentially great on a rising generation which lacks the warmth of Jewish tradition and the intellectual vigor of Jewish scholarship.

The majority of world Jewry subscribes to a more moderate position—what might be called a religio-nationalist philosophy of Jewish life and culture. While allowing for a considerable variety of opinions and degrees of performance, this philosophy satisfies the majority of Diaspora Jews and their 800,000 children who attend Jewish schools.

In the scale of priorities, parents accord first place to general education without which, they feel, their children will not find their place in modern society. In countries like the United States where Jews are free to provide both general and Jewish education, the majority of parents tend toward a religious orientation, reserving the right to decide the degree of observance of specific rituals. They also seek to cultivate among their children a concern for their fellow Jews wherever they may be and particularly for Israel. While parents as a rule do not seek an intensive Hebrew education for their children, they wish them to acquire some knowledge of Hebrew as the language of the prophets and of Israel reborn. A goodly number of Jewish communities have been turning in recent years to day schools which combine general education with Jewish subjects. These are sponsored as a rule by Orthodox groups and place considerable emphasis upon Judaic and Hebraic studies.

Despite this consensus, there are no indications that even the minimum objectives are being attained for the majority of Jewish children. This is due to the lack of properly organized Jewish schools, the critical shortage of educational personnel, and above all to the failure on the part of Jewish communal leadership to appreciate the crucial importance of Jewish education.

In recent years, voices have been raised to restore to Jewish education a modicum of the priority it enjoyed in Jewish tradition. To attain this end, Jewry will have to recapture the spirit of devotion and reverence associated with the study of Torah.

Ludwig Lewisohn, in his *Expression in America*, makes the plea that since Scripture has become literature for modern man, it is incumbent upon literature to imbibe the spirit of purposefulness and sacredness associated with Scripture. Similarly, one might say that since Torah has become Jewish education for the modern Jew, those concerned with Jewish education must imbue it with the earnestness, dedication and sacredness associated with Torah.

FOR FURTHER READING

ACKERMAN, Walter, "Jewish Education Today" *The American Jewish Yearbook*, Volume 80, (New York: American Jewish Committee, 1980). A now standard review of the present reality in Jewish education.

ADAR, Zvi, *Jewish Education in Israel and the United States* (Jerusalem: Melton Research Center for Jewish Education, Hebrew University). A wide ranging review and assessment of the current state of Jewish educational affairs in Israel and the United States.

BOCK, Geoffrey, *Does Jewish Schooling Matter* (New York: American Jewish Committee, 1972). A detailed study of one impact of Jewish schooling on Jewish identity formation.

SPIRO, Jack D., *To Learn and to Teach* (New York: Philosophical Library, 1983). A well known figure in the world of Jewish education suggests an existential approach to modern Jewish education, especially in the face of the competing pressures of contemporary society.

PILCH, Judah, Editor, *A History of Jewish Education in America* (New York: American Association for Jewish Education, 1969). An anthology of informative essays on one evolving pattern of Jewish education in America.

THE JEWISH
VISION OF
GOD AND MAN

The modern Jew is definitely in a challenging mood. The Darwinian revolution has led him to question the Biblical story of creation as literal truth. His general scientific education has undermined his belief in the historicity of the miracles of the Bible. He questions the efficacy of prayer. Having lived through the Nazi horror, he asks: How could a merciful God "hide His face" from the slaughter of millions of innocent men, women and children? Indeed, how can there be evil, sin and suffering in a world created by the God of love and mercy? Some modern Jews go further: they question the existence of an imminent, personal God.

Since the modern Jew has lost the main props of his world outlook, how can he tell with confidence what is morally right or wrong, what is the good life and what is or should be the goal of humanity? To be sure, there are some Jews who have managed to maintain a sense of certainty despite the rapidly changing world. They hold on to the traditional answers about God and man. But such Jews are relatively few. The majority are confused and troubled, very much as was the famous disciple of Maimonides for whom the master wrote his *Guide for the Perplexed*.

Unfortunately, too, the image of Judaism has been distorted. The Christian environment in which Jews are nurtured has warped the content of the Jewish faith. Exposed to assertions of Judaism's inferiority, and deficient in his Jewish education, the thoughtful Jew seeks reliable information to enable him to attain a few certainties upon which to build a sound world outlook and a firm religious commitment.

The third section of this book aims at giving authentic and reliable information to help the modern Jew to rethink his uncertainties and arrive at some tenable truths. The essays in this section will not provide categorical answers to any theological questions; they will, however, present authentic Jewish theological views. Since the authors do not belong to one school of thought, their emphases differ. The reader will therefore be challenged to weigh and evaluate the different approaches within Judaism.

Chapters Eleven and Thirteen were adapted from longer manuscripts submitted by their respective authors.

9 . *God and Man*

LOU H. SILBERMAN

T H E relationship between God and man that lies at the center of Judaism is most clearly articulated in that cluster of prayers, the *K'riat Shema,*[1] made up of three Biblical passages and the benedictions preceding and following them, found in the prayer book (*Siddur*).[2]

The Yoke of the Kingship

The heart of this formulation is the Biblical imperative: "Hear, O Israel, the Lord is our God, the Lord is one." Traditionally, the reciting of this sentence from Deuteronomy (6:4) is known as "receiving the yoke of the Kingship." For rabbinic Judaism, the crucial idea was found in the word "Kingship," *Malkhut,* for the recitation of this sentence was intended to proclaim, on the one hand, the sovereignty of God, and, on the other, the rejection of any divided authority.

The *Shema* thus understood was an affirmation of the providence of God, not of His existence.[3] In the Greco-Roman world in which rabbinic Judaism flourished, many gods were believed in but they were thought of by their devotees as totally indifferent to the world or unconnected with it. In the Aramaic translation of Genesis 4:8, Cain is made to echo this attitude in these words: "There is neither law nor judge; neither future world nor reward for the righteous and punishment for the wicked. He did not create the world in mercy nor does He rule in mercy." It was against such a position that the Rabbis saw the phrase "the Lord is our God" directed. They were able to do this because they understood the divine name *Elohim* to refer to God as He manifests Himself in justice; just as they understood the Tetragrammaton, the Name of Four Letters, to refer to God's manifestation in love and compassion. Thus, they understood the Biblical phrase to mean: "the Lord is our Judge." The recitation of the *Shema* was then the acknowledgment of divine rule and judgment. The God of Israel was intimately and actively concerned with the world and with man.

The crucial sentence was not an abstract philosophical statement about the metaphysical being of God. It was a passionate proclamation of His providential activity in the world; at the same time it denied reality to the multiplicity of deities ardently believed in by the ancient world.

In medieval times, this particular emphasis seems to have faded. In its place, the oneness of God as a philosophical idea, that of metaphysical unity, came to the fore to counter the Christian doctrine of the Trinity. This doctrine had been defined even more precisely by Church theologians in metaphysical terms, thus making it necessary for their Jewish counterparts to interpret the phrase, "the Lord is one," in the language of speculative philosophy.

The later Middle Ages saw the rise of mystical thought within the Jewish community. The adherents of this mode of thought were, as Gershom Scholem has written, fascinated by the implications of this verse that was the center of worship. They speculated about the kind of unity it proclaimed, attempting to relate it to their understanding of divine emanation.[4]

In our own century, the German philosopher Hermann Cohen pondered whether monotheism was concerned with unity or with uniqueness. The former clearly indicated opposition to the multiplicity of deities. For Cohen, however, polytheism was something more than a plurality of deities. It involved the relationship of the latter to the universe and its forces. Monotheism could then not be understood as merely setting one over against many. It demanded an understanding of the relationship of one to nature in all its forms and with all its forces. Cohen argued that monotheism was concerned not merely with a contrast between one God and many deities, but with the uniqueness of God, the contrast between Him and the world.[5] It is this same idea that the contemporary Biblical scholar Yehezkel Kaufmann claims is the original meaning of Israelite monotheism. ". . . it is a mistake to think that a merely arithmetical difference sets off Israel's religion from paganism . . . The Israelite conception of God's unity entails His sovereign transcendence over all . . ." [6]

The proclamation of the *Shema* has thus been the vehicle for a variety of ideas over the centuries, and this variety carries over into the understanding of the Biblical passage which follows it:

> And thou shalt love the Lord thy God with all thy heart, and with all thy soul, and with all thy might. And these words, which I command thee this day, shall be upon thy heart; and thou shalt teach them diligently unto thy children, and shalt talk of them when thou sittest in thy house, and when thou walkest by the way, and when thou liest down and when thou risest up. And thou shalt bind them for a sign upon thy hand, and they shall be for frontlets between thine eyes. And thou shalt write them upon the door-posts of thy house, and upon thy gates.

This passage (Deuteronomy 6:5-9), still in the imperative mood, confronts us with the response divine sovereignty calls forth from man. The proclamation of God's Kingship requires not fear or reverence, but love and obedience.

The second section (Deuteronomy 11:13-21), though worded in terms of an agricultural community ("I will give the rain of your land in its season . . . grass in thy fields, for thy cattle . . . ," etc.), deals with the interrelation of man's obedience and God's providence. It contains God's response to man's conduct: "It shall come to pass, if ye shall harken diligently . . ."

The third passage (Numbers 15:37-41), while specifying a particular commandment (the wearing of fringes at the corners of garments), is clearly thought of as summarizing man's responsibility toward all the commandments. Its conclusion once again recalls God's sovereignty and love through the remembrance of the founding event of the people of Israel, the going-forth-from-Egypt, as an expression of the love binding Israel and God.

Here, within these Biblical passages, are the crucial affirmations of Judaism, not spelled out, yet fully present. In the *b'rakhot*, the benedictions or blessings that introduce and conclude the recitation of these passages, the implications of these affirmations are made clear.

God and the World

The Mishnah (*B'rakhot* 1:4) prescribes that two benedictions be recited before the Biblical passages discussed above and one after. The *G'mara*,[7] assuming widespread knowledge of them, briefly notes their content in discussing certain questions raised about them. In their original forms these benedictions were shorter than those found in our present-day *Siddur*, as the analysis of the nineteenth-century scholar Leopold Zunz indicated and the textual research of later scholars like Solomon Schechter demonstrated. Although they were added to in the course of the centuries, incorporating new material to illuminate the central theme of each, they preserved their basic ideas while at the same time illustrating the way in which succeeding generations understood them.

The first benediction, called *Yotzer*, takes up the theme of the relationship between God and the world. It does so by quoting in a slightly altered form a verse from Isaiah (45:7): "Who forms light and creates darkness; who makes peace and creates all." The original text reads "evil" or "adversity" in place of "all" and the *G'mara*[8] discusses the substitution. The reason given suggests that the change was made only for suitability in prayer and that a change of meaning was not meant. It is clear, however, that behind the change there must have been considerable discussion concerning the question of the theological implications of the original phrase. The benediction underscores the relation of God to the world as that of Creator to creation with the added insight that His activity is not of the past but is ongoing and continuous, for He "makes new continually, each day, the work of creation." Not only does He "enlighten the earth" but in compassion He enlightens "the dwellers upon it."

These short phrases contain a whole complex of meaning. There is further emphasis upon the uniqueness of God, for He is other than His creation. As a rabbinic statement puts it: "He is the place (*makom*) of the world, but the world is not His place" (*Genesis Rabbah* 68:9). He is, says the text, more than First Cause. He is intimately related with the world and with "those who dwell upon it." He is always and altogether involved in that which he created although not subject to it. He solely is its Creator and Sovereign, for both "light and darkness, peace and adversity" come from Him. These are all themes found in the Biblical passages and their interpretations. Creation has but one sovereign power, not two or many. The variety of forms and forces man experiences in his life have, however difficult it may be for him to comprehend this, one source, one ultimate.

This emphatic insistence raises difficult problems, perceived and pondered by the Rabbis. If God is sole sovereign, how is it possible to explain pain and suffering? Judaism has had to learn to live with the paradox of suffering and sovereignty, of pain and providence, for it could not have endured a partial God.

This first benediction also teaches us about man, the "dweller on earth" who is the object of God's compassion. The relation of *raḥamin*, the Hebrew word for "compassion" to the word *reḥem*, meaning "womb," may suggest that the bestowal of God's compassion is to be thought of as analogous to the relation of mother to child, the bestowal of existence. The world's very existence, says the benediction, is dependent upon God's compassion, through which alone man can endure. Even when man is disobedient and strict justice makes its demands, the earth and its dwellers continue to exist; the creative act is renewed; divine sovereignty manifests itself in the entire structure of the universe, in an intricate order permeating the great and the small. This is a dimension of God's compassion, an aspect of His goodness. It discloses the most abstract, impersonal side of His being. But this revelation of God through His creative act, by its very abstractness, its impersonality, points beyond itself.

God, Israel, Torah

The second benediction is called *Birkat ha-Torah*, "the Torah Benediction." It develops in another way our understanding of God's compassion and goodness. "Great love," "everlasting love," "with abundant compassion hast Thou been compassionate," "Thou wilt be gracious," "Thou art He who performs saving acts," "Thou hast chosen . . . in love," "Thou hast drawn near"—these are the words and phrases that spell out God's gifts of compassion and goodness, opening up new dimensions of understanding the relationship between God and man.

If creation itself is the initial act of sovereign compassion, it is not the last. Its renewal provides opportunity for man's response, and makes possible other levels into which universal compassion penetrates. The goodness disclosed in creation calls forth trust in the human heart. Just as the bestowal of physical light was an act of compassion in creation, so the bestowal of spiritual and moral light is a continuing act of love.

God is Teacher as well as Creator. His teaching (Torah) is the life-giving law bestowed graciously upon man. The Creator is not a distant God; He is a very present God who acts in the life of mankind, performing saving deeds. He has, says the benediction, chosen from among men those who are to stand in a particular relationship to Him, who are to declare His existence and uniqueness to those who have not yet recognized or understood Him. He is the God of Israel, having called this people from "among every people and tongue" and brought it near, so that it might by its acknowledgment of Him and its fervent proclamation of His uniqueness make Him known to all mankind.

Here are further dimensions of Judaism's understanding of God. He is the source of obligation and responsibility, for He has given to man in love and grace the means by which he may live. Man, as he responds in love and awe to the gift of Torah and commandments, becomes a meaningful being, unashamed to be a man. Most particularly has the giving of Torah determined the nature of Israel. It is through the choice of and the witnessing, through the way of life of this people that the ethical demand of God is made evident to all mankind.

Judaism's understanding of the concept of God as "He who chose His people Israel in love" through His gift of Torah and commandments is found imbedded in the idea itself. In Deuteronomy (7:7 and 8) we read: "It was not because you were more in number than any other people that the Lord set His love upon you and chose you, for you were the fewest of all peoples; but it is because the Lord loves you, and is keeping the oath which He swore to your fathers." The source of the love is within God Himself. Solomon Schechter emphasized this:

. . . even those Rabbis who tried to establish Israel's special claim on their exceptional merits were not altogether unconscious of the insufficiency of the reasons of works in this respect, and therefore had also recourse to the love of God, which is not given as a reward, but is offered freely.[9]

Here we meet with the idea of covenant, *b'rit,* called by Leo Baeck "the idea of the great relationship, the great unity of all, the unity of hiddenness and certainty. Here the divine order that binds together time and eternity, near and far, heaven and earth seeks to express itself." [10] Thus God's act of love in choosing Israel is the act of giving to Israel and through Israel to mankind the Teaching, Torah, that which established and sustains man.

Man's Love and Obedience

As has already been pointed out, in the ancient world there were many who accepted the idea of a creator God, but who consigned Him to a pallid existence, unrelated, or nearly so, to His creation. He was uninvolved in and unconnected with the unfolding history of man. For them, history was devoid of meaning or structure. Ethical demands were entirely relative; none was binding upon mankind. Others, perplexed by variety and multiplicity, by contradiction and conflict, were led to affirm more than one deity. If creation was the work of a good divinity, it had fallen into the hands of a perverse one.

Jewish thought rejected all such propositions. The Creator and the Source of obligation are one. Recognizing God as Creator and Teacher, Judaism unequivocally proclaimed the unity of His sovereignty and uniqueness: "The Lord is our God, the Lord is one." He who created the world in justice and compassion gave Torah to man in love.

This twofold affirmation about God found its parallel in man's twofold response. Thus, the last word of the second benediction, "Who has chosen His people Israel in love," continues to sound during the proclamation of the Kingship, "Hear, O Israel . . ." It finds its answer in the Biblical imperative: "Love the Lord, your God, with all your heart, with all your soul, with all your might." Using modern counterparts to the Hebrew terms one might say: love Him with your entire mind, all your emotions and every fraction of your physical power. For as God loves, so is He to be loved by the totality of each man. And that totality of man's responsive love is now spelled out. "These words," that is, the teaching, are to be in man's mind. He is obligated to teach them to his children and be occupied with them in all his activities, even while walking by the way, lying down, rising up. This is the human side of the covenant—total involvement and total responsibility. There is no part of a man's existence that is unrelated to God as man obediently lives in accord with the requirements of the covenant.

What then is the nature of man, typified by Israel? He is capable of love, understood as a function not of a partial aspect but of his entire being. He is called upon to love in accordance with that relationship. He thinks; he feels; he acts in response to the presence of God. But he can be disobedient as well. That possibility appearing as a cloud on the horizon quickly gathers as a dark storm: "Guard yourselves, lest your heart (i.e., your mind) be persuaded and you turn" (Deuteronomy 11:16).

The tradition early recognized the tremendous tensions in which man is caught up. Thus in the *G'mara* (*B'rakhot* 54a) the writing of the Hebrew word which we translate "all your heart" in Deuteronomy (6:5) with two *vets* rather than the more common one, *l'vav'khah* rather than *lib'khah*, is understood to indicate the twofold mind of man. He is possessed of power either to love God or to turn from Him. He obeys God because he loves Him. If he turns from this passionate total response, if he disobeys, then the relationship is shattered.

Jewish tradition as expressed in the prayer book has no illusions about man. While insisting that "the soul which Thou placed within me is pure," it nonetheless could declare, "not in reliance upon our righteousness do we cast down our supplications before Thee." Its questions are sharp: "What are we? What our lives? What our righteousness? What our strength? What our power?" Man requires God's compassion. Neither influence, dignity, learning nor wisdom suffice. Man is superior to the beast only because he has been called into the covenant through God's love.

God's Justice

We have seen that according to Jewish tradition the world exists because of God's compassion, and man has come to know the way of life through His love. Man's disobedience raises the thorny problem of the justice of God. The love of God expressed in the covenant is the very basis of the order required of man. Man's failure, a failure not blinked away by the tradition, turns our attention to a consideration of God's justice.

The second Biblical selection in the *Shema* declares that man's love and the obedience that flows from it are rewarded. While the language used is the simple figure of agricultural life, its intention reaches beyond. The reward of obedience is the preservation of order so that the community and its individual members find wholeness in life. On the other hand, disobedience which is fundamentally rebellion against the sovereignty of God, the "breaking of the yoke," shatters order so that the community is overwhelmed by adversity. With the passage of time, the original formulation was not able to satisfy more sophisticated minds, but the basic principle remained. In the face of such perplexities as, why do the righteous suffer? why do the wicked prosper?, there was the affirmation that there is law! there is the Judge!

Man's attempt to understand this side of the nature of God demands response. He is called to obedience once again. Man's responsibility in the presence of divine justice, even when it is not understood, is still the total commitment of the self through both study and act, Torah and *mitzvah*. "The reward of *mitzvah* is *mitzvah*," said Ben Azzai, "and the reward of transgression is transgression" (*Ethics of the Fathers* 4:2). The justice of God calls man to turn back from rebellion to a new affirmation of divine sovereignty.

God the Redeemer

The source of man's renewal, of his return to and reaffirmation of God's redemptive act, is clear from the final words of the third Biblical passage (Numbers 15:37-41), which deals with the remembering and doing of the commandments: "I the Lord am your God, who brought you out of the land of Egypt to be your God; I, the Lord your God." The Jew fulfills the commandments because God by freeing him has made it possible. Thus the third and concluding benediction *Geullah*, following these words, emphasizes that He who is Creator and Lawgiver is Redeemer. Once again the theme of divine unity resounds and the continuity of divine sovereignty is reaffirmed: "our Redeemer, Redeemer of our fathers . . . there is no deity other than Thee." The Exodus from Egypt, the central experience of the people of Israel, is understood as both fulfillment and promise. Through it the ultimate meaning of the covenant between God and the people of Israel was disclosed. The past thus foreshadows the hope of Israel and of mankind, and reveals God both as Judge and as Redeemer. It is promise as well, for it provides the assurance that when man turns back from rebellion he will be met and accepted in love.

Wholly Other and Nearer than Near

The ideas sketched here represent the formulation of belief that unites all parts of the Jewish community. Yet, as we have seen above, each generation has had to understand anew the meaning of these crucial words. In this way the wonderings of many centuries have gone into the building of Judaism's affirmations.

In discussing the nature of God as Creator, we pointed out that this concept involves a remote, almost impersonal side of His being. In the Book of Job, for example, the Creator is portrayed as overwhelming Job. The fearsome "otherness" of God, His holiness, is emphasized as well in the threefold shout of the seraphim: "Holy! Holy! Holy!" in the Book of Isaiah. Expressions such as these seem to underscore the utter separateness and inviolability of the God of Israel. It was after hearing the chanting of "*Kadosh! Kadosh! Kadosh!*" in a Moroccan synagogue that the German Protestant theologian Rudolph Otto arrived at his understanding of God as the "tremendously mysterious."

Jewish tradition has demonstrated God's separateness by the way in which it has treated the divine name. In place of the Tetragrammaton, the Name of Four Letters, it substituted *Adonai*, "Lord," and even this substitute has been protected from familiarity by the further substitution of other forms. The phrase *Avinu Malkenu*, "our Father, our King," for example, seems to have been introduced as a substitute for the Biblical usage *Adonai Elohenu*, "Lord our God." Other surrogate names were invented by the tradition as it attempted to preserve the sense of the otherness of God. Refusal to allow casual use of the divine name pointed to God's "otherness."

Yet the tradition affirmed at the same time the absolute nearness, the ever-presentness of God. It did so, for example, by the use of the name *Sh'khinah*, the Present One." Since the Hebrew root of this name *shkh'n* means "to dwell," God is thus referred to as "He who dwells with us." God causes His presence, His glory, His Name to dwell continuously in the midst of His people. God's nearness is emphasized in history by the Exodus from Egypt in which God Himself was an active participant. It is illustrated also in the life of each individual to whom God is, in the words of the Palestinian Talmud, as near as lips to ear when one whispers to his neighbor.

This concept of God as the Present One, the *Sh'khinah*, finds its expression most particularly in the familiar pronoun, *Attah*, "Thou." Over and over again man has found himself in the presence of God and dares to address Him who is Creator, Teacher, Redeemer, He who has made Himself known in Israel's history and in each man's life, as He who stands over against the community and the individual as living Person, not theological abstraction. It is in this relationship, discussed so beautifully in Martin Buber's *I and Thou*, that remoteness is overcome and presentness is established. It is this relationship that illumines creation, that gives meaning to Torah, that promises redemption, for here man comes to know the meaning of love.

It is the "Thou" God who spoke, speaks and will speak to man that makes him man and enables him to address "Thou" to God. As Franz Rosenzweig wrote in a note to a hymn by Judah Halevi, "Man is able to cry 'Here am I,' for the echo of these words comes back to him from God's mouth." [11] God, unique in His oneness, calls each man to his own unique oneness as He called and calls Israel to its unique oneness in history.

"Thou" is thus the name that undergirds all the names of God the Jewish tradition has dared to use. It is the name that shines through every other name, uniting man to God and God to man.

Concluding Words

In the preceding sections we have pointed to some of the ways, perhaps the most decisive ways, in which the people Israel has endeavored to express its understanding of the un-fathomable power and structure made known to it in its history. It has spoken to the Creator, Teacher, Redeemer, Him who is incomprehensible yet close at hand. It has proclaimed both His vast remoteness and His ultimate presence. It has dared to address Him with the most intimate word man can use, "Thou." It has said all this and more besides, yet it has recognized as well the failure of any and all words.

This is expressed poignantly by an episode reported in the Talmud. In it a teacher chides a student for having used more adjectives in praising God than the three used by Moses in Deuteronomy 10:17, the three taken over into the prayer book: "great, mighty, revered." It is more than a warning about wordiness in prayer; it underscores our inability to do more than begin to understand God who in His love has made it possible for us to say even what we have said. And yet, the inability does not excuse us from the undertaking. The great medieval exegete Rashi, commenting on the first words of Scripture, wrote: "This verse says but one thing, understand me!" That remains our task as well.

FOR FURTHER READING

BOROWITZ, Eugene, *Liberal Judaism* (New York: UAHC, 1984). An articulate and modern exegesis of the dialogue between God and man from the perspective of Reform Jewry.

JACOBS, Louis, *A Jewish Theology* (New York: Behrman, 1973). A comprehensive discussion of the main building blocks of the Jewish tradition, especially in its specifically theological dimensions by a distinguished contemporary scholar.

SHAPIRO, Davis S., "God, Man & Creation," in *Tradition* Vol. 15, (spring–summer, 1975). The significance of man's status in creation is reviewed by a major orthodox rabbi.

SOLOVEITCHIK, Joseph, "The Lonely Man of Faith", in *Tradition* Vol. 1, one of the few authentically "classic" statements in modern Jewish thought by one of the few authentic Jewish luminaries of our time.

SOLOVEITCHIK, Joseph, *On Repentance*, edited by Pinchas Peli (Ramsey, N.J.; Paulist Press, 1984). An English translation of Soloveitchik's remarkable lectures on this most basic of Jewish theological doctrines relating to man's encounters with God.

SPERO, S., "Selfhood & Godhood in Jewish Thought and Modern Philosophy" in *Tradition* Vol. 18 (summer, 1980). One of Orthodox Jewry's leading contemporary thinkers reflects on one basic polarity of God and Man, and their interrelationship.

STEINSALTZ, Adin, "Worlds, Angels & Men", in *SHEFA,* Vol. 1 (summer, 1978). A neomystical meditation on the meaning of human life, and its place in the cosmic hierarchy by one of the most remarkable Jewish thinkers of our time.

10 . The Nature of Man

LEVI A. OLAN

T H E primary question of our time is the cry of the psalmist. "What is man, O God, that Thou art mindful of him?" (Psalms 8:4). In the face of decades of mass cruelty and destruction, of Nazi gas chambers and the nuclear bomb terror, the problem is not only one of believing in God: it is also a despair about the nature of the human creature, a mood of pessimism about man's moral possibilities. This disenchantment, bordering on the misanthropic, is expressed in novels, on the stage and in the popular arts. From Franz Kafka to Mickey Spillane, man is pictured either as an insensitive brute or a helpless victim of demonic powers.

Unlike other faiths, however, Judaism stands firmly against any philosophy or creed which is rooted in the soil of despair about man's possibilities. Though basically a God-centered religion, it patiently accepts man's failure to believe in God. But it can never countenance a lack of faith in man. The Rabbis make this point clearly in their Midrashic explanation of Moses' failure to enter the Promised Land: "You doubted me," God tells the lawgiver, "but I forgive you that doubt. You doubted your own self and failed to believe in your own powers as a leader, and I forgave that also. But you lost faith in this people and doubted the divine possibilities of human nature. That I cannot forgive. That loss of faith makes it impossible for you to enter the Promised Land." However divergent the theological doctrines in Judaism, on the matter of hope for man there is almost unanimity of belief from Sinai to our own day.

Man's significance in the scheme of the universe is announced with the account of Creation, where great preparations take place before the first human being is introduced. Said one of the Rabbis: "It is like an earthly king who built a palace . . . prepared a banquet and then invited guests." [1] Man is a creation of the one and only God who made the heavens and the earth and all that is in them. In this sense he shares his creatureliness with the animals and with matter. But he is also unique, being supreme over all of creation: he is God's special concern through whom the divine purpose is to be fulfilled.

In examining Genesis, the sages found that in only two phases of creation does God perform the deed directly, in the beginning when "God created the heavens and the earth" (Genesis 1:1), and at the end when "God created man in His own image" (1:27). In all the rest of creation it was the word of God: "Let there be." When Philo, under Greek influence, suggested that Adam was partly or wholly created by angels, that "man was not made by the hand of God, but is the work of invisible nature," [2] Jewish tradition asserted itself strongly in favor of a direct creation by the "hand of God." The Midrash relates that the angels argued among themselves as to whether man should or should not be created. In the heat of their discussion God says, "Why are you arguing? Man has already been created." [3]

Man's Place in the Universe

It is a distortion to suggest that Judaism sees man as the center of history. The tradition's basic affirmation is that God and His will are both the beginning and the end. But Judaism does give the human creature a place right next to the divine, "a little lower than the angels" (Psalm 8:6). One of the Rabbis went so far as to state that the Torah really begins with the fifth chapter of Genesis: "This is the book of the generation of man. In the day that God created man, in the likeness of God made He him." [4] Not only does all of creation find its climax in man: but he is distinguished in the very nature of creation. God forms him "of the dust of the ground," like all other creatures. But then He "breathed into his nostrils the breath of life, and man became a living soul" (Genesis 2:7). In other religious cultures God fulfills His purpose without man, but in Judaism God and man are partners, co-workers in the building of the Kingdom.

The supreme place of man in the universe is further emphasized by the worth given each person. "One man is equal to the whole creation," says one of the sages.[5] God created one man, a single individual, in order to teach us that whoever destroys one life is guilty of destroying the whole world; and whoever saves one life, it is as though he had saved the whole world.[6] Furthermore, there is a uniqueness in the appearance of each person, for though all are descended from Adam, there are no two alike. Thus every human creature can say, "For my sake was the world created" (*Sanhedrin* 37).

In Jewish thought this high estimate of man's significance in God's universe maintains an unquestioned place, second in importance only to belief in the unity of God. Faith in the importance of man has been maintained despite the Jewish historic experience of terror and brutal persecution. Saadia, writing in the tenth century, ranked men above the spheres and all other existences: "He is the axis of the world and its foundation." [7] In this beautiful sentence he caught the dominance of Jewish faith in man: "Though his body be small, his soul is larger than heaven and earth, for through it he reaches even what is above them and the cause of them, the Creator Himself." [8]

The entire structure of Jewish ethics and its fundamental belief in human dignity may be said to rest upon the doctrine enunciated in the sentence: "And God created man in His own image, in the image of God created He him" (Genesis 1:27). Just what is meant by "image" has long been a matter of discussion. It suggested to some commentators a physical likeness: Adam "begat [a son] in his own likeness after his image" (Genesis 5:3). But Jewish tradition early in its history discarded all corporeal interpretations, ascribing to the "image" those qualities of conscious reason which lift man above the animal world. Man alone is gifted with intellectual faculties and a creative capacity which gives him the means of developing the sciences, philosophies and arts. He is endowed with a moral sensitivity enabling him to differentiate between right and wrong and to concern himself with the welfare of other men. Man's distinguishing characteristic is that he can know God if he will seek Him, and thus find the way that he should walk. Man's uniqueness lies in the fact that, formed of matter like all of creation, he alone is allied to the divine by his nature.

This divine quality is characteristic of all men at all times. Each person is therefore due reverence and respect because he bears the stamp of God. Even the gentle cynic Ecclesiastes found that "God made man upright" (Ecclesiastes 7:29), a creature of dignity with aspirations for the good, the true and beautiful. He is not to be ashamed or humiliated; he is not to be exploited, cheated or used for another man's pleasure or profit. There can be no exceptions because of race, creed, national origin or station in life. Rabbi Meir, with sensitive insight, declared that if a man is convicted to die for a crime he is to be buried the same day, lest by hanging in public view he bring shame to his Maker in whose image he is formed.[9]

The test of whether an individual or a society is moral must, in the final analysis, be determined by its treatment of each creature made in God's image. The justification for any economic system is not whether it produces the most goods or the greatest prosperity, but whether it serves to dignify the person who works and gives him an opportunity to fulfill himself. A political order is good not when it is efficient and powerful but when it makes room for the expression and achievement of every person as a free, dignified child of God. In the Jewish tradition what is immoral is basically a blasphemy, *ḥillul ha-Shem*, a profanation of the name of God. Race prejudice, economic injustice and war are condemned because they deny the innate worth of man. By the same token, what a man owes to his fellow man he must ask for and give to himself. As Hillel said, "If I am not for myself, who is for me?" (*Ethics of the Fathers* 1:14). This implies that a person must respect himself for he too is formed in the divine image. This basic Jewish idea of man is the cornerstone upon which rests man's moral destiny on earth.

Unity of Man's Nature

Judaism has vigorously resisted all threats to its basic monotheistic faith and with equal persistence has maintained its belief in the unity of the human creature. Paul, basing himself upon Platonic thought, posited an inevitable conflict between body and soul, in which the soul must struggle to release itself from the unclean body.[10] Such dualism is alien to Jewish tradition, which believes in the essential unity of man. He is formed of two elements, dust and the breath of life, which are united into a single animated being. The Bible presents man as an entity in God's mind before creation, and rejects the suggestion of the transmigration of souls and their pre-existence before birth.

Man's body and soul are envisioned together and created together. In a poetic passage the Midrash relates that everything which came into being was alternately formed of heaven and of earth. When the time came to create man, there was a tie between the terrestrial and the celestial creatures; God therefore made man's soul of heaven and his body of earth. In so doing, He established the harmony of the universe.[11]

Though body and soul are distinguishable one from the other, the distinction is not one between good and evil. The soul is the animating principle of the body; as the Rabbis described it, "What God is to the world, the soul is to man." [12] Three Hebrew words describe various attributes of the soul: *nefesh*, *neshamah* and *ruah*, to which later philosophies ascribed the qualities of reason, passion and appetite. Essentially, however, they describe what the Biblical writer intended by the "image of God," or by "breath of God." This was the distinguishing characteristic which set man apart from the animal kingdom: coming in purity from God, the soul enters upon the everlasting life when the body dies. The real difference is that the flesh is perishable and the soul eternal. Man's obligation is to preserve the purity of his soul; if he fails in this, "behold, I will take it from you" (*Nidah* 30b).

The majority of Jewish philosophers in the Middle Ages accepted Aristotle's definition of the soul as "a substance which actualizes a natural organic body, potentially having life." With Ibn Daud, they characterized it as an "immaterial substance," which is not matter but form. Maimonides found within the unit such diverse faculties and activities as nutritive, sensitive, imaginative, appetitive and rational. To him the "form" of the soul is reason. "If the form (reason) does not communicate its impression to the soul, then the disposition existing in the soul to receive that form is of no avail and exists to no purpose." [13] One recognizes in all this the attempt to describe substantively the nature of the soul. The philosophers got no further than the modern psychic researchers. It is probable that we cannot go beyond the Biblical belief that the soul is the divine essence which gives to matter the quality of "life."

The body of man, the material substance, though perishable is not in opposition to his spirit, nor does it pull him toward sin. *Basar*, "flesh," is neither unclean nor unholy, and it is not the seat of corruption. The body, as much the handiwork of God as are the heavens and the earth, is worthy of reverence and respect. It is related that Hillel once told his pupils that he must leave them to perform a religious duty, "to bathe in the bath house." "If somebody is appointed to scrape and clean the statues of the king which are set up in the theaters and the circuses, and is paid to do the work, and furthermore associates with the nobility," he explained, "how much more should I, who am created in the divine image and likeness, take care of my body?" (*Midrash Leviticus Rabbah* 34). Akiba showed the same respect when he used the little water given him as a prisoner of the Romans to wash his hands rather than for drink.[14]

In Jewish teaching, man is a microcosm in whom is reflected the whole creation of God. The sages went so far as to work out an analogy: man's hair corresponds to the forests, his lips to the walls, his teeth to the doors, his neck to towers, his fingers to nails.[15] Though their knowledge of physiology was limited, the Rabbis demonstrated that every organ of man was designed by God to enhance and prolong his life. The psalmist says of the body, "I will give thanks unto Thee, for I am fearfully and wonderfully made; wonderful are Thy works, and that my soul knoweth well" (Psalm 139:4). Far from accepting the Pauline doctrine of the wickedness of the flesh, and the description of it as the "prison house of the soul," Judaism looked upon man's physical nature as divinely formed and worthy of respect. This gave the Jew the foundation for his rejection of asceticism as a way of life. What God created is for man's enjoyment so long as he does not abuse the privilege. If he has an opportunity to enjoy something and refuses it, he is denying what God created for his benefit. Thus food and clothing are normal interests for a healthy person. Sex is not a sin since God created it, and man may enjoy its benefits. The material world is not evil; on the contrary, it is good, as God declared when He created and looked upon it.

The Hellenic doctrine of a corrupt flesh imprisoning a pure soul came into Western culture through Paulinian Christianity and has played an important role ever since. The Puritan strain was, and still is, a significant factor in our civilization. It had its appeal to Jews even though it was alien to their tradition. Thus a writer in the first century B.C.E. could say, "The corrupt body oppresses the soul, the worldly skeleton is a burden for the soul which has many worries." [16] There are some prescriptions about sex in the *Shulḥan Arukh* which reflect more of Paul than of Moses. These are exceptions, however; as derivatives from the dualism rooted in Hellenism, they are alien to Jewish tradition. The question of the source of evil remains to be answered, but Judaism rejects as an explanation the existence of a dichotomy between a good soul and an evil body.

The modern emphasis upon the interdependence of mind and body, of thought and sense, is a development of studies in physiology and psychology. Though the Rabbis were not scientists, they insisted upon the principle of unity in the nature of man. A well-known Midrash answers the question of whether the body or the soul is to blame for sin.[17] It is only by placing the lame man upon the shoulders of the blind man that the fruit of the king's orchard was stolen. Thus God judges man by putting the soul back in the body and holding them responsible together. Judaism is rooted in monotheism—which is not only the belief that God is one, but the corollary affirmation that man too is one.

Man Is But Flesh and Blood

That man is mortal and finite, and his end dust and ashes, is the predominant view of the Bible. In Daniel and the apocalyptic writings, the concern appears with what lies beyond death. The prayer included in the *Yom Kippur* service embodies the Jewish view of man's limited nature: "for they are but flesh and blood. Man's origin is dust and his end is dust . . . he is like a fragile potsherd, like the grass that withereth; like the flower that fadeth; like the cloud that passeth; like the wind that bloweth; like dust that is blown away; and like a dream that vanisheth." It was Rabbi Joḥanan who said that death is the inevitable end of all creatures.[18] There is a strong tradition that God created man knowing that he is destined to die; the Rabbis say that the angel of death was created on the first day, long before Adam and Eve sinned in the Garden of Eden. While death is the inevitable destiny of every human creature, it is at the same time a punishment for sin and rejection of God's commandments. Failure to obey God is punishable in many cases with death, but it is always premature death. Living the good life is to be rewarded with a long life, aging in health and peace and then being gathered to the fathers.

Judaism drew a vital distinction between the infinite God and the finite creature. The Pharisaic doctrine of bodily resurrection and the more Platonic idea of the immortality of the soul, both of which have their place in Jewish theology, did not save man from his mortality. Only God is eternal; man must die. In commenting on the Rabbis' sentence, "*Tov, zeh ha-ḥayim; tov m'od, zeh ha-mavet*" ("And God saw that it was *good*" refers to life; "And God saw that it was *very good*" refers to death),[19] Chaim Zhetlowsky[20] suggests that it points to the basic Jewish idea that in a conflict between the life of the individual and the life of the species man, the latter must win. Death is important to the evolution of life; we must die so that higher forms may appear. That man is mortal should not dismay us because God's purpose is good, even though man must die to achieve it. Our task is to know that life is good and to make it a blessing by seeking God's will and obeying His commandments. Those of us who have faith may leave the rest to God.

Man Not Innately Sinful

There is a seeming revival today of the doctrine of man's innate sinfulness and the need for his redemption by the grace of God. The enlightenment program, which optimistically looked forward to the steady advance of man and society, has failed. We are told that man has forgotten that he is human and therefore a sinner, and no matter how hard he may try to save himself he is doomed to failure because of the original sin. This doctrine seems to be receiving increased emphasis by theologians, and is reflected in the arts, politics and the social sciences. The doctrine of original sin has become a convenient explanation for the failure of nineteenth- and twentieth-century optimism.

Judaism rejects the suggestion that man is a sinner at birth because he is stamped with the fall of Adam. While there are scattered statements in rabbinic literature which suggest the belief that in the sin of the first man all human beings come into life with an original sin, Ezekiel reflects the major view of the tradition: "The soul that sinneth, it shall die" (Ezekiel 18:4). This is clearly indicated in the imaginative account which makes all men face Adam before they die in order to prove that they die for their own sins, not for the sin of Adam. The first man says to them: "My child, I only committed one sin and was punished for it. You who have committed many transgressions certainly deserve to be punished." [21] The sin in the Garden of Eden may have brought physical consequences, and death is accepted by some sages as the most serious. But it does not announce the belief that man inherits sin. He may be burdened by the fruit of the wrongdoing of his forefathers, but Judaism does not assent to the doctrine that a man can do a wrong for which he is not personally responsible. That man is happy, according to the tradition, whose hour of death is like the hour of birth—that is, free of sin.

In the Jewish view of the nature of man he is endowed with two *yetzarim* ("tendencies" or "inclinations"), one toward evil and the other toward good.[22] The temptation to sin is real, and the desire on man's part to follow it stronger than his desire to choose the good. The Biblical insistence that "sin coucheth at the door" (Genesis 4:7), was interpreted to mean that at birth a child already has the impulse toward evil; indeed, it is his only desire until he is thirteen years old, when the *yetzer tov*, the inclination to do good, is born. Judaism is not naive about the nature of evil and man's propensities toward it. Indeed, evil is part of God's creation and is therefore endowed with purpose. In monotheism one God is responsible for all of creation, for evil as well as good. There is a strong indication that the *yetzer ra*, the inclination toward sin, is a necessary ingredient in life, for through its controlled and wise use the race is perpetuated and civilization made possible.[23]

Sin begins when men abuse the sanctity of life. A Rabbi, commenting on the injunction, "Thou shalt love the Lord thy God with all thy heart" (Deuteronomy 6:5), said it means to love

Him with both impulses, the good and the evil.[24] Even the evil inclination can be employed to serve God and become a means of demonstrating love for Him.

The Jewish tradition does not minimize man's capacity to do evil, but it rejects as false the idea that he is stamped with an ineradicable moral depravity. There is a *yetzer tov* which man can follow, and in which God helps when he so acts. God gave man the Torah as a strong antidote against the evil desire. With control, man can govern the evil inclination. The tradition defines a mighty man as one who conquers his impulses: as he can sweeten a bitter herb so he can turn the *yetzer ra* into the good. Judaism is under no delusion about the power of man's tendency toward sin, but man's task is to oppose it with his gift of the *yetzer tov*. If he has a difficult time, he may study Torah and pray; if he is still in trouble, "let him reflect upon death" (*B'rakhot* 5a).

Doctrine of Free Will

This doctrine that man is endowed with two natural impulses rests upon a belief in moral freedom. In fact, the whole structure of the covenanted relationship between man and God, basic to Judaism, is inconceivable without the affirmation that the human creature is free to choose whether or not he shall obey the commandments. The Biblical formulation of this belief is almost naive in its directness: "I have set before thee life and death, the blessing and the curse; therefore choose life" (Deuteronomy 30:19). No matter how difficult the problems of free will, which later Jewish teachers recognized, Judaism is unwavering in its rejection of any kind of moral fatalism or predestination. The fact that God hardened Pharaoh's heart presents the dilemma of man's freedom and God's prescience. The Rabbis recognized the difficulty, and the *minim* (sectarians) exploited it in their efforts to tear down their basic belief in man's moral freedom. But they could not swerve them from the essential human quality of free will.

The seeming contradiction of man's finitude and his moral freedom was resolved by Akiba with the declaration that "everything is foreseen, yet free will is given" (*Ethics of the Fathers* 3:19). Much of man's life is predestined; it is decreed at birth whether he will be strong or weak, wise or foolish, rich or poor. But in the matter of morality he is master and must choose and take the consequences. "Everything is in the power of Heaven, except the fear of Heaven" (*B'rakhot* 33b)—this is the generally accepted Jewish view from Moses to our own day. Heredity and environment as conditioning factors in man's behavior were understood by the Rabbis, who suggested that the human race originated from one man. Thus the righteous can not claim that they are descended from a righteous ancestor, and the wicked that they are the offspring of a wicked one. If there is any limitation upon God's omnipotence in Judaism, it is in the nature of man's moral freedom.

But freedom demands responsibility, and the burden of it is often too much for man. The doctrine of fate in any of its forms is easier to bear, and cultures which teach it relieve man of the necessity to make moral decisions. Judaism, mindful from its earliest days of man's need for help in this area, presented him with the Torah as a guide and source of strength. God the Creator is the creator of the *yetzer ra*, and seemingly should not punish man for yielding to it. But He also is the author of the Torah, which He fashioned as a counter spirit to it. Let man study the Torah and live by it, and he will overcome the inclination to do evil.

In the charming imagery of the Midrash, the sages resolve the problem of freedom and guilt. The angels object when God gives the Torah to man because he is, after all, only flesh and blood, and in the instance of the generation of the Flood he revealed his wickedness. God tells these heavenly creatures that were they to live on earth they would be even worse. Two of them go down and cannot resist the temptation of women.[25] Moses is made to reply even more poignantly when he asks God questions: Did He bring angels out of Egypt? Did they serve Pharaoh? Do they live among heathens and are they tempted to serve other Gods? Do they work all week so that they need rest? Are they in business and therefore tempted to take false oaths? What good is the Torah for angels? The nature of man is such that he needs the Law as a guide in making his moral decisions.[26]

God's grace is available to man; he may depend upon it in his struggle with freedom. But grace is no substitute for the responsibility of choosing between good and evil. Although the desire to yield to evil is ever before man, he is told, "but thou mayest rule over it" (Genesis 4:7). Torah is an ever-present help for man in the hour of his decision: if he chooses to defile himself the door is wide open; but when he wants to purify himself he receives help from heaven. The desire to violate the law of God is a real and essential part of man's moral nature. The merit of an act lies not in the fact that man has no desire for what is forbidden but that he withstood it because it is prohibited despite his strong desire. In the Jewish tradition man's freedom is expressed in his choosing to live by God's commandments. Liberty is not license; it is reflected in God's exhortation: "let My people go that they may serve Me" (Exodus 10:3). Man's choice is not between freedom and slavery; the highest definition of man's freedom is caught in the sentence, "obedience to law is liberty."

Rabbinic thought was mindful of the theological difficulties involved in the proposition that God is omnipotent and omniscient, and man His creature is morally free. One Rabbi said, "Man does not strike his fingers here below without a decree from above, for it is said: 'A man's goings are of the Lord; how then can man look to his ways?' " [27] But despite the difficulties, they accepted the formula of Akiba which preserved man's moral independence in a world where much was determined. This basic doctrine withstood the influences of Hellenic fatalism, Christian original sin and modern materialism. Ben Sira, for example, declares: "God's wisdom is boundless. He is omnipotent and He sees all. He knows every action of man, but He commanded no man to err." [28] He understands the *yetzer* in a neutral sense, with the power to choose between right and wrong. Philo speaks of God as "a pilot who manages the universe with saving care" and provides for all, yet posits freedom as the very essence of man's nature. This was said against the background of the Stoics, whose materialistic pantheism left no room for man's free will. Josephus, the first-century Jewish historian, in recording the differences between the Jewish sects of his day recognized that the matter of freedom was a major point of debate. The Pharisees, who represent the native tradition of Judaism, are described by him as believing that "it has pleased God to mix up the decrees of fate and man's will, so that man can act virtuously or viciously."

Jewish philosophic speculation is more characteristic of the

Middle Ages than of any other era of its history. This was the natural reaction to Christian Scholasticism and Mohammedan theological discussions. The problem of God's providence and man's freedom was a central issue, and the differences inherent in rabbinic literature came forcefully to the forefront among the Jewish philosophers. Saadia, following the Pharisaic tradition, argued that the omnipotent sovereignty of God does not exclude human freedom. God's foreknowledge of coming events is not the cause of their happening. In fact, the manifestation of divine providence is that man is endowed with the power of mind to choose the right path. Freedom, as Maimonides later defined it, is rooted in reason. Man is morally free because he is a rational creature; this is his distinguishing characteristic, separating him from all other creatures. Maimonides gave the fullest expression to this doctrine:

> God does not decree that a man should be good or evil. It is only fools among gentiles and Jews who maintain that God decrees at birth whether he shall be wicked or righteous. Any man born is free to become righteous as Moses, wicked as Jereboam, a student or an ignoramus, kind or cruel, generous or niggardly. The subject of man's freedom and God's foreknowledge is profoundly difficult for man to grasp, as difficult as it is for man to understand God. We believe that the actions of man are in God's hands, and yet God does not coerce a man or direct him to act one way or another.[29]

In this general vein Judah Halevi suggests that if man is an object of absolute necessity he will merely submit and not do anything about the hunger he feels or the enemy who threatens him. Halevi speculates that man's decision precedes God's knowledge, and that free will is an intermediary cause which traces itself back to the First Cause. The cause, however, is not compulsion; there is a contingency permitting the mind to waver and choose between differing opinions, and is therefore worthy of reward or punishment because of its choice. Ibn Daud added to this by maintaining that God Himself created this contingency of man's freedom. God knows what possibilities exist, but not the actual outcome, and He has willed it so. The general tendency was thus to preserve man's moral freedom even if it called for a limitation of God's power.

There were some dissenting opinions. Hasdai Crescas, alone

among the philosophers, was moved to limit man's freedom in order to preserve God's absolute sovereignty. God's foreknowledge is in a different time sense than man's, and all the future is to God as present knowledge. There is an open possibility for man to choose because what is essential is man's will, not the act; and in this, man's freedom is primary. But even Crescas, troubled about God's omnipotence, could not escape the basic Jewish demand for man's free will in the moral realm, limited as he found it to be. Only Baruch Spinoza dared depart from the basic Jewish tradition and confined man's freedom to the laws of his own nature. His was a deterministic materialism which left no room for either an absolute mind or a free will. "But the mind is determined for willing this or that, by a cause which is determined in its turn by another cause, and this one again by another and so on to eternity." [30] This fatalism in the moral realm is alien to Judaism. The concept of freedom of the will, guarded jealously by Jewish theologians and philosophers of the past, remains central in present-day Jewish thought.

In the nineteenth century Judaism was challenged by the doctrine of idealism, represented by Kant, Hegel, Schelling and others. Jewish thinkers were influenced to a significant degree. But in the matter of freedom and its nature, Jewish philosophers departed from the Hegelian pattern wherein nature and God are inextricably identified. In the Jewish view, man and God are one in that both are free. Man's freedom is a gift of God, which distinguishes him from everything else in nature and brings him closer to God, who is Himself free. This was in a sense a protest against Hegel, who had raised the doctrine of original sin to a metaphysical reality by insisting that God's freedom is expressed in the hard and unbreakable laws of nature: God is free only as He is true to the laws of His being; man is free only when he accepts the will of God as his own will. All Jewish thinkers rebelled against this as a threat to the concept of man as a free moral agent capable of choosing between alternatives. The danger of deification of nature was real to them, and though they reflected much of the German idealistic philosophy, they departed, without exception, on the nature of man's moral freedom. Ethical monotheism is impossible with a human creature who is not free to choose between good and evil.

The modern climate of thought on the matter of free will discloses a strange paradox. The natural sciences, which recently seemed to support a mechanistic view of man holding all of life within rigid laws of causation, have given way to such terms as "the law of probability" and the "principle of indeterminacy." It may be premature to label this as evidence of man's moral freedom, but we are warranted in believing that the possibility for it is real. The Freudian concept of man whose conscious life is governed by animal instinct, hidden and embedded in the unconscious, has given way to the belief that man is endowed with the capacity to conquer his evil impulses. Indeed, the most recent developments in biology and anthropology present a picture of man free from the chains of original sin and endowed with the capacity to change his characteristics and to learn from experience. They reveal a creature free enough in his nature to fashion the instruments which form his cultural milieu and thus help determine his own destiny. Indeed, the sciences tend to confirm the Jewish affirmation that man is a morally free agent within a universe which is fixed at many points.

The capstone of the Jewish view of man is his ever-present opportunity for repentance and forgiveness.[31] No matter how far he may fall, man is always free to knock on the gates which lead to God's mercy. If he repents in sincerity he is immediately forgiven. This is so integral to the whole structure of Jewish theology that it runs in an unbroken line from the Bible to the most modern prayer of the synagogue. Its necessity stems from the frank recognition that man was created with an evil impulse which makes him prone to sin. Justice, then, demands that the antidote of repentance be provided for his salvation. Thus the Rabbis suggested that *t'shuvah* or penitence was created even before the world itself was formed. In fact, they project the thought that *t'shuvah* is the cement which keeps the world from falling apart.[32]

The act of atonement runs the gamut from the priestly drama of sacrifice to the prophetic moral prescription of turning from evil and seeking good. At no time is man deprived of the privilege and opportunity to reject his choice of the wrong path and to retrieve his steps and put himself on the right one. The prophets often sound heartless in their pronouncement of judgment for the sins of the people. No other people in history has dared to catalogue and canonize the evil-doings of the people and the punishments which must follow, as does the Bible. At no point is the door closed to salvation. The call of God to man, which Moses recorded, is the central doctrine of Judaism: "Return O Israel, unto the Lord thy God; For thou hast stumbled in thine iniquity" (Hosea 14:2).

The belief that God is a merciful Father who must judge with kindness His children whom He loves is a pronounced doctrine in the Bible. Nowhere is this more forcefully presented than in the covenanting statement: "The Lord, the Lord God, merciful and gracious, long-suffering, and abundant in goodness and truth; keeping mercy unto the thousandth generation, forgiving iniquity and transgression and sin" (Exodus 34:6). Iniquity must be punished in any universe of moral content, lest everything turn to chaos, yet it must be tempered by mercy and the ever-present possibility of reform and forgiveness. In one of the rabbinic legends, the Torah speaks to God as He is preparing to create the first man. "O Lord of the world! The world is Thine, Thou canst do with it as seemeth good in Thine eyes. But the man Thou art now creating will be of few days and full of trouble and sin. If it be not Thy purpose to have forbearance and patience with him, it will be better not to call him into being." To which God replies: "Is it for naught I am called long-suffering and merciful?"

Basically, Judaism affirms its faith in the possibility of man's moral and spiritual maturation. The perfectibility of human nature is not a problem to Jewish thought. "In the end of days it shall come to pass"—but that is God's time, not man's. For the human creature there is the assurance that his effort to change is supported by the reality of the world and assured by the promise of God. Step by step man moves nearer to the Kingdom of God. Progress is an ever-present potential which man can help along by his own moral growth. Against all philosophies of fate or doom, Judaism stands firmly and unitedly. There may be differences among Jews about traditional observances or the concept of resurrection. But about the possibility of moral growth for man there is unquestioned unanimity. It may be said with justice that the strength of Judaism rests on its belief in a realistic hope for man.

FOR FURTHER READING

HESCHEL, Abraham Joshua, *Who is Man* (Stanford, Stanford University Press, 1965). See next entry.

HESCHEL, Abraham Joshua, *The Insecurity of Freedom* (New York: Schocken, 1966). This collection of essays, together with the first title above contain key statements by A.J. Heschel on the human condition in our time. As one of the seminal thinkers of our era they are a "must" for anyone interested in this issue.

JACOBS, Louis, *A Jewish Theology* (New York: Behrman House, 1973). A modern review of the individual elements which comprise the totality of Jewish anthropology.

KAPLAN, Mordecai M., *The Purpose & Meaning of Jewish Existence*, (Philadelphia, Jewish Publication Society, 1971). Kaplan's reconstruction of Jewish life after the model of Hermann Cohen's neo-Kantianism, though touched with his own special anthropologist genius.

SOLOVEITCHIK, Joseph, (a) "Catharsis" (b) "Humility & Majesty", in *Tradition* Vol. 17 (Spring 1978). The reflections of the Rav, American Orthodoxy's leading thinker, on the meaning of inner spiritual transformation and man's essential character.

STITSKIN, Leon, *Jewish Philosophy A Study in Personalism* (New York: Yeshiva University Press, 1976). A somewhat mixed attempt to restate Orthodox Jewish beliefs in a modern personalist philosophical idiom.

11 . *When Man Fails God*

ELIEZER BERKOVITS

I N D I S C U S S I N G man's nature and his relationship to God, we make the basic assumption that law prescribes man's behavior. While violation of man-made laws is criminal, the disobedience of divine law is a sin against God. In this framework, the concept of sin implies human responsibility and freedom. Obedience to a law or principle of behavior can properly be expected only of a person free to choose between alternatives and thus responsible for his choice. The breaking of a divine law can be done only by a man who could have acted differently if he wanted to.

Judaism distinguishes between sins against God (*ben adam lamakom*) and sins against man (*ben adam l'ḥavero*). The latter comprehend violations of ethical laws, while the former are infractions of the purely religious commandments that deal with faith, observance and ritual. Judaism considers both codes divine, deriving validity from God. A wrong done to a man is a sin because the moral code is established by God. "Thou shalt not murder" is God's command. "Thou shalt not bear false witness against thy neighbor" is no less part of the Decalogue than "Thou shalt have no other gods before Me." "Thou shalt love the Lord thy God with all thy heart, and with all thy soul, and with all thy might" is a divine commandment as is "Thou shalt love thy neighbor as thyself." A sin against man is equally a sin against God. The prophet Malachi speaks for God (3:5):

And I will come near to you to judgment;
And I will be a swift witness

Against the sorcerers, and against the adulterers,
And against false swearers.
And against those that oppress the hireling in his wages,
The widow, and the fatherless,
And that turn aside the stranger from his right,
And fear Me not.

At times it would seem easier to find atonement for sins against God than for those against man. God will forgive sins against Himself, but He will not pardon sins against another man unless the offender first receives forgiveness from whomever he wronged.[1] A Midrashic interpretation by Rabbi Eliezer holds that the generation of the Flood was annihilated by God as punishment for the sin of robbery. But the generation that built the tower of Babel rebelled against God Himself, and was dispersed rather than destroyed. Why this mercy? "Because they loved each other, for so it is said of them: 'And the whole earth was of one language and of one speech'" (*Genesis Rabbah* 38). The phrase is understood to mean that they lived in peace with each other. They were therefore less strictly punished than if they had sinned against one another.

If sin depends on human decision and a choice between alternative courses of action, one can never consider the deed alone, unrelated to the man who performs it. One may transgress a law intentionally or unintentionally, as an act of defiance against the lawgiver or in spite of full acknowledgment of the law's authority, giving in to human weakness and placing one's own wishes ahead of a divine command. For example, a Jew may desecrate the Sabbath unintentionally, unaware that a certain activity is forbidden. Or he may transgress in full awareness of the laws of the Sabbath, yet disregard them out of expediency. Or he may consciously reject the concept of a sanctified day. Thus Jewish tradition distinguishes between *ḥet*, unintentional sin; *avon*, intentional sin; and *pesha*, acts of deliberate rebellion.[2] The resulting deed may be the same in each case, but the nature of the sin differs. The determining factor is the attitude in which it is executed.

Judgment takes account of the individual sinner and his special circumstances. The Talmud teaches that the unintentional transgressions of the *talmid ḥakham* (the man learned in the Torah) are accounted as if they were deliberate sins, whereas even the intentional transgressions of an *am ha'aretz* (a man ignorant of the Torah) are judged as if they were unintentional violations.[3] A human being may be responsible for his unintentional acts. An oversight may be due to avoidable lack of attention; an act performed in ignorance may be reprehensible if the transgressor's state of ignorance is itself not justifiable.

Much more is demanded of a *talmid ḥakham*. Since he is fully aware of the importance of the divine injunctions, he must always act with sufficient deliberation so as to avoid even unintentional transgressions. If he fails in this respect, his failure may be due to carelessness. On the other hand, the *am ha'aretz* may act deliberately, without full awareness of the meaning and consequences of his actions. Since he does not know what he is doing, even his deliberate transgression may have the quality of an unintentional sin.

The closer a person is to God, the more severely is his transgression judged.[4] The nature of a sin is inseparable from the nature of the sinner. Sin is not an action which takes place exclusively outside of man. What goes on within his heart and soul determines its most significant feature.

Since transgression can never be evaluated independently of the doer, it is difficult to establish an objective order of gravity among sinful acts. But attempts have been made in the Talmud. One method of classifying sins is to distinguish between those committed by an actual deed (*lav sheyesh bo ma'aseh*) and those committed by inaction (*lav she'ein bo ma'aseh*). Sins of omission are considered less serious than those of commission. Nevertheless, the story is told that once, as Rabbi Judah Hanassi was occupied with study of the Torah, a calf was led by to be slaughtered. The animal, frenzied with fear and trying to escape, ran to the rabbi bleating as if to ask for protection. But Rabbi Judah did not intervene, as if saying to the animal: "What can I do for you? It is for this that you have been created." Immediately, he was punished with a sickness of the mouth from which he suffered for thirteen years.[5] Objectively, Rabbi Judah was blameless, in the sense that slaughtering the calf for food is permissible. Nevertheless, Rabbi Judah was censured for not having shown mercy to the animal. It was the animal's destiny to be slaughtered, but its terror should have been assuaged because the mercies of God are bestowed on all His creatures.

Although Judaism classifies idolatry, sexual immorality and murder as the three deadly sins,[6] hatred between men is equally heinous. For example, it is stated that the First Temple was destroyed because of the aforementioned sins. But at the time of the Second Temple, the people were very virtuous, occupying themselves with the Torah and the commandments and practicing charity. When it was asked why then was that Temple destroyed, the Rabbis answered: ". . . because of the causeless hatred that was rampant among them. This teaches you that causeless hatred between a man and his fellow weighs as heavily as the three deadly sins put together" (*Yoma* 9b). Though it may be difficult to judge hating another person as being worse than murdering him, the moral degeneration of a man motivated by such causeless hatred may render him more censurable than a murderer. Rabbi Joḥanan exclaims:

> Come and see how grievous are the consequences of violence! The generation of the Flood committed all the sins under the sun, yet their doom was not sealed until they put their hands to robbery as well, for so it is written: "For the earth is filled with violence through them; and behold, I will destroy them with the earth."
>
> (*Sanhedrin* 108a)

Acts of violence indicate a mean and corrupt society and doom it.

In this same sense, pride is sometimes considered a sin equal to idolatry and the denial of God; slander may even surpass the deadly sins in gravity.[7] According to the Talmud, a person who commits adultery has not forfeited his share in the world-to-come; one who insults his fellow man in public has done so.[8]

The Evil Inclination

What is the cause of sin in man? In the language of Jewish tradition, the answer is the *yetzer hara*, the evil inclination, from which there is no escape. God calls the *yetzer* of man's heart "evil from his youth" (Genesis 8:21) and the Rabbis maintain that the youth of a man begins with the separation from his mother's womb.[9] Is it then useless to expect man to refrain from evil? Is his only hope for God's compassion: "for He knoweth our *yetzer*; He remembereth that we are dust" (Psalms 103:14)?

Since the force for evil in the human heart is so powerful that man is often ruled by it, does it become meaningless to speak of sin? A deed may be sinful only if performed by man himself and not by some natural power that uses him as a helpless instrument. In the Midrash and Talmud there are sayings which indicate that, though "it is difficult to say so and impossible for the mouth to elaborate," perhaps not all the blame should be placed on man. The nature with which he is born has some responsibility for his failings. As Rabbi Joḥanan puts it: "if it were not for that, there would be no ground on which man in his sinfulness could stand at all." [10] What then is this *yetzer*, the cause of man's failings in the sight of God?

In a Midrashic interpretation, Rabbi Samuel, the son of Naḥman, called "good" the *yetzer tov* or good inclination, and "very good" the *yetzer ra* or evil inclination. ". . . Were it not for the evil inclination man would not build a house for himself or get married; he would neither beget children, nor ply a trade or pursue a profession" (*Genesis Rabbah* 9:9). The evil inclination is here recognized as a necessary ingredient of life itself, the Jewish concept of the *élan vital*, the individual's desire to live and survive. It is the affirmation of one's personal existence and the drive for self-fulfillment. It is not evil in itself but only the potential source of evil. The vital forces of individual existence which maintain a man in the world are the same which may carry a man against the world. The desire to survive may engender ruthlessness; man's justified desire to be himself may become the source of pride and rebellion against God.

What then is to be done with the "inclination of the heart"? One must teach it to respect the boundaries. Man is sufficiently free to acquire a high measure of control over his heart's inclination. "If you really want it, you can rule over it," says the Talmud (*Kiddushin* 30b).

Judaism has no illusion regarding man's difficulty in gaining control over the inclination of his heart. It is a never-ending struggle, and what is gained today may easily be lost tomorrow. As Rabbi Yitz'hak puts it, "The *yetzer* of a man renews itself daily against him (*Kiddushin* 30b).

Man may gain control over his evil inclination, but the next instant is a new moment and the beginning of a new struggle. Mastery over the evil inclination is never a condition which a man reaches; it is an event through which he passes, a station from which he has to move on to the next phase. "Do not trust yourself till the day of your death," says Hillel (*Ethics of the Fathers* 2:5).

This is the plight of all men, without regard of person or status. Indeed, the more saintly the man, the more severe his battle for self-control and self-mastery; as the Talmud says, the greater a man, the more powerful his evil inclination, the closer he is to the possibility of spiritual disaster.[11] This follows from the Jewish understanding that the more endowed a man is, the greater the resources of his individual vitality, and the fiercer the struggle he has to wage in order to control his drives for self-realization and to keep them within the boundaries set by the laws of men or the Law of God. In this sense Rabbi Johanan, in the unique style of Midrashic exegesis, raises a question, "Why was death decreed for the *tzaddikim* (saints)?," which he answers: "As long as the *tzaddikim* live, they struggle with their *yetzer*. When they die, they are at rest" (*Genesis Rabbah* 9:7).

Another Midrash says: "The Holy One, blessed be He, does not call a *tzaddik* a saint until he has been put into the grave. Why? Because all the days of his life he is beset by the evil inclination and God does not trust him in this world till the day of his death." Not even the patriarchs, the "fathers of the world," are an exception.[12]

The resources at man's disposal to help him in his struggle with the inclination of his heart are in man himself, the Torah and God. God created man with two inclinations, teaches the Talmud, one good and one bad.[13] While the term *yetzer tov* is used often, there is little elaboration in Talmudic or Midrashic literature on its meaning. Presumably it can be understood as an elementary vital urge, similar to that of the *yetzer hara*, but one acknowledging the existence of the other, seeking out the non-ego. Urges and drives in themselves are neither moral nor immoral; they are natural manifestations of being alive. If without the evil inclination a man would neither build a house nor marry or beget children, without the good inclination he might build a house but not a city; he might beget children and yet be no father. In other words, life needs both self-affirmation and other-affirmation. In order to exist, one must desire to be oneself and one must desire to be oneself with others.

Yet if one compares the two drives, the *yetzer hara* or vital drive for self-affirmation is much more powerful than that for other-affirmation. Fully aware of this discrepancy, the Talmud compares the evil inclination to a mighty king who lays siege to a city, and the good inclination to a meek man inside it.[14] What hope is there for that city? According to the Talmud, the meek man becomes the savior of the city because he is not only meek but also wise. What is his wisdom? His wisdom is the Torah, which Jewish tradition calls *tavlin* or "seasoning" for the evil inclination.[15] The Torah is not only the Law of God but it also teaches all-embracing discipline that helps the Jew to deal effectively with his evil inclination. The task is not to eradicate the *yetzer hara* from the heart of man, but to soften its rawness, to tame its elementary force for its legitimate function of helping man to live in the presence of God.

Two sources of strength are thus accessible to man, the good within him and the good within the Torah. But he still needs divine assistance. Rabbi Shimon ben Lakish has reason to declare: "Daily man's evil inclination threatens to overwhelm and to destroy him. Were it not for God's help, man would not be able to stand up to it" (*Kiddushin* 30b).

If man sins because of his evil inclinations, he is misusing his *yetzer hara* and at the same time denying expression to his *yetzer tov*. By thus misdirecting and betraying his vital inclinations, man confounds himself. According to the Rabbis, a sin stupefies the human heart[16] and defiles the soul.[17] Every sin undermines a man's moral strength and diminishes his chances to meet the next temptation more hopefully. The Rabbis taught that a man's soul is the witness against him;[18] whatever a man does, he does first of all to himself. A sin implies an act of self-defeat.

Reward and Punishment[19]

Whatever reward or punishment there may be and whatever their meaning, Jewish tradition holds that they result from the account a man has to render and from God's judgment based on that reckoning: *din ve'ḥeshbon* (judgment and reckoning). God judges man and the world, and at the same time He is merciful and loving. How may judgment be reconciled with the idea of mercy and love? Job asked: "If I have sinned, what do

I unto Thee, O Thou Watcher of man?" (Job 7:20) Elihu raised a similar question: "If thou hast sinned, what doest thou against Him? If thou be righteous, what givest thou unto Him? Or what receiveth He of thy hand?" (Job 35:6-7) Judgment is completely compatible wtih love and mercy because God's law is for the sake of man. God wills life for man:

> I have set before thee this day life and good, and death and evil . . . I have set before thee life and death, the blessing and the curse; therefore choose life, that thou mayest live, thou and thy seed; to love the Eternal One thy God, to hearken to His voice, and to cleave unto Him: for that is thy life, and the length of thy days.
>
> (Deuteronomy 31:15, 19-20)

In giving the Torah of Life (*Torat Ḥayim*) to the Jewish people, God gave them a law for their own sake to teach them how to live. God in His love and mercy gave Israel the Torah, as expressed in the evening prayer: "With everlasting love Thou hast loved the house of Israel, thy people; Torah and commandments, statutes and judgments hast Thou taught us." That God's law for man is a manifestation of His love is basic to the Jewish attitude toward judgment, forgiveness and *t'shuvah* (return).

Since the Law is God's gift to man for his own sake, God's forgiveness too is granted for man's sake. Having failed, having lost a share in the kind of life that God has meant for him, man would not profit by unconditional forgiveness. Like a good father who judges his child and, when necessary, punishes him out of love for the child's sake, God judges men in a manifestation of His mercy. A Midrash elaborates on the phrase: "The Eternal One is for me my helper" (Psalms 118:7).

> The meaning of this should be compared to some who appeared before a judge in fear of the verdict. But they were told: do not fear the judgment but be of strong heart. Similarly, Israel has to stand in judgment before the Holy One, blessed be He, and they are afraid of the verdict. However, the angels of God say to them: Do not fear the verdict. Don't you know Him? He is from your city . . . He is your brother . . . Indeed, He is your Father, as it is written: "Is not He thy Father that has gotten thee?"
>
> (Midrash *Shoḥer Tov 118:10*)

Since man is capable of choosing, he is responsible for his choices and may at any time be called upon to justify them. He is thus judged for his own sake, and, according to the verdict, receives reward or punishment. The whole Biblical history of Israel is represented as a rhythmical movement between the people's loyalty and their disloyalty, and the corresponding grace and anger of God. The prophets interpreted events in the life of numerous other nations in the same manner.

But post-Biblical history up to our own day defies interpretation in terms of reward and punishment. If we consider the annihilation of six million Jews under the Nazis, no concept of punishment can conceivably yield an explanation. Nor is the problem different in the question of reward. Can we really say that success and happiness are given to the deserving?

As old as man himself is the problem of the justness of divine rule. Are reward and punishment apportioned to men and nations according to their merits? The Talmud has Moses asking: "How is it that there is a *tzaddik* and it goes well with him, and another *tzaddik* and he fares ill? In the same way, there is a *rasha* (wicked person) who does well and another *rasha* who is plagued by misfortune?" The Talmudic response is: "A *tzaddik* and it is well with him? A perfect *tzaddik!* A *tzaddik* who fares ill? An imperfect *tzaddik!* A *rasha* and he is well off? Not a complete *rasha*. A *rasha* and unfortunate? A perfect *rasha*" (*B'rakhot* 7a). The answer implies that an imperfect *rasha* fares better than an imperfect *tzaddik*. Another Talmudic opinion holds that the *tzaddik* is punished in this world for his few sins so that he may reap only reward for his many good deeds in the world-to-come; the *rasha* is rewarded in this world for his few good deeds, so that in the world to come only punishment should await him.[20]

Together the two passages suggest that the perfect *tzaddik*, having committed no sins at all, would know no evil, either in this world or in the future one. The perfect *rasha*, having no good deeds to his credit, will know only punishment. The imperfect *tzaddik* will suffer on earth for the few sins of his imperfection and will thus fare worse than the imperfect *rasha*, who is rewarded here for the few good deeds which save him from total wickedness. This theory barred the suggestion of indifference toward good and evil. Jewish tradition always took its stand on an axiom of God's justice. The tradition went so far as to state: "Know that the reward of the *tzaddikim* is in the world-to-come" (*Ethics of the Fathers* 2:26).

The Rabbis went even further: "There is no reward for a *mitzvah* in this world." [21] In another approach, Rabbi Abba said in the name of Rabbi Kahana: "The Holy One, blessed be He, has removed the reward for *mitzvot* from this world, so that Israel may contemplate them and do them wholeheartedly (for their own sake)." [22] If reward consistently followed fulfillment of God's commandments, one might do them not for merit but for gain. Judaism teaches: "Be not like servants who serve their master on condition of being rewarded, but like servants who serve their master not on condition of being rewarded" (*Ethics of the Fathers* 6:3).

To serve God without ulterior motive, reward in this world must be disposed with. So too if punishment automatically followed sin, people would refrain from evil in fear of punishment, not in devotion to God's law. Man would lose his freedom to choose between good and evil and become a puppet of the Almighty: the Torah would cease being a way of life. Reward and punishment are required of justice, but—for the sake of man—its divine dispensation is not revealed.

Since Judaism sees the world-to-come as purely spiritual, [23] reward must be of a spiritual nature. In what could such a reward consist? [24] Some envision it as being permitted to behold the truth close to its source and enjoying the glory of the Divine Presence. But it is taught that it is wrong to serve God in anticipation of even such rewards.

If one serves God not for the sake of reward, not even for the sake of a share in the world-to-come, then clearly the service of God itself is man's highest goal and greatest value. Judaism teaches life as God intended it to be lived by man. In fulfilling the will of God, man fulfills himself; in rejecting it, he loses himself. Therefore, service of God carries its own reward and rejection its own punishment. Thus Ben Azzai maintained: "The reward of a *mitzvah* is a *mitzvah* and the reward of an *averah* (a sin) is an *averah*" (*Ethics of the Fathers* 4:2). Whatever other reward and punishment there may be, they are not known to man.

The believing Jew ends all speculation by standing with Judah Halevi in affirming his faith in the justice of God.[25] He considers the problem of reward and punishment in the light of the whole life of the individual, of which only the phase spent in this world is known to him. The spectacle of the innocent, the meek and God-fearing suffering and the arrogant prospering could destroy religious faith in a supreme just providence, if human existence ended with death. Even though a father hopes to live on in his children, can his own undeserved suffering be justified? Can attainment of progress toward a better world give answer to those untold millions crushed in the meantime? Will the suffering of the individual remain forever unredeemed? Not in the order of a just God, one surmises. For injustice and suffering endured by the individual, one must comfort the individual. If God is just, man must be immortal.

The philosopher Immanuel Kant called the belief in personal immortality "a postulate of practical reason." He meant that a man's moral perfection could never be reached in his short lifetime but only in a world of infinity. He assumed that infinity exists and man is immortal. Judaism's faith in immortality stands not on the demand of "practical reason" that man be perfect, but on the truth that God is perfect. God is the guarantor that the imbalance of human history is somehow righted.

T'shuvah

If judgment follows sin, the sinner finds his hope in God. Said the Rabbis: "Let a man not say, since I have sinned, there is no hope for me; but let him set his trust in the Holy One, blessed be He. Let him do *t'shuvah* and He will receive him. And let him not say: if so, what becomes of my dignity? Let him hate dignity and humble himself and change in *t'shuvah*" (Midrash Shoher Tov 40:3).

T'shuvah, a uniquely Jewish concept, means literally "response" or "return." Repentance and "renewal" of faith are only one phase of *t'shuvah*. Isaiah said: "Let the wicked forsake his way, and the man of iniquity his thoughts; and let him return unto the Eternal and He will have compassion on him, and to our God, for He will abundantly pardon" (Isaiah 55:7). The return to God is not merely "a change of heart," but a change in one's way of life. Ezekiel deals with *t'shuvah* by declaring: "As I live, saith the Lord God, I have no pleasure in the death of the wicked, but that the wicked turn from his way and live; turn ye, turn ye from your evil ways, for why will ye die, O house of Israel" (Ezekiel 33:11). *T'shuvah* is a turning away and a turning toward—a matter of believing and of altering one's daily living.

The turning away begins with a realization of having sinned. At times, that realization and confession of sin are enough to bring God's forgiveness. When King David confesses to the prophet Nathan, "I have sinned against the Eternal One," the prophet reassures him: "The Eternal hath put away thy sin; thou shalt not die" (II Samuel 12:13). David demonstrates his greatness by renouncing royal dignity and pride in his confession of sin.

But realization of guilt is not enough. The sinner must also forsake his way. "He that covereth his transgressions shall not prosper; but whoso confesseth and forsaketh them shall obtain mercy" (Proverbs 28:13).

Jewish tradition recognizes four conditions necessary for *t'shuvah:* regret for the past, desisting from objectionable conduct, confession and the firm resolution never to backslide.[26] Repentance is the first phase and regeneration the second. The first is only the preliminary condition necessary for leading a man up to the second, the turning toward God. Every sin undermines the spiritual strength of the sinner; his regeneration is required. Thus the psalmist exclaims: "As for me, I said: 'O Eternal One, be gracious unto me; heal my soul; for I have sinned against Thee'" (Psalms 41:5). *T'shuvah* is called healing,[27] and is also seen as purification. The psalmist prays:

Wash me thoroughly from mine iniquity, and cleanse me from my sin . . . Behold! Thou desirest truth in the inward parts; make me, therefore, to know wisdom in mine inmost heart. Purge me with hyssop, and I shall be clean; wash me, and I shall be whiter than snow . . . Create me a clean heart, O God; and renew a steadfast spirit within me.

(Psalms 57:4-12)

The Talmud draws a sharp distinction between those motivated by *t'shuvah m'yirah,* "return out of fear" (of punishment), and *t'shuvah me-ahavah*, "return out of love" (of God). Of the former it is said that their intentional sins are accounted as if they were unintentional; of those who return out of love, their intentional transgressions become like merits.[28] At the source is a concept of the human personality as dynamic, spontaneous and capable of regeneration and renewal.

T'shuvah is thus an experience of personality transformation. When performed out of fear, it lessens the burden of sin but does not remove it; intentional transgressions become unintentional ones. *T'shuvah* undertaken out of love accomplishes a fundamental transformation, in which healing and purification are complete. Intentional sins of the past function almost as meritorious deeds in their impact and significance for the new personality. Past failures may serve as new sources of spiritual strength and security for the *ba'al t'shuvah*, "the man who returned."

Transformation through personality renewal may be completely spontaneous. "Even if he was an inveterate *rasha* (wicked person) all his days, but returns at the very end," says the Talmud, "they will not remind him of his wickedness" (*Kiddushin* 40b). *T'shuvah* as transformation is like creation; it requires a return to God in love, a timeless moment.

King David turns to God for the healing of his soul. He pleads for God to "create" in him a clean heart and "renew" his spirit. The fulfillment of *t'shuvah* is a new birth wrought by the mercy of God. "God receives those who return and creates them a new creation (*Leviticus Rabbah* 30). "Because they renew their deeds, the Holy One, Blessed be He, creates them a new creation" (Midrash *Shoher Tov* 102:3).

Turning away is performed by an individual. Turning toward God implies mutuality: one returns to God because He is willing to turn to man. "Return unto Me, and I will return unto you, saith the Eternal One of hosts" (Malachi 3:7). As Israel, turning from its ways, turns to God, so God, turning from His anger, turns to Israel. "Thou hast withdrawn all Thy wrath; Thou hast turned from the fierceness of Thine anger" (Psalms 85:4,7). The ultimate appeal of the psalmist is: "Wilt Thou not quicken us again, that Thy people may rejoice in Thee?" A better rendering of the reference to *t'shuvah* might be: "Wilt Thou not return-quicken us?" Inherent in the text is the thought that

God's return to Israel and His quickening of Israel are a single action. In God's return to Israel, Israel is brought to new life.

Sin is estrangement between man and God: "But your iniquities have separated you and your God, and your sins have hid His face from you, that He will not hear" (Isaiah 59:2). As man turns from his sin toward God, God turns toward man. In the restored relationship of love and mercy, man gains a clean heart and comes to a new life.

A Midrashic comment reads: "The Holy One, blessed be He, does not reject any creature. He is willing to receive them all. The gates are always open and all who desire may enter" (*Exodus Rabbah* 19). Open gates are of no avail to those who have no desire to enter. *T'shuvah* begins with man and is completed by God: "Happy are ye, Israel! Before whom do you purify yourself and who purifies you? Your Father in Heaven," Rabbi Akiba exclaimed (*Yoma* 85b; Mishnah). God is Israel's hope and the ever-present well of Israel's eternal renewal.

FOR FURTHER READING

HESCHEL, Abraham Joshua, "The Concept of Man in Jewish Thought," in *The Concept of Man* edited by S. Radhakrishnan and P.T. Raju (London: Allen & Unwin, 1960). pp. 108–157. A wonderful, if very Heschel-like, statement on the Jewish view of the human condition.

JACOBS, Louis, *A Jewish Theology* (New York: Behrman House, 1973). Contains helpful summary chapters, organized chronologically, on the themes of 'Sin & Repentance' (ch. 7) and 'Reward & Punishment' (ch. 18).

KOOK, Abraham, *Philosophy of Repentance* (New York: Yeshiva University Press, 1968). Typically difficult, profound, reflections by this great mystic-rabbinic figure and first chief Rabbi of Modern Palestine.

PELI, Pinchas H., *Soloveitchik: On Repentance* (Jerusalem: Orot Publishing Company, 1980). A classic collection of oral discourses by Rav Joseph Soloveitchik on the theme of *teshuvah*.

PETUCHOWSKI, Jacob, "The Concept of Teshuvah in the Bible and Talmud," in *Judaism*, Vol. 17 (1968), pp. 175–185. A helpful introduction to and summary of basic ideas.

URBACH, Ephraim, *The Sages* (Jerusalem: Magnes Press, 1975). A distinguished scholarly review of talmudic conceptions of man, sin, repentance, among other related doctrines.

12 . *Suffering and Evil*

HAROLD M. SCHULWEIS

> If a bird's nest chance to be before thee in the way, in any tree or
> on the ground, with young ones or eggs, and the mother-bird
> sitting upon the young, or upon the eggs, thou shalt not take the
> mother-bird with the young; thou shalt in any wise let the mother-
> bird go, but the young thou mayest take unto thyself, that it may
> be well with thee and that thou mayest prolong thy days.
>
> (Deuteronomy 22:6)

ELISHA ben Abuya, observing a child climbing a tree to gather
eggs from a nest in obedience of both his father's request and
the cited Scriptural ordinance, saw the youngster fall from the
tree and die. The shock of the death of such an innocent who
dutifully followed the prescriptions of the Torah led this second
century rabbi to the painful conclusion: "There is no judge and
no justice." It was such an event, the Rabbis speculated, that
caused him to turn apostate. Other accounts explaining his loss
of faith suggest analogous cases involving the suffering and death
of the righteous.[1]

No event sears the soul of the believer more deeply than the
discrepancy between an act and its consequence, whether that
discrepancy be among the righteous who suffer or the wicked
who prosper. And no problem clings more tenaciously to the
whole of Jewish literature than the apparent contradiction between the existence of evil and the presence of a wise, powerful
and just God.

Many Jewish solutions to the problem of evil have been put
forward. But for reasons that may become apparent, a justifica-

tion of God's ways or a theodicy is much harder to come by in Judaism than in other theologies.

"*Unde malum?*"—"from whence evil"—if there be a God? The Greek philosopher Epicurus formulated the problem as a tight dilemma: "God either wishes to take away evils and is unable; or He is able but unwilling; or He is neither willing nor able."

It would seem that to resolve the dilemma, one or more of the traditional attributes of God—wisdom, power, benevolence—needs to be deleted or seriously curtailed. Traditional theologies of all faiths have been aware of the consequence of reducing God's attributes, and have acted to protect the status of the deity.

In arguments used by traditional theologians, what man calls evil sometimes turns out to be good in God's eyes. And suffering, pain and death occasionally end up as the consequences of man's erring belief or behavior, and are therefore just punishments. Invariably and inevitably, the divine image is sustained, and it is man who is diminished. God's omniscience, omnipotence and benevolence can seemingly be held inviolate only at the expense of man's ignorance, impotence or malevolence. For this reason, traditional justifications of God's ways tend to read like cases of conflicting interests, clashes of personalities in which God and man are adversaries.

Jewish religious literature incorporates each and every argument employed in these traditional expositions. But there is one significant, indeed revolutionary, difference. This is the cry of resistance, never completely stifled, which echoes from the earliest Biblical documents down to contemporary writings, and by which the Jew openly resists being shoved downward in the balancing between him and his God. It is the unprecedented struggle in which the Jew asserts nothing less than his moral equality with his Father.

The Moral Partnership

And Abraham drew near, and said: "Wilt Thou indeed sweep away the righteous with the wicked? Peradventure there are fifty righteous within the city; wilt Thou indeed sweep away and not forgive the place for the fifty righteous that are therein? That be far from Thee to do after this manner, to slay the righteous

with the wicked, that so the righteous should be as the wicked;
that be far from Thee; shall not the Judge of all the earth do
justly?

(Genesis 18:23-25)

Right wouldest Thou be, O Lord,
Were I to contend with Thee,
Yet will I reason with Thee:
Wherefore doth the way of the wicked prosper?
Wherefore are all they secure that deal very treacherously?
Thou has planted them, yea, they have taken root;
They grow, yea, they bring forth fruit;
Thou art near in their mouth,
And far from their reins.

(Jeremiah 12:1-2)

Awake, why sleepest Thou, O Lord?
Arouse Thyself, cast not off forever.
Wherefore hidest Thou Thy face,
And forgettest our affliction and our oppression?
For our soul is bowed down to the dust;
Our belly cleaveth unto the earth.
Arise for our help.
And redeem us for Thy mercy's sake.

(Psalms 44:24-27)

How long, O Lord, shall I cry,
And Thou wilt not hear?
I cry out unto Thee of violence,
And Thou wilt not save.
Why dost Thou show me iniquity,
And beholdest mischief?
And why are spoiling and violence before me?
So that there is strife, and contention ariseth.

(Habakkuk 1:2-3)

Thou that art of eyes too pure to behold evil,
And that canst not look on mischief,
Wherefore lookest Thou, when they deal treacherously,
And holdest Thy peace, when the wicked swalloweth up
The man that is more righteous than he?

(Habakkuk 1:13)

As God liveth, who hath taken away my right;
And the Almighty, who hath dealt bitterly with me;
All the while my breath is in me,
And the spirit of God is in my nostrils,
Surely my lips shall not speak unrighteousness,
Neither shall my tongue utter deceit;

Far be it from me that I should justify you;
Till I die I will not put away mine integrity from me.
My righteousness I hold fast, and will not let it go;
My heart shall not reproach me so long as I live.

(Job 27:2-6)

The vast protest literature in the Bible, of which the above are samples, is echoed throughout Jewish writings, through the Midrash and Talmud, medieval poetry, the parables of the *Hasidim*, through the intimate conversations with God of Levi Yitz'hak of Berditchev to the fierce anger of Yossel Rakover writing his last testament amidst the flames of the Warsaw ghetto: "I believe in the God of Israel even though He has done everything to destroy my belief in Him. I believe in His laws even though I cannot justify His ways . . . I bow before His majesty, but I will not kiss the rod with which He chastises me." [2]

The religious audacity first articulated in the Biblical hero may come as a shock to those whose image of the believer is of one who always submits to the will of God.[3] Traditionally, the man of faith may be depicted as once-born or twice-born; he may be subject to doubt or conflict; but once in the presence of God, kneeling is his posture.

The voice of rebellion in Jewish literature, however, is authentic. It is not considered blasphemous; indeed, it is canonized. The indignation rises from within the religious framework. Expressions of its tensions are therefore not debates but internal conflicts. Out of personal anguish, the sufferer defies but does not deny.

From where stems the moral courage of the Jew, the right to resent? That privilege is based on an unusual arrangement between God and Israel, in which both parties agree to a unique set of terms. The everlasting covenant, entered into by Abraham and his seed with God, unites the two in a moral partnership. Man is to keep the commandments of the Lord, true; but it is also understood that the pact of "righteousness and justice" is undertaken with the Lord.

Both sides are mutually responsible, and a miscarriage calls forth sanctions against either transgressor.[4] This covenant, setting forth the moral responsibilities of both parties, gives Abraham and his descendants heart to dissent even against so awesome a co-signatory as God. So long as man is a partner with God in sustaining the moral universe, protests can be hurled from below as well as from above.

Man's Moral Competence: Religious Audacity

Man's status as a moral agent is thus asserted along with his capacity to distinguish good from bad, happiness from adversity, saintliness from sin. Both man and God are released from the amoral decrees of fate, the *moira* of the pagan world.

God is free to change His decrees, to repent of His decisions, to alter the course of events. And man is freed from passive silence: he may now appeal from God to God. "I will flee from Thee to Thyself, and I will shelter myself from Thy wrath in Thy shadow; and to the skirts of Thy mercies I will lay hold until Thou hast had mercy on me. I will not let Thee go until Thou hast blessed me." [5]

The God of Israel can be thus addressed because He is not only the metaphysical God of power and wisdom but also the moral God of justice and mercy. In his anger the religious rebel does not turn away from God but toward Him. God Himself prays, "May it be My will that My mercy may suppress My anger, and that My mercy may prevail over My other attributes" (*B'rakhot 7a*).

The same defiance is kept alive in the post-Biblical tradition. It is not Noah, accepting the decree of the deluge and hiding his impotence in a shelter for himself, who is admired by the Rabbis. They praise instead Abraham and Moses, who draw near to God and contend with Him on the grounds of justice. Abraham challenges God's exile of his people, demands confrontation with those who have accused Israel of sin, and successfully silences the Torah from testifying against them.[6] Moses rebukes God for keeping silent before the slaughter of mothers and children.

Rachel dares contrast her compassion and forbearance with God's zealousness so as to move God toward charity.[6] Even Elijah "speaks insolently towards Heaven," accusing God of wronging the sinners; and the Holy One admits His responsibility and error.

In another rabbinic interpretation, Moses is seen as figuratively seizing hold of God's cloak and refusing to let go until "the

Lord repented of the evil which He said He would do unto His errant people" (Exodus 32:14).[7] On another occasion Moses "hurls words against the Heavens" and "remits God's vow for Him," for, while the Lord cannot break His word, the righteous may break it on His behalf.[8]

The extraordinary intimacy and audacity allowable within the relationship between Israel and the deity is incomprehensible without a clear perception of their covenant. This unique "contract" explains the Jew's respect for man's moral dignity as well as his more revolutionary faith in God's responsiveness to the call of justice. Moses in prayer attributed to God greatness, might and awesomeness. But the prophet Jeremiah deleted the attribute of awesomeness from God because "aliens are destroying His temple"; Daniel, observing the captivity of the people, similarly reduced the attribute of might from God. The Rabbis were perplexed. How could Jeremiah and Daniel abolish the attributes established by Moses? Rabbi Eliezer offered an explanation: "Since they know that the Holy One insists on truth, they would not ascribe false attributes to Him" (*Yoma* 69b).

What is more, in the *Din Torah*, the tribunal of justice to which the Holy One is summoned by man, God cannot lose. For when justice triumphs God is the victor. In His apparent defeat, when the voice of law and righteousness is heeded and the Heavenly Echo is ignored, He rejoices, *"Nitz'huni Banai:* My children have defeated Me" (*Bava M'tzia* 59b). In Israel, man does not acquiesce as do the angels, but like Abraham's grandson Jacob-Israel, he girds his loins to wrestle with God and is allowed to prevail (Genesis 33).

Rabbinic tradition holds fast to the basic thrust of Biblical literature—the moral impulse. A rich storehouse of speculations concerning God and man is found in the Talmud and other rabbinic writings such as the *Midrashim*, in their informal, discursive and often conversational commentaries. Of course, the unsystematic and digressive style makes it difficult to cull a well-ordered consistent rabbinic position on given topics. Nevertheless, it is beyond dispute that the Rabbis sought a personal God, one directly and primarily involved with man, and whose purpose for the universe is integrally related to man's salvation. Their major concern was with God's providence, justice, love and mercy.

The Rationalist Influence of Medieval Philosophy

It was not until the advent of medieval Jewish thought that a metaphysical view of the universe was introduced, which in turn had great effect on the efforts of Jewish philosophers to justify God's ways. Under the influence of medieval interpretations of Aristotelian philosophy, the goal of theologians like Abraham Ibn Ezra, Abraham Ibn Daud, Gersonides, Hasdai Crescas and Moses Maimonides was to search out God as the principle of explanation of the universe, the very essence of the nature of the world. They paid most attention to God's unity, His incorporeality, His power, eternity and wisdom.

The special challenge of medieval philosophic Jewry was to square the rationalistic philosophy of Aristotle with the claims of Biblical revelation and Talmudic authority. They tried to harmonize the logical, objective orientation of Greek philosophy with the personal and ethical approach of the Biblical-rabbinic tradition. God and man are no longer equal partners in running the universe. Gersonides, intent on retaining human free will, limited God's foreknowledge to the universal laws of nature and excluded His knowledge of particular events. He thus attempted to keep the scales balanced. While man as an individual is free, his freedom is severely limited as a member of the species man. And God's wisdom and providence are restricted to the human species as a whole.

Though Maimonides states that when individual man exercises his intelligence he receives divine providence, this is a far cry from the Biblical and rabbinic idea of God's conscious and deliberate extension of His personal mercy. Once again human freedom and divine control need to be accommodated. Crescas moves to protect the absolute sovereignty of God in a system of determinism which virtually eliminates man's free will.

In all these medieval thinkers, God and man are cast as rivals, each contending for natural or supernatural rights, as if the attributes of one can only be attained at the cost of the other.

Judah Halevi aptly labeled the difference between metaphysical and moral theology as that between the "God of Abraham and the God of Aristotle." "There is a broad difference indeed between the believer in religion and the philosopher. The believer seeks God for the sake of various benefits, apart from the benefit of knowing Him; the philosopher seeks Him only that he may describe Him accurately, as he would describe the earth . . ." [9]

There is, of course, considerable overlapping between both approaches in Jewish writings. But it is instructive to note that the Rabbis saw in God the guarantor of the values revealed to and accepted by man. From this stance, the resolution of the problem of evil touches the very heart of faith. In metaphysical theology, however, the problems wrought by evil are secondary to sustaining the logic of the world order.

The Logic of Evil

Medieval Jewish philosophers frequently distinguish between two kinds of evil which befall man—moral and physical. Moral evils include those which people willfully inflict upon each other —robbery, murder, war, excessive eating, drinking and passion.[10] They are taken to be a function of man's free will when exercised in ignorance. Were man to use his reason to the fullest, he would maintain the correct course of behavior in harmony with the ultimate principles of the universe.

Physical evils afflict man from sources outside himself, such as earthquake, storm and disease. Here free will does not seem involved. A scientific account of the origin of illness appears to ignore the hand of God in all things. The medieval religious philosophers have two favored vindications of God's role in the presence of such physical evil. First is the principle of privation,[11] the analysis of evil as a negative term and non-existent.

Evils such as blindness and death are not positive attributes of life, and God had nothing to do with them in a direct manner. God creates only positive properties. Blindness is the absence of sight; deafness, a failure to hear; disease, the absence of health; muteness, the privation of speech. He who blows out the light creates nothing. Metaphysically, evil, like darkness, is what is not. God, who makes and forms, is therefore responsible only for what is.

The second oft-invoked metaphysical principle chides the human being for his egocentrism in believing that the world was created for his benefit. Many a medieval metaphysician, noting the fullness of God's universe, invokes the principle of plenitude.

Out of God's infinite being and inexhaustible perfection there flows a chain of being in which every conceivable diversity and potentiality of kinds exist. Man's self-centered view of the universe would have it limited to those things which are serviceable for him. His metaphysical astigmatism, thereby, robs the universe of its pluralism, the grandeur of its perfection. If lions and snakes and bacteria were not to exist, the universe would be an impoverished structure. Better that one animal should eat another than that a unique creature be denied and a vacuum exist in the universe.

The twelfth-century Jewish philosopher Abraham Ibn Daud uses this principle when he argues that without a graded series of being our world could not have emerged; for all minerals would have been plants, all plants, animals; all animals, men; all men, angels. Without imperfection there would be a universe only of God and angels.[12]

And Maimonides, using another variety of the same principle of plenitude, shows how metaphysical wisdom can offer its own solace. Man calls death a destructive evil. Such a misleading error could be avoided would we but understand: "In accordance with the divine wisdom genesis can only take place through destruction, and without destruction of the individual members of the species the species themselves would not exist permanently." [13]

In general, for these philosophers the issues of morality appear secondary. They are prepared to concede that there are limitations in the ordering and preserving of the world. Left alone, the contrary elements in the sublunar world might destroy each other. The "higher causes" of the heavenly spheres maintain an equilibrium which may unavoidably bring about some accidental evil to some element in the universe—to man, as much as to any other form in the great chain of being. These are the inevitable consequences of running the best of all logically possible worlds. But the original intent in the creation of the universe is good; and the physical evils are accidental by-products of divine beneficence and wisdom.[14]

Both the righteous and the wicked man are viewed as subject to the general providence which God exerts. But the righteous have a special stance which they earn in proportion to the exercise of the divine faculty of reason. The righteous man who actively employs his intellect has the instrument with which to control even those harmful events determined by indiscriminate laws of the universe. Wisdom is the salvation attained by the righteous man.[15] Interestingly, both Maimonides and Gersonides maintain that while Job was a great man, he is not to be described as intelligent, wise or clever.[16] "It is of great advantage that man should know his station and not erroneously imagine that the whole universe exists only for him."[17] David Hume, in his *Natural History of Religion,* observes the changing weights placed upon God's attributes as a result of differing ends: "The higher the Deity is exalted in power and knowledge, the lower of course is He depressed in goodness and benevolence."

The Rabbinic View

For the Rabbis, the impersonal, objective explanations of evil offered by the systematic philosophers would be wholly inadequate to explain individual or collective history. Causal laws, like blind fate, are devoid of moral intent; therefore their importance in understanding the world is superficial. If man searches deeply, he discovers that nothing simply happens; tragedy is not the result of a morally capricious or indifferent cause. There is an ultimate explanation of events which lies in a purposeful God. "All is in the hands of Heaven, except the fear of Heaven."[18]

Most of the Rabbis seek explanations of suffering that free God from the possibility of indictment by man. If man suffers, there is good reason. "If a man sees that painful sufferings visit him, let him examine his conduct" (*B'rakhot* 5a). "There is no death without sin and no suffering without transgression" (*Shabbat* 55b).[19] And if self-examination fails to reveal man's moral failure, let him attribute his suffering to neglect of the study of Torah. Moreover, even if he is a diligent student, he may attribute his pain to God's "chastisements of love."

Many are the modes of punishment for transgression, such as disease, war, accident, sentence by a tribunal; but all can be traced to the just exercise of divine will. When, after the destruction of the Temple, capital punishment could no longer be decreed by the Jewish courts, many Rabbis contended that the punishment continues through natural agencies: "He who would have been sentenced to stoning, falls from the roof; he who would have been decapitated is either delivered to the (Roman) government or robbers come upon him; he who would be sentenced to strangulation is either drowned or dies from suffocation" (*K'tuvot* 30ab). This insistence on the just hand of God behind all events encouraged many Rabbis to find ways of erasing apparent moral inconsistencies or injustices in life. Should we discover a righteous man suffering, we need not deny either his goodness or his suffering. We may explain the punishment of the righteous as evidence of the wickedness of his father. Inversely, if an evil man prosper, it may be the merit he inherits from his parents' good deeds.[20]

Other Rabbis repudiate the doctrine of reward or punishment as running counter to their sense of justice. They vindicate God by assigning higher meaning to the circumstance. The suffering of the righteous is, in fact, a badge of honor, not a stigma of transgression. "The Holy One brings suffering upon the righteous of the world in order that they may inherit the future world" (*Kiddushin* 40b). Sickness and death help purge the lesser iniquities of the righteous so that "the abounding happiness that is treasured up for them shall be unalloyed." [21]

Saadia Gaon, the tenth-century theologian, explains the case for unpunished evil: God pays off evil men for their petty virtues with trifling this-worldly rewards. Even the devil must be given his due. But this transaction in the outer vestibule of the universe only helps clear the path for the full measure of justice to be exercised against the evil-doers in the nethermost rung of the next world.[22]

Extending their horizons to include both worlds, some of the Rabbis thereby can assure ultimate justice. The topsy-turvy moral disorder of this world must not lead us to despair of God's ultimate righteousness. "God does not deprive any being of his full reward." "He who says that God remits only part of a punishment will himself be punished" (*P'sahin* 118a; Midrash *Genesis Rabbah* 9).

While some Biblical explanations treat Israel's expulsion from the Land as divine punishment for its iniquitous ways, rabbinic theology lifts that disaster to the higher dimension of martyrdom. Israel is exiled for God's sake and suffers because it is witness on His behalf. "For Thy sake are we killed all day long" (Psalms 44:22; Isaiah 43:12). Collective suffering is a badge of courage and a religious testimony: "God's rod comes only upon those whose heart is soft like the lily"; the yoke is placed upon "the strong and not the weak"; the potter does not test defective vessels lest with one blow he shatter them. Suffering is the mark of Israel's election.[23]

Taken as a whole, rabbinic theodicy adheres to the basic principle that the world is well conducted by a supernatural moral power. Suffering is either a disguised blessing or an overt malediction.[24] The face of justice embarrassed in this world may be saved in the tribunal of the other world.

Rabbinic Uneasiness with Traditional Theodicies

The Biblical view which holds man to be *shutaf lakadosh barukh hu,* a partner with God, is a magnificent conception, but it generates unique irritants. The partnership between God and man, working together to improve the world and dually accepting responsibility for it, frequently involves conflict over jurisdiction. What if God and man disagree as to who is innocent or what suffering is? If a righteous man suffers grievously, is God to be accused or is some way to be found to indict man?

Rabbi Meir, upholding the sovereignty of the divine will, states that God "will be gracious unto whom He will be gracious," and may reward or punish the undeserving. But such an appeal to the inscrutable ways of God did not satisfy everyone. If God alone knows who is truly evil and if God alone can judge man, then the unique moral structure of Jewish religious civilization collapses. If man is morally incompetent to distinguish the righteous act from the wicked one, he is also legally incompetent. Many Rabbis were fearful of such an anarchic situation.

"Should someone whisper to you: But is it not written, 'contend not with evil-doers . . . ,' then you may tell them: Only one whose conscience smites him says so" (*B'rakhot* 7b). A man of good conscience must contend with the wicked and judge them. He cannot bury his head in the skirts of God's otherworldly justice. "They that forsake the Law, praise the wicked; but such as keep the Law contend with them" (Proverbs 28:4).

The rabbinic tendency to take what appears evil and see it

as disguised good may quiet the rages of a Job; but it suggests equally a suspension of all human judgment. Involuntarily, such a theodicy is akin to the false prophecy against which Isaiah inveighed: "Woe unto them who say of evil, it is good, and of good, it is evil; that change darkness into light and light into darkness; that change bitter into sweet and sweet into bitter" (Isaiah 5:20).

Common-Sense Realism in Rabbinic Tradition

Nurtured in a tradition which provided them experience in making moral judgments and decisions, some Rabbis refused to surrender reasonable common sense and this-worldly ways of estimating good and evil. They refused to see in suffering and death anything but affliction, or to transform righteousness from an intrinsic good into sin. They refused to deny that evil can occur without sin.

"Are your sufferings welcome to you?" ask some Rabbis. "Neither they (the sufferings) nor their reward," respond their colleagues. With deliberate repetitiveness and dramatic irony, the Talmud reveals how the very Rabbis who earlier had preached the doctrine of divine chastisements of love (*y'surim shel ahavah*) to comfort sufferers were unable to accept it when they themselves were stricken.[25] Maimonides too found this doctrine of the afflictions of love offensive both to the intellect and the emotions. God does not cause those He loves to suffer, nor does He test the loyalty of the believers with trials of pain. Such doctrines, he argues, are unscriptural, ignorant and absurd.[26]

Similarly, evidence arguing strongly against the notion of inherited punishment is adduced from the Bible itself. "The fathers shall not be put to death for the children, neither shall the children be put to death for the fathers; every man shall be put to death for his own sin" (Deuteronomy 24:16).[27]

Nor are all the Rabbis willing to transform martyrdom into a blessing. When Rabbi Hanina ben Teradyon defied the Roman authorities by reading the Torah in public, Rabbi Jose chastised him for his carelessness. "I talk common sense to you, and you say 'God will have mercy' " (*Avodah Zarah* 18a).

In 135 C.E., during the Hadrianic persecutions, wild and capricious decrees called for such a widespread risk of life that the Rabbis were moved to define mandatory martyrdom. At the same time, they discussed criteria for exempting men from such a fate. Distinctions were drawn between decrees which called for private as opposed to publicly coerced transgressions. The source and motivation of the decrees were likewise taken into account before martyrdom was chosen over accommodation.[28]

Death may testify to man's saintliness or heroism, but its evil is neither to be denied nor absolved. Death, counselled Ben Sira (*Exodus Rabbah* 29b), may be preferable to a lingering disease, but it is not thereby transformed into an intrinsic good. If adversity is good, what sense is there to pray and work for its elimination in the Messianic era?

Why portray the world of the future in which there will be no need to require blessings over evil tidings, since there will be no evil (*P'saḥim* 50a)? How could death be other than evil if God Himself will slaughter the angel of death? [29]

Original Sin and Its Inheritance

Many of the Rabbis also refused to accept a verdict against man. Did Moses and Aaron deserve to die, even if they were not perfect? Does God punish twice for the same sin? Therefore, concluded the Rabbis, "there is death without sin, and there is suffering without transgression" (*Shabbat* 55b).

While some Rabbis accepted the explanation that death is born of Adam's sin and that we all participate in his original sin, others denied its moral implications. The angel of death, the latter argued, was created on the first day, before Adam was even fashioned.[30]

In another Midrash it is stated that Adam himself did not deserve to die for his transgression. He died because God, foreseeing that Hiram and Nebuchadnezzar would declare themselves gods, decreed their death and thereby rendered all men mortal. Why then were not the innocent, such as Adam, exempted from this punishment? The answer: lest the wicked, observing the immortality of the righteous, feign piety and perform insincere repentance for ulterior motives (*Genesis Rabbah* 9:5). These fragments of moral philosophy repudiate the notion of original sin and the claim that death is the just punishment of the evil.[31]

As if to insure the equality of the Heavenly Tribunal with that of the earthly court, there are Rabbis who insisted that God Himself does not take advantage of His perception of the secret, inner intentions of man's heart. He restricts His own judgments to the public, overt acts of man. "The Holy One combines only intention which bears fruit with deeds (i.e., intentions which are followed by action); but intention which does not bear fruit, He does not combine with deed" (*Kiddushin* 40a). The human court can take heart from such knowledge of the jurisdictional propriety of the Divine Court and with confidence judge the publicly observable acts of men.[32]

In summary, rabbinic theodicy, which is predicated upon the divine, moral causation of all events, in which man is also a free moral agent, carries with it the warmth and intimacy of a personal God who is the author of justice in the world. But it also bears the sign of strain. The moral dialogue of Biblical Judaism can—and often does—emerge as a clash of forces.

Consciously or not, Jewish justification of God's ways are torn between two ideas that they wish to maintain equally: *the sovereignty of God* and *the dignity of man*. How well the Rabbis recognized this conflict can be seen in their characterization of prophecy. Elijah's prophecy is unsatisfactory in that, while he insists upon defending the honor of God, he ignores the dignity of man. Jonah's prophetic stance seeks to defend the son but ignores the claim of the Father. Jeremiah is the ideal prophet, for he insists on the honor of both Father and son— God and man. He achieves this delicate equilibrium by simultaneously chastising and exonerating the ways of God and man (*Mekhilta* to Exodus 12:1).

A God endowed with the traits of personality—acting, willing, loving, judging—is both wonderfully approachable and painfully vulnerable. Job's familiarity with God is so close as to enable him to speak of Him as "mine adversary" and to demand that "He set aright a man contending with God as a son of man setteth aright his neighbor" (Job 16:20-21; 31-35). The simile is striking: God and man are both persons, and each has moral claims upon the other.

After Auschwitz: The Challenge of Adversity

While easy converse between God and man presents no problems in times of peace and tranquillity, in times of adversity that very intimacy jeopardizes the sovereign perfection of God. The personal God is too close for comfort in moments of despair. If God is to be protected from Jobian critique, His relationship with man must be formalized. Job must be put in his place and the forthrightness of the earlier dialogue broken off. God, in the epilogue, does indeed appear to Job, out of the whirlwind, with all His awesome omnipotence: "Hast thou an arm like God? And canst thou thunder with a voice like Him?" (Job 40:9 f). God is thereby lifted to the heights of inviolability and Job discovers the limitations of dialogue. He now knows that, at best, he can only be a silent partner and he learns to lay his hand upon his mouth forever.[33]

Similarly, in modern times, Martin Buber's human-divine encounter is severely shaken by the atrocities of the Nazi holocaust. He is led to ask: "Can one still speak to God after Oswiecim and Auschwitz? Can one still, as an individual and as a people, enter at all into a dialogue relationship with Him? . . . Dare we recommend to the survivors of Oswiecim, the Jobs of the gas chambers, 'Call to Him, for He is kind, for His mercy endureth forever?' "[34]

The confidence and trust of the original dialogue shrivel into paradox. Buber advises us to await the voice of "our cruel and merciful Lord."[35] We are presented not with a theological diffidence which limits man's knowledge of God's attributes but with the shocking assertion that the moral character of God is unknowable in principle. God is no longer simply "righteous and just" in the manner that Abraham knew Him, in the manner which assured him that God and he shared the same moral universe of discourse. Now Buber speaks of God as "super-good."[36] We have reason to wonder whether our moral language is the same as that which God employs. Stripped of the moral certainty axiomatic in the Biblical dialogue, we may well panic. We do not know whether it is God or Moloch who addresses us.[37] After Auschwitz, Buber entertains a God who is "Absolute Personality,"[38] what he himself calls a "paradox of paradoxes" because an absolute has no personality and is beyond love, desire and will. And yet without personality there can be no dialogue with the Absolute God. The original innocence of the dialogue fades before the scandal of outrageous injustice. God is said to be "hiding" and man is counselled patience until His unpredictable revelation. What He may say we cannot know, for "His coming appearance resembles no earlier one . . ." [39]

The painful truth appears to be that the Nazi atrocity has severed the dialogue. In its place, a mysterious monologue is awaited. After Auschwitz, only one voice speaks, and man is reduced to listener.

A Personal God: Stumbling Block or Rock of Comfort?

As in Job and Buber, so Jewish theodicy is tossed, like a shuttlecock, from a personal to an impersonal God. Yet whether we turn to God as Super-person or Person, toward a good God or one who is super-good, whether the goodness is understood or mysterious, all the traditional explanations invoke a personal God. All events occur through the agency of a deliberate, personal will. Metaphysical and moral theologians may quarrel as to the intent of that will—whether the world is created for the sake of man or not—but all agree that true explanation entails a purposive agent, a personal cause.

The insistence upon a personal God is held to guarantee the objective status of moral values. Feared most are the twin heresies of atheism and pantheism, which are inimical to Judaism. Atheism proposes a rudderless world, wherein God is irrelevant to any proper explanation of history. In pantheism, where God is identified with nature, evils of all kinds are assimilated into the natural system, and nature reigns with an indiscriminate hand. Moral distinctions between good and evil, order and confusion are dismissed as human biases, as functions of man's self-centeredness.[40]

If good and evil are not to be blurred, as they are in pantheism, their separate reality must be maintained. The distinctions drawn between them seem best to be kept intact by finding their sources. Good is most readily personified as flowing from a divine power; but the tendency to personify experience suggests an analogous path to the source of evil: Satanic power. Each seems as real as the other.

Behind every experience to which moral adjectives are assigned, there lies a substantive noun to which it properly belongs. The inclination to forge experiences, events, transactions into things and nouns has an ancient and modern history to which philosophy will readily attest. "Good" and "bad" are transformed into "the good" and "the bad," and further transformed into "God" and "Satan." This metamorphosis generates demons as readily as angels. Little wonder then that the rabbinic tradition felt the need to combat the doctrine of *Shtei R'shuyot*, of two competing divine powers.[41] However, it is no light task to trace good and evil to a common divine matrix so as to avoid the heresy of dualism, while adhering at the same time to the real distinctions between these two aspects of moral behavior. Where distinctions are held to be objective, differences frequently give birth to contending deities.[42]

"Why?" Is Not the Same as "What-For?"

Why does theology bog down when confronted by the challenge to explain evil? Scientific answers will be accepted for questions concerning impersonal events—"Why did the metal expand?" But where personal events are involved, we insist upon a different type of explanation. Birth, sickness or death demand explanations heavy with personal intent. To answer a question such as "Why was my child blinded?" with a medical report appears to demean the seriousness of the tragedy. The objective answer will be met with another, "But why did it happen to *my* child?" This sort of question is limitless, and each scientific answer only postpones a further one. Only that answer which is compatible with the tacit assumption of the question is acceptable. The question grows out of a mode of thinking wherein serious events can be explained only by conscious, purposively causal agents. Only a universe peopled with motivations, deliberate actions and purposes is regarded adequate to account for important personal affairs. Hence, we speak of an "act of God" or the "will of God." While such an explanation of adversity may have its initial advantage, it frequently leads to resentment against the One Person who, if He were but willing, could have averted the disaster.

It is self-evident that traditional theodicy limits its scope to one kind of theological view: God is a Person who punishes and rewards with sickness and death, with health and long life. Unless we are willing to challenge that underlying assumption, the gnawing problem of evil in God's world remains insoluble.

Toward an Alternate Theodicy

Traditional Jewish theology does not equate God with nature nor does it set God apart from nature. Rather, it allows God to incorporate and transcend nature. A view of God's envelopment of nature is felt necessary to assure belief in His power and control of the universe. In the rabbinic approach, this total embrace of nature implicates God as responsible for all natural events, including disease and nature's disasters. He is involved in every natural catastrophe.[43]

A new approach to the relationship between God and nature sees the latter as belonging to the realm of *ḥol* or the non-holy. Nature itself is morally neutral, neither hostile nor friendly to the realm of values. Understood as a system of morally ambivalent energies, it is beyond the judgment of evil or good. "The world pursues its natural course and stolen seed sprouts as luxuriantly as seed honestly acquired (*Avodah Zarah* 54b). To conceive of God's running nature as we conduct our affairs only leads to the embarrassment of defending God each time lightning strikes or gales devastate the innocent. It leads us to strain for occult moral purposes behind every natural tragedy, and to associate God's activity with havoc and catastrophe.

God is not nature. Physical evils require no justification of His ways, for the ways of nature are not identified with the ways of God. There is no need to search for "deeper" explanations for drought or flood in defense of God.

In this view, nature is the source of potentialities for man's sustenance, health and security. Nature is not a conscious moral force, but it can be used for conscious moral ends. With natural piety we seize hold of nature. "Is it not our own substance? Are we made of other clay? All our possibilities lie from eternity hidden in its bosom . . . we may address it without superstitious terrors; it is not wicked. It follows its own habits abstractedly." [44] And the Jew follows God, not nature. Divinity is not larger than nature, but is discovered *within* nature, in the acts of men who transform the uncommitted powers of nature to consecrated ends.

This position suggests an interesting analogue with that of Gersonides' critique of Maimonides. Maimonides had insisted that God created matter out of nothing, and that were matter co-eternal with God, existing before creation, it would limit God's power and freedom. But Gersonides disagreed. Eternity, he argued, does not constitute divinity. Therefore, let matter be eternal; it does not reduce the majesty of divine creation. Creativity is not in the manufacture of matter, but in the shaping of its raw, chaotic substance into an intelligible universe. As Gersonides was convinced that longevity is no mark of divinity, we are convinced that largeness is equally irrelevant to the character of divinity. In separating God from nature, we do not reduce divinity but clarify its essential meaning.

Physical evil requires no justification. This does not mean that the tragedies wrought by nature are not real. But unfortunate physical accidents which befall man ought not to be converted into events derived from cosmic purpose. If we trace our tragedies to hidden divine causes, we cast a shadow of disillusionment upon an omnipotent personal God who has betrayed us. Such resentment and frustration are needless; because God conceived as Person fails us, we need not repudiate divinity.

God Creates the World Incomplete

A more positive approach is to see that man and the universe are incomplete. Nature is not law to be followed; it is power to be controlled and organized for moral ends. Endowed with freedom of will man encounters divinity in his effort to overcome sickness, ignorance and greed. In his transactions with his environment he discovers the attributes of divinity which are essential to his health and moral maturity—love, justice, knowledge and compassion.

These predicates of divinity are real and effective. But the ideals of peace and love, while they move men to action, are yet to be realized. In what soil can these values be rooted so that their significance is preserved? And what will endow these values with power? The Greeks secured them in a world of ideas, and the Jews in a Person, God. A potentially split world ensues, leading to a strained relation between the secular and the sacred, between person and Person. When man heals and cures, the glory is God's: when man hurts and destroys, the blame is his alone. To praise God as a Person distinct from man for the good achieved by human effort and benevolence appears artificial; and the assignment of evil to man exclusively appears unjust.

The Nazi holocaust dramatizes our dilemma. That men who sin are punished is understandable; but that millions of innocent should be destroyed is not. What role does God play here? Is His permissiveness morally justifiable? If the monumental catastrophe belongs to man, what relevance does God have if He washes His hands of the whole matter and sets Himself apart as a spectator?

To save His relevance and to give dimension to our tragedy, it is felt that God should be called upon as the controlling Cause of all significant events. But to do so is to rip open the wounds of Job and then to fall back upon the God that hides His face. But the concealed God holds a double-edged sword. In the defense of Nazi leader Adolf Eichmann, his lawyer Dr. Robert Servatius used classic theological overtones when he raised the question: "Do you not believe that irrational factors, transcending human understanding, are responsible for the fate of the Jewish people?" That which is meant to justify God's ways is now used to justify man's. The wicked, as easily as the good, can hide behind the Hiding God.

"Tikun Olam": Perfecting the World

Depicted as Person, endowed with the traits of personality—willing, desiring, punishing, rewarding—divinity will forever require defense. We call for a different conception of God. We experience divinity not as a Person or "He who" but as "That which." *That which* cures the sick, loosens the bonds of the fettered, upholds the fallen, supports the poor, we identify as Godly. These revelations are not arbitrary, neither being cast earthward from heaven nor capriciously invented. They are discovered, tested and affirmed in this world through our individual and collective interactions with nature, human and non-human. Activities are Godly and real without being objects, things or persons. Evil and good are encountered in the world, not as the effects of contending supernatural powers, but as distinguishable events which frustrate or contribute to our moral maturity.

The moral dualism in the world we experience is the tension between what is and what ought to be—between *hol* (neutral and uncommitted energy) and *kadosh* (energy dedicated to ideal ends). The monotheism of Jewish tradition is expectant. The world is incomplete. "The Lord shall be King over all the earth; on that day the Lord shall be One and His name One" (Zechariah 14:9).

That which works to overcome the tension which ruptures the moral world is divine. Godliness is revealed to us in terms of values we can understand as human beings. Godliness is that feature of the world which penetrates the dumbness of nature and makes it speak the language of moral intent.

In our view, no segregated area exists where divinity may not be found. Moral evil and moral good are not supernaturalized. They are both in the same world, where men may be blameworthy or praiseworthy, but divinity is blameless. For divinity is neither person nor omnipotent will. Divinity, by our meaning, designates those energies and activities which sustain and elevate our lives. Such an understanding of divinity requires no justification in the presence of evil.

FOR FURTHER READING

BERKOVITS, Eliezer, *Faith After the Holocaust* (Hoboken, NJ: Ktav, 1973). A distinguished attempt to defend God and present a modern version of the "free-will" defense after the Holocaust.

HICK, John, *Evil and the God of Love* (New York: Harper & Row, 1966). The most wide-ranging, general, contemporary philosophical introduction to this enduring problem. Though its author is Christian, the issues he raises and his handling of them are largely nondenominational.

KUSHNER, Harold, *When Bad Things Happen to Good People* (New York: Schocken Books, 1981). An immensely popular attempt to answer the question posed in the title. Its theology may be dubious, but it has proved thought-provoking to many.

GLATZER, Nahum, Editor, *The Dimensions of Job* (New York: Schocken Books, 1969). A collection of seminal reflections on the perennial issues concerning theodicy raised by the biblical book of Job.

SANDERS, Edward, "Rabbi Akiba's View of Suffering" in *Jewish Quarterly Review* pp. 332–351 (Philadelphia, 1972). A helpful discussion by a leading Christian scholar on one key rabbinic attitude towards the problem of suffering.

13 . The Meaning of Prayer

JACOB B. AGUS

IN PRAYER the ultimate mystery of existence is invoked and addressed as if it shared in the life of humanity. There is an outreaching to that which is beyond human reach and a straining to extend the domain of meaning to that mystery. Prayer is an agonizing awareness of limitation together with an inner assurance of breaking through the barriers of finitude. It is a paradoxical combination of anguish and faith, anxiety and hope, submission and action.

The all-enveloping mystery may be most powerfully represented in some impressive force or event. The human mind does not dare to dwell long on abstractions. Thus, in the history of humanity, the occult power becomes associated first with a life-giving stream, a massive rock, the summit of a mountain or a grove of trees. As man grows in keenness of perception and clarity of thought, the divine mystery becomes detached from concrete things. From fetishism or the worship of "sticks and stones," man rises to animism, the belief that an indwelling occult force, generalized and impersonal, is concentrated in certain places. Next comes polytheism, the notion that certain gods control the diverse forces of nature. The final stage is monotheism, the worship of the one God, when prayer acquires its full authentic stature.

Prayer—An Exercise in Spiritual Growth

The difference between monotheism and polytheism is not just a matter of arithmetic. The world that is apprehended by our senses is a medley of contrasts in which diversity and conflict prevail. To believe in one God, a unity of will and design transcending the range of man's total experience, is to set cumulative wisdom against the evidence of the senses.

> How great are Thy works, O Lord!
> Thy thoughts are very deep.
> A brutish man knoweth not,
> Neither doth a fool understand this.
>
> (Psalms 92:6-7)

The concept of one God makes Him different from all else that enters our ken. His unity and uniqueness signify that there is more to heaven and earth than is revealed to our senses. His wisdom imposes a structure of meaning upon all things and events, compelling them to serve His all-embracing purpose. To reach Him, man must achieve a high degree of inner harmony and an elevation of purpose. Above all, man must reach beyond his own being. Prayer becomes an exercise in the growth of the spirit, a continuous effort at self-transcendence. It consists of the passive phase of *appreciation* followed by an active phase of *aspiration*, and a final *transfiguration* or the articulation of a new spirit, heart and mind.

Appreciating the Symphony of Creation

In the Jewish tradition the worshipper begins by calling to mind the manifold beauties of divine creation. As he looks at the universe filled with the glory of God, shame overwhelms him for being concerned with his puny self.

> When I behold Thy heavens, the work of Thy fingers,
> The moon and the stars, which Thou has established;
> What is man, that Thou art mindful of him?
> And the son of man, that Thou thinkest of him?
>
> (Psalms 8:4-5)

But man cannot admire the awesome majesty of creation without sensing the wonder of the divine image in the heart of man.

> Yet Thou hast made him but little lower than the angels,
> And hast crowned him with glory and honor.

Thou hast made him to have dominion over the works of Thy
    hands . . .
How glorious is Thy name in all the earth!

(Psalms 8:7-10)

Continuing this lyrical song of praise, the worshipper extols
the glory of God.

Praise the Lord, O my soul! . . .
I will praise the Lord as long as I live;
I will sing praises to my God while I have being.

(Psalms 104:1, 33)

The entire range of creation is suffused with a radiance which
compels man's assent and admiration.

The heavens declare the glory of God,
And the firmament showeth His handiwork.

(Psalms 19:2)

In our day, we are just beginning to acquire knowledge of the
vastness of the expanding universe. The ancients had some idea
of the immense range of the universe, but they peopled the
emptiness of space with angels and seraphim, all of whom served
God in some mysterious way. Through prayer it is man's
privilege to articulate the symphony of creation and to join the
universal chorus in singing God's praise.

The theme of this cosmic symphony is given by Isaiah in the
formula repeated several times in the daily prayers: *Kadosh,
kadosh, kadosh, m'lo khol ha-aretz k'vodo* (Holy, holy, holy is
the Lord, the whole earth is full of His glory).[1] Holiness is
man's feeling of the realm of mystery, extending beyond the
reach of his faculties. He reaches out to the divine by thought,
feeling and ethical action.

In prayer man brings himself to see all things in the divine
perspective, where "evil is the base of the good." [2] In the Thir-
tieth Psalm, which is read daily, the recitation of catastrophes is
firmly fixed within the framework of an optimistic expectancy.

I will extol Thee, O Lord, for Thou hast raised me up,
And hast not suffered mine enemies to rejoice over me.
O Lord, my God,
I cried unto Thee, and Thou didst heal me;

O Lord, Thou broughtest up my soul from the nether-world
    (Sheol);
Thou didst keep me alive, that I should not go down to the
    pit . . .
Thou didst turn my mourning into dancing;
Thou didst loose my sack cloth, and gird me with gladness;
So that my glory may sing to Thee, praise and not be silent;
O Lord my God, I will give thanks unto Thee forever.

The optimism of Judaism is a deliberate decision of heart and
mind. Though the outer reaches of the universe are unknown to
us and the inner depths of our existence are too opaque to see
clearly, we throw our weight on the side of hope and faith.

This optimism is directed to man as well as to the universe. As
the will of God is to prevail in history, so man's will for good
can overcome the depths of evil in his being. He is not the helpless victim of dark and deadly forces. Man's capacity to lift himself spiritually has always been stressed in Judaism. God says to
Cain, the first murderer, "Sin lies at the door, but you can master
it" (Genesis 4:7). To be sure, man needs the help of God if he
is to climb out of the morass of sin, and this help is always available to those "who seek it with all their heart and soul and
might."

Aspiring to Reach Fulfillment

The sages put the first phase of prayer—*appreciation*—ahead
of the second phase of *aspiration:* "Always, a person should
first bring to mind the many praises of the Ever-Present, and
only then should he ask for his needs" (*B'rakhot* 32a). Man
understands his failures and shortcomings only as he sees them
against the background of divine power and mercy. He chafes
against the obstructions which bar his way and prevent him from
joining fully in the song of creation.

Man is a transient, mortal creature. Death is the ultimate privation, symbolizing the many deprivations to which his life is subject: the sudden malignancies of disease, the grinding struggle
for a livelihood, the many frictions which sap human strength.
It is only in rare moments that the boundaries of man's horizon
open and he beholds the radiance of the infinite. Once he
glimpses the Eternal, he knows better what to ask for; his desires

and necessities fall into patterns. He wants to be embraced in the grand design of the Almighty and to make his presence felt in God's eternal plan. God's image is in his soul, attaining its fullest potential only through his own efforts.

"Beside every blade of grass, stands an angel, who beats it and cries, grow up!" Prayer enables man to feel the beating wings of the angel. Thus, man petitions the Almighty for his personal needs, asking for "children, life and livelihood," but only after he has learned to see his needs in the light of God's design. "Make thy will be like His will, that He might make His will to be like thy will," say the sages (*Ethics of the Fathers* 2:4).

Two opposing views are often voiced regarding such petitionary prayer. Some feel that requests of a personal nature belong to an earlier, more primitive stage of religion and have no place in modern worship. Others hold that petitions are meaningful only if we believe that they will be "granted," in a direct, immediate, literal sense. Reflection would reveal that both of the above views are too narrow to embrace the full meaning of prayer.

If the religious dimension is to be maintained amid the actual pressures of life, then its high moments must be integrated with the harsh realities of human existence. Religious contemplation and worship must not become an ethereal domain of solitary and timeless reflection, insulated from the burdens of daily existence. Hence, the supreme importance of including our personal needs, in all their paltriness, within the perspective of our yearning to become part of His design. It is not as a disembodied soul that man stands in prayer, but as a living human being, with needs and responsibilities. The individual also remains mindful that wholeness in prayer encompasses a selfhood not detached from his community seeking the God of the universe.

The consummation of self-surrender in prayer is made more meaningful when we bring to mind the many ways in which the divine image is imprisoned within us. Religion is the cutting edge of the soul as it seeks reality; man's soul is, at the same time, the reflection of his feeble, earth-bound personality.

To go from the contemplation of the divine to concern with personal needs is not anti-climactic. On the contrary, it is the only way to make religion meaningful. The individual, frail and sinful though he be, is yet the purpose of all creation. The divine image is reflected not in the "soul of the world," but in the soul of man. Boundless and eternal as is the cosmos, the soul of man is closer to the Supreme Being than the universe with its billions of galaxies.

In the Jewish faith the concrete individual mirrors the divine being. In primitive societies and totalitarian countries the individual is submerged by the mass, but in Scriptures he is the supreme concern of the Almighty. Abraham arises to defy the entire pagan world. Jeremiah is made into "a fortified wall" and a "pillar of brass" that would resist the surging mob. Moses is told that God prefers him to all the children of Israel.[3] A great *Ḥasidic* teacher said that a person should aways bear two verses in mind: "it is for my sake that the world was created" and "I am but dust and ashes." [4]

If the individual is of supreme importance, the worshipper may well feel that his efforts to deal with his problems and concerns form part of the movement of the world toward the perfection of the "Kingdom of Heaven." As Hillel put it, "If I am not for myself, who will be for me? But if I am for myself only, what am I?" (*Ethics of the Fathers* 1:14).

A person should see his own needs in the light of his over-riding concern for self-fulfillment, and understand that the fulfillment of his self is attained through his integration within the purpose and design of God.

Are Personal Prayers Answered?

Are our petitions granted? We must believe that they *may* be granted, but we cannot assert that they *will* be granted. It is not permitted to pray for the impossible (*t'fillat shav*), and the unpredictable may well happen. Hope belongs in the life of human beings.

Two points can be made in regard to the efficacy of prayer. As to the granting of specific petitions, it is obvious that only poets and prophets can pretend to describe events from the standpoint of God. Their parables and metaphors may be taken literally by children and persons of childlike mentality, for whom prayers are meaningful if they work "miracles." In Judaism we are called upon to acquire a mature faith which reverences the divine miracle of the ever-renewed "fountain of life." But we are not asked to accept specific "miracles"—that is, suspensions of the laws of nature. Thus we say in the *Amidah*: "In every generation, we shall thank Thee and recount Thy praise—for our lives which are in Thy charge, for our souls which are in Thy care, for Thy miracles, wonders and favors which are with us daily, evening, morning and noon." [5]

In prayer, we learn to feel the reality of that which is not immediately apparent—the past, the future and the open-ended dimension of mystery in nature and in human nature. In contradistinction to inanimate matter, living things possess the dimension of the potential: the oak is in the acorn; the man is in the child. But this dimension is extended in several directions by our religious reflections. In this sense all experience takes on the aspect of the miraculous. We come to feel that spirit is a deep and abiding reality—the power which makes the walls of Jericho, wherever they may be, crumble into dust.

One miraculous event to which attention is drawn again and again in our prayers is the Exodus from Egypt. Indeed, the Talmud declares it mandatory for us to recall the Exodus every day.[6] That story is a remarkable illustration of the feeling of standing on the boundary line between the known and the unknown, between the calculable and the unpredictable, between the natural and the supernatural. Each one of the plagues is a physical phenomenon, rare but not impossible. The "Sea of Reeds" was dried at the right time by a wind which blew all night, and then the direction of the wind was reversed so that the Egyptians were drowned.[7] The food of the desert, *manna*, a secretion of a sugar-like substance by insects, was then particularly abundant; a flock of birds in flight happened to descend within reach of the starving camp; brackish water was turned sweet when some wood was put in it; the Amalekites were vanquished by Joshua because Moses prayed on the mountain with hands uplifted.[8]

In this entire sequence of miracles, the life of the Israelites was made possible by their straining to live on the edge of the transnatural and miraculous. Indeed, the miracle of the Exodus was the indomitable spirit of the erstwhile slaves—who risked their lives for freedom by braving the treacherous passage of the Sea of Reeds, subsisting on the niggardly gifts of the desert and attributing their victories to the hands of Moses raised in prayer. The true miracle of the Exodus, the archetype of all miracles, is man's indomitable quest for freedom and higher levels of dignity.

In this second phase of prayer man assumes an active posture. He now seeks to assert the fullness of his own being, petitioning for the things and events that he requires for the complete realization of his self. He reaches out for the goals that are beyond his grasp, asking for a miraculous extension of his powers.

Transfiguration

The third phase of prayer is a climax that is rarely attained, which may be designated *transfiguration*. In this *transfiguration*[9] the worshipper feels himself lifted to a higher level—transformed into another being. His self expands horizontally to include the spiritual community of which he is part, and it rises vertically to embrace the ideals of God. As the wish of naive prayer is transmuted into the self-fulfillment of mature worship, so the ideal of self-fulfillment acquires a new range of meaning when the self comes to embrace God.

The term *transfiguration* is suggested by the account of Moses returning from the mountain with the second set of tablets of the Law in his hands. His prayer on behalf of his people had been answered; they were forgiven for the sin of worshipping the golden calf. We are told that his face shone, with beams of light radiating from it. His personality was extended, as it were, beyond its physical limitations.[10]

The worshipper acquires that illumination which enables him to look upon himself as "the messenger of the community." He is no longer simply an individual; he is now identified with the community as it addresses itself to God. This is the climactic meaning of genuine prayer. Thus, the Rabbis ordained that we must stand in reverence when we see a person engaged in prayer. Even if he is an ordinary person, the Divine Presence rests upon him. In great moments of prayer, the self transcends its normal boundaries, becoming one with the spirit of the community and the Divine Presence.

Transfiguration is a natural state of mind, not a mystical or even a mysterious phenomenon. Our personality is brought into being through our many relations to people and to the realm of ideas. We attain human dignity only when we come to value freedom, integrity and truth. And the dimensions of our life are in direct ratio to the ideas and the ideals that nourish us. The persons we love, the purposes we cherish, the standards of excellence which we set for ourselves comprise collectively that increment of selfhood which is spiritual growth. In the prayer of transfiguration our selfhood achieves a cosmic enlargement.

Through prayer, the blessing of transfiguration comes to us as an enduring treasure. To be sure, we cannot by our volition stretch our souls as we can stretch our muscles. But when our prayer is deep and meaningful, we can hope to experience moments of transfiguration. "The eternal God is your dwelling place, and underneath are the everlasting arms" (Deuteronomy 33:27).

When the sages stated in the Passover *Haggadah* that "in every generation, every man is obliged to see himself as if he had gone out of Egypt," they articulated the feeling reflected throughout the prayer book. The history and destiny of the Jewish people become part of our own experience.

It Is "We" Who Pray

To aid in the achievement of transfiguration, the Jewish prayer book phrases nearly all petitions in the first person plural. It is "we" who pray, we who are part of the community of Israel. The *Amidah* begins with the reference to the patriarchs. We address the Lord of the universe as "the God of Abraham, Isaac, and Jacob." Then we continue with the second benediction, giving thanks for the miracle of the revival of the dead. Quite apart from the validity of this dogma as a hope for the future, it symbolizes the concept that the dead are alive in us when we turn to God in prayer.[11]

God is remote and holy, but He is the source of *our* knowledge, *our* healings, *our* prosperity, *our* redemption, *our* vindication in the wonder of the Davidic restoration and *our* peace.[12] It is only after the Eighteen Benedictions are concluded that the first person singular is resumed briefly: "O Lord, guard my tongue from evil . . ."[13]

Identification with the Jewish people is only the first step. The next step is to seek identification with the ideals that derive from God and lead to Him. To merge and dissolve into the community is in itself a dubious good: in weak and anxious moments, we may want to surrender our individuality and "escape from freedom." These are the primitive feelings that flare up in mobs and transform human beings into brutal, blind beasts.

In transfiguration it is not with the ethnic community of Israel that we unite, but rather with the "congregation of Israel" (*K'nesset Yisrael*). In this sense, the community, with all its historic travail and undying hopes, is but a stepping-stone to the larger community of mankind redeemed. The events and visions of the Jewish people are the collective telescope; we look through them and see the slow, stumbling advance of the nations toward one God.

Thus, in the *Alenu* prayer, which ends every daily service, we joyfully accept our destiny as Jews in the first paragraph, freely translated:

> Let us praise Him, Lord over all the world;
> Let us acclaim Him, Author of all creation.
> He made our lot unlike that of other peoples;
> He assigned to us a unique destiny.
> We bend the knee, worship and acknowledge
> The King of kings, the Holy One, praised is He.[14]

The second paragraph states the universal purpose of Israel's existence.

> We therefore hope in You, O Lord our God,
> That we shall soon see the triumph of Your might,
> That idolatry shall be removed from the earth,
> And false gods shall be utterly destroyed.
> Then will the world be a true Kingdom of God,
> When all mankind will invoke Your name,
> And all the earth's wicked will return to You.
> Then all the inhabitants of the world will surely know
> That to You every knee must bend,
> Every tongue pledge loyalty.
> Before you, O Lord, let them bow in worship,
> Let them give honor to Your glory.
> May they all accept the rule of Your Kingdom.
> May You reign over them soon through all time.

The Jewish people is not set apart from the nations, made different and unique for its own sake, as if it were a special category of humanity. Rather, it was *called* to serve in the cause of all men—the continuous shattering of the idols of the market-place. This is an ongoing task, for progress consists in tearing down old idols and outworn goals to create a fresh vision of the good. The idols of the pagan religions were replaced by the Caesar-worship of the Roman Empire; that in its turn was succeeded by the adoration of the Papacy. In the modern period, the rejection of the idols of institutional religion led to the introduction of new idols—the nation, the state, economic classes, race and superman.

It is our tragic fate as human beings, organized in mass societies, first to bring abstractions down to earth in the form of concrete symbols, rites and institutions, and then to adore these agencies as if they were divine in their own right. It is the task of Israel and all who turn to God to transcend the idols of the moment by means of new insights and fresh fervor, "preparing the way in the wilderness for the path to the Lord" (Isaiah 40:3). This idol-shattering task is that of Israel, not because the Jewish people is *exceptional* in some cosmic way, but because all who live on the frontier of faith ought to be *exemplary*.[15]

Learning and Reflection: Central Aspects of Worship[16]

Perhaps the most characteristic quality of Jewish prayer is its emphasis on Torah-learning. In the daily morning services, the benediction for Torah follows immediately after the benedictions expressing gratitude for the varied gifts of life. And the faithful Jew is expected to read selected passages from Scripture and the writings of the sages before he begins his prayers. The central focus of the morning service is the ceremonial reading of the Torah-portion, followed on the Sabbath by the chanting of the prophetic *Haftarah*.

Torah-learning is the essence of prayer. "He who turns his head in order not to hear Torah, his prayer too is an abomination" (Proverbs 28:9). In this connection, Torah assumes an additional meaning, that of rational reflection and self-criticism, "the accounting of the soul." Says the Talmud, "the first *Hasidim* would wait one hour (and meditate), and only then would they pray" (*B'rakhot* 30a). When Rava saw that Rav Huna was engaged in prayer for a long time, he said: "Alas, he forsakes the world of eternity and engages in the life of the hour" (*Shabbat* 10a). Describing the ideal form of prayer, Maimonides says:

> Our purpose . . . is to caution man to concentrate his love on His Name, only after long and careful reflection, for the service of God is dependent on a true conception of Him. The more we think and refine our understanding, the greater is our service. But if one should remember Him, without the labor of wise thought, relying upon the fancies of imagination and the beliefs that others have bequeathed to him, then he is outside the palace of the King and far from Him, not serving Him at all but some unreal, mythical illusion.[17]

The importance of rational reflection in Jewish prayer is readily understood when we contemplate the pitfalls that abound in every phase of worship. In the stage of *appreciation*, we have to distinguish the abounding glory of God from the various forms of nature-mysticism. Nature affords us infinite illustrations of divine mercy and power, but only after we have learned to identify the divine with the noblest expressions of human nature. By itself, nature is a poor teacher, often leading man back to the law of the fang and the claw. The Nazi mass-murderers of modern times drew their teachings from perverted concepts of biology. In Judaism, spirit is distinguished from nature on the principle that the will of God and His work are not identical. The marks of infinite spirit must be discovered in the beauty and majesty of the ever-changing face of nature.

The intellectual component is even more prominent in the second stage of prayer, *aspiration*, for man must know his failures and limitations if he is to overcome them. Thus, in the *Amidah*, he prays first for knowledge and second for Torah-piety before he asks for the forgiveness of his sins.

The plaintive notes of repentance, heard in all daily prayers, are particularly prominent during the High Holidays. On the Day of Atonement, the mood of penitence attains its climax, and the recitation of sins is repeated several times. It is remarkable that the individual sins recited on the ten days of penitence refer only to moral transgressions, in particular the so-called "duties of the heart." There is no mention of ritualistic violations —non-kosher food, non-observance of "purity" laws, desecration of the Sabbath and the holidays. Rites and ceremonies are aids to piety, not surrogates for the spirit of humility, generosity and wisdom. The prayer book focuses attention on the dimension of depth in piety, challenging the reader to repent for such failures as "the hardening of our hearts," "wronging our neighbor," "sinful meditation of the heart," "confession of the lips," "impure speech," "haughty eyes," "confusion of the mind."

The rational component of religious aspiration prevents us from succumbing to the doctrine that the sinner is a "fallen" creature who is no longer able to help himself. This belief that the sinner is dehumanized and incapable of finding his own way to God removes the power of decision from the human sphere. People are not responsible agents but marionettes; their actions are neither good nor bad, but either blessed or accursed. The real battle is between God and the devil, with all human history being a "battle between the children of light and the children of darkness."

In Judaism *all* men face God directly, and *all* can turn to Him at any moment. The Talmud tells of the conversion and penitence of Nero, the arch-villain of the ancient world, adding that Rabbi Meir was descended from him.[18] Nebuzaraddon was the master-butcher who massacred thousands of people in Jerusalem. Of him the Talmud says—"his descendants taught Torah in the Sanhedrin" (*Gittin* 55a). Menasseh, the evil king of Judah, whose sins brought about the destruction of the Holy Temple, repented in the last years of his life, and the Lord reinstated him in His good graces.[19]

Man cannot sink so low in sin as to be deprived of the capacity to mirror the divine in his soul. This is why Jewish law ruled that the bodies of condemned criminals had to be removed from the gallows before sundown.

This feeling of fellowship with the sinner is particularly important because we are all sinners. "There is no one, not a righteous man upon earth, that does good and does not sin" (Ecclesiastes 7:20).

"That His Name Be Beloved"

In the third stage of prayer, *transfiguration,* the role of rational reflection is decisive. As we enlarge ourselves to embrace the divine we must take care not to identify the divine with ourselves. It is at this point, when religion attains its most potent impact, that the disastrous inversion of piety is most likely to be manifested.

We must learn to distinguish between the piety of crusades and the rational-moral-religious art of transfiguration. In the former, the crusader imagines that he knows the will of God—he *has* it, sealed and delivered. In the latter, the divine is sought as a goal, not grasped as a possession; the person devotes himself to the cause of God and pledges his life to its service, as in the concentration of Jewish fervor on the goal of becoming a "people of priests and a holy nation" (Exodus 19:6).

It would seem at first glance that the crusading mentality is essentially selfless. Did not the medieval knights surrender all to the cause of God? Yet the religious crusaders of the Middle Ages brought untold desolation and horror to the European world.

The crusading spirit was not encouraged in Judaism. At Sinai, the Jewish people became a covenant-people, pledged to bring the love of God into human life. They were not to be a missionary nation, pledged to spreading the word by fire and sword. They were to begin by improving themselves, their family, their community.

While the romantic-mystical phase of transfiguration makes us feel as if we were one with God's redeeming power, the rational-moral phase warns us that we are far from this consummation. The Kabbalists admonished us to pray "with both fear and love" (*Bid'ḥilu ur'ḥimu*). While love draws man toward union and identification, fear pulls him back, reminding him of his failings. Yet fear and love together are "the wings of the soul."

The Three Stages of Prayer—An Example

Psalm Twenty-three reflects the three stages of prayer in simple and moving language. It begins by sounding the note of grateful appreciation:

The Lord is my shepherd; I shall not want.
He maketh me to lie down in green pastures;
He leadeth me beside the still waters.

The mood of passive trust and self-surrender to the Ruler of the universe is articulated here in the image of the shepherd, his green pastures and still waters.

Then the psalmist calls attention to a feeling of finitude, a fear of death. Man can never forget the overhanging sword, the brevity of his stay on earth. This feeling of finitude is countered by the determination to walk with Him in "circles of righteousness"—a literal translation of *ma'aglai tzedek*, a phrase which reminds us that the right road is not always the straight and obvious one. The vision of divine goodness is present not simply to be enjoyed, but also to be introduced into life. The "valley of the shadow of death" symbolizes the many unfinished areas where evil and privation still prevail. Man's task is to advance in the knowledge that God is his companion.

This thought leads directly to transfiguration, the third phase of prayer. The metaphor changes: the worshipper is no longer a lamb, looking up to the shepherd; he has become an honored guest, a son in the house of His Creator.

Thou preparest a table before me in the presence of mine enemies;
Thou hast anointed my head with oil; my cup runneth over.
Surely goodness and mercy shall follow me all the days of my life;
And I shall dwell in the house of the Lord for ever.

The triumphant note of transfiguration is clear and resonant. God is within us as well as beyond us. He is our Father as well as our King. We serve Him as sons, not merely as slaves.

The Kaddish—Prayer of Transfiguration

The *Kaddish*, recited by mourners, is the special prayer of transfiguration. The mourner comes to the synagogue for eleven months and at every *yahrzeit*, testifying by his presence that he appreciates the blessings of God in spite of his loss. In effect, his attendance is a silent articulation of the standard formula— "The Lord has given, the Lord has taken; may the Name of the Lord be blessed."

He does more than accept the judgment of God: he undertakes to fill the place of the deceased and to become part of the company which is eternal, engaged in the redemptive labor of the Eternal. His personal self is now part of the collective soul of Israel, the congregation of men and women who help to build the Kingdom of God on earth.

The *Kaddish* begins with the plea, "Magnified and sanctified be His great Name . . ." The Name of God is the totality of all the events which bespeak His presence and His power. Whenever a person departs from this world, the divine name is diminished, and the work of building His Kingdom on earth slowed down. The mourner undertakes to step into that breach and fill the lacuna. He becomes part of the task performed by the procession of the builders of the Kingdom.

The mourner finds that this transfigured self is blessed by the feeling of peace. "He who ordains peace in the uttermost ends of the universe will embrace us and grant all Israel His peace."

The mourner feels himself taken up in the larger harmony of existence. His life and the life of the deceased have meaning and purpose within a larger context. His grief is not dulled or numbed but it is brought to a higher plane where the majesty of the divine purpose is felt without being understood.

The Symbolism of Prayer

All prayer is symbolic. On the High Holidays, the blasts of the *shofar* provide deeply moving moments; this, too, is the effect of the action-symbols of *tallit* and *t'fillin,* of the ceremonial reading of the Torah and the carrying of the Scrolls in procession. The sense of being part of a living congregation, acting, responding and moving in concert, is of great value in promoting the enlargement of the self and its transfiguration.

To encourage communal worship, the sages ruled that the *mitzvah* of saying certain prayers can be fulfilled only in the presence of ten men (*minyan*). In one sense, "the Divine Presence (*Sh'khinah*) does not rest on fewer than twenty-two thousand people" (*Y'vamot* 64a). But for ordinary worship the Divine Presence is assumed whenever ten men gather in prayer, since at any moment at least one of them directs his thought and love to God.

The perennial problem of worship is to utilize a concrete action as a vehicle of the transcendent, and at the same time not to forget that this is no more than a symbol. Hence, the various

Names of God that we have in the prayer book, though the most all-embracing Name (YHVH) is never pronounced directly but only by the substitution of *Adonai*, Master. The Tetragrammaton (YHVH), whatever its original meaning and pronunciation, is understood to be a formula, combining the future, the past and the present; Moses Mendelssohn translated it as the Eternal, but it might also be interpreted as Ultimate Being. The injunction against pronouncing God's Name was a reminder that He could not be named. "He is called according to His deeds." Thus we address Him as the Merciful (*Raḥman*), the Good (*Tov*), the Almighty (*Shaddai*), the Lord of Nature (*Elohim*), or as our Father (*Avinu*) and our King (*Malkenu*).

In the opening paragraph of the *Amidah*, the Lord is described as "the God of Abraham, the God of Isaac, and the God of Jacob." In the days of Moses this designation meant the God who had revealed Himself to the patriarchs and who had concluded a covenant with them. Later, the phrase took on deeper meaning, signifying the providence revealed in the entire range of Jewish history. Later still, the difference between the three self-revelations was stressed. To Abraham God was revealed under the aspect of steadfast love (*ḥesed*); to Isaac He appeared in overwhelming awe (*paḥad*); and to Jacob He was shown in the quest of truth (*emet*).

So too, Zion, Israel and the Messiah were endowed with universal meanings. Zion is the symbol of the Divine Presence which fills the earth; Israel is the ideal community, invisible yet encompassing all who serve God with heart and mind; and the Messiah is the symbol of ultimate redemption.

Though they imaged Thee through many guises,
Thou Art One, in all disguises.[20]

FOR FURTHER READING

ARTZ, Max, *Justice and Mercy* (New York: Burning Bush Press, 1963). A well-designed guide for novices to the high-holiday services.

DONIN, Hayim H., *To Pray as a Jew* (New York: Basic Books, 1980). A step-by-step guide to all elements practical, as well as theoretical in Jewish prayer. A literal "how-to-do-it" manual for all occasions.

MILLGRAM, Abraham, *Jewish Worship* (Philadelphia: Jewish Publication Society, 1971). A comprehensive, non-technial, introduction to Jewish prayer.

MINTZ, Alan, "Prayer and the Prayerbook," in Barry Holtz, editor, *Back to the Sources: Reading the Classic Jewish Texts* (New York: Summit Books, 1984). A fine summary and guide to the nature and inner meaning of Jewish prayer. A good place to begin.

PETUCHOWSKY, Jacob, J., editor, *Understanding Jewish Prayer* (Hoboken, NJ: Ktav Publishing, 1972). A helpful, accessible, exploration of many central aspects of the litergy.

SCHACHTER, Zalman, "A First Step: A Devotional Guide" in *The First Jewish Catalogue* (Philadelphia: Jewish Publication Society, 1973): One of contemporary Jewries' spiritual innovators helps bring to the surface the inner significance of prayer for those to whom it is a foreign reality and practice.

14 . The Messianic Doctrine in Contemporary Jewish Thought

STEVEN S. SCHWARZSCHILD

F O R T H E Jews of Eastern Europe who went to their martyrs' death at the cruel hands of the Nazis, on the walls of the Warsaw ghetto or in the gas-ovens of Treblinka, the song *Ani Ma'amin* became something approximating a national anthem. Its text consists of the twelfth of Maimonides' Thirteen Principles of Faith, the classic formulation of the beliefs which every Jew is expected to hold and which, in poetic form, has also been turned into one of the most popular hymns of the synagogue to this day, *Yigdal Elokim Hai.* This Twelfth Principle, in penultimate place (not unrelated to the last which deals with resurrection) and, therefore, very near the climactic pinnacle of Jewish faith according to Maimonides, reads: "I believe with complete faith in the coming of the Messiah—and, though he may tarry, yet will I wait for him every day on which he may come." [1]

The surviving Jewish people have acclaimed this song a symbol of unshakable Jewish confidence in the righteousness of its cause and in the eventual triumph of divine goodness, because its melody and its words swelled up out of Jewish throats in the midst of the most destructive storm of human wickedness and in the face of the most horrible wave of mass-murder. But *Ani Ma'amin* was more than a symbol. To make it merely a symbol tends to sentimentalize it: we admire the generalized attitude of hopefulness which we fancy we detect in its use; we remember the melody and forget the import of the words. The fact is that to the mass of martyrized Jewish people the text of the *Ani Ma'amin* conveyed literal truth: they really believed that their suffering, and all of the evil that was then ruling the world, were the *Ḥevley Mashiaḥ*, "the birth-pangs of the Messiah." For it is established Jewish doctrine that, even as a woman who is about to give birth and thus to perform the most marvelous act of human creation must first undergo great pain, so also the world will be torn by terrible wars, the wars of Gog and Magog, of which the prophet Ezekiel spoke (chapters 38, 39)—cruelty and ugliness, catastrophes and malice—immediately before the Kingdom of God will be established on earth by the Messiah, with its eternal peace and love, truth and justice. Therefore, throughout Jewish history, whenever Israel seemed to have reached a new nadir of misfortune and persecution, it was believed that this, surely, must be—to use another traditional metaphor for this conception—"the footsteps of the Messiah"; this was a last and terrible trial through which Jews had to go in order to come out into a world of light and gladness. Thus the horrors of every single generation were endowed with cosmic significance for all of mankind, and apparently irrational, immoral experiences were transformed into useful and even creative human acts: suffering made sense; pain had a purpose.

It was in this light that the Jews of Europe endeavored to see their fate. When they sang *Ani Ma'amin* they were engaging in no juvenile optimism. They truly thought that through their own convulsions they were helping to give birth to a radically new and better world under the immediate sovereignty of God, and they firmly expected the person of the Messiah to appear shortly to usher in this new age. In the book *Emunat Yisrael*,[2] for example, the last moments in the life of Rabbi Israel Shapira of Gradsiks are described by his son in these words:

When the people of the camp, by the thousands, were brought into the forecourt of the chambers of destruction in Treblinka, they turned to the rabbi and said: "Our rabbi, what do you say now?" The holy rabbi answered them quietly: "Hearken, my brothers and my sisters, O people of God! We may not criticize God's deeds. If it has been determined that in this time, at this stage of the process of redemption, we are to be sacrifices of the agonies of the Messiah, that we are to go on the stake, happy are we that we have been given such meritorious opportunity. When our sages said: 'May he come, but let me not see!,' this one may say only before the event—but we who have reached this stage must rejoice that our ashes will purify all Israel. I command you not to panic and not to weep as you go into the oven but rather to be joyous, with the song *Ani Ma'amin*, and like Rabbi Akiba to die with the word 'one' of the *Shema* on your lips." The people obeyed the words of the holy one, and singing *Ani Ma'amin* and reciting the *Shema Yisrael* they publicly sanctified God. May God keep them, and may their memory be blessed.

This personal commitment to the belief in the expected coming of the person of the Messiah prevailed throughout religiously sensitive circles of European Jewry directly in the hour of their doom. What was true of the masses of Orthodox Jewry of Eastern Europe was also true among the ranks of acculturated German Jewry. Ernst Simon of The Hebrew University has movingly demonstrated [3] that a series of popular booklets published by and for German Jews beginning in 1933, by the selection of its subjects and their treatment, gave expression to the tenor, ethos and spirituality of that community throughout the years of its constriction and into the final hour of its death. "The Messianic note barely struck soon rises to a Messianic folk-song translated from the Yiddish and to *Hasidic* stories 'about the Messiah' which Martin Buber related." Professor Simon could have pointed out that this series of booklets came to its conclusion when the pogroms of 1938 incinerated the synagogues and incarcerated and murdered the people, in the next-to-the-last volume, a double number, entitled *Gottes Gesalbter Der Messias und die messianische Zeit in Talmud und Midrasch* (*God's Anointed—The Messiah and the Messianic Age in Talmud and Midrash*). The booklet, beautifully and chastely published at the very moment that the world around was literally going up in flames, is still the best compilation of many of the relevant literary texts. It does not breathe a word about the conditions under which it came into existence; it does not homiletically apply what it talks about to the urgent contemporary situation; it simply states the classic Jewish case, soberly cites Bible, Talmud and medieval thinkers—forgetting all about the modern apparatus of culture, philosophy and science, for these were doing their vicious work in the outside world—and let the reader draw his own conclusions!

Clearly, then, in the Jewish doctrine of the Messiah we are not dealing with a *theologumen*, an abstract and irrelevant theoretical proposition of religion, but rather with a living faith, an active force in the most crucial hours of the lives of men and of Jewish history. This does not mean that the doctrine cannot or should not be subjected to rational analysis and interpretation, but it should at least make us wary of dry, academic quibbles as to whether the Messiah is a person or the symbol of a stage in human development—whether belief in him will lead to quietism or to activism—whether abuses and misinterpretations by pseudo-Messiahs refute the belief—and similar disputes that have occurred in the past. Some of these discussions were valid expressions of the problems that afflicted earlier generations: Joseph Albo in the late Middle Ages had to worry about the use made of the belief in the Messiah by Christian polemicists and, therefore, relegated the doctrine to a subordinate place; in the early nineteenth century emancipated Jews pressed for complete social enfranchisement and fancied that they could bring about the utopian society by the work of their own hands, with the help of other men of good will, and that, therefore, the Kingdom of God was about the evolve in the natural course of human events; in the early twentieth century, Zionists trying to build up the land of the promised Messianic future ran into resistance by some Orthodox Jews who felt that such an undertaking was an impertinent usurpation of divine providence by fatally ambitious men. The strong disagreements which arose under such circumstances about the value of the Messianic doctrine were natural and cogent, and we of a later period have learned much from them. But we may also conclude, on the basis of the evidence of our generation, that we have espied the outlines of the figure of the Messiah in the highest, faintest wisps of smoke over the chimneys of Auschwitz and on the skyline of Jerusalem-rebuilding. In our time we must either fall into utter despair at the sight of Jewish distress and imminent universal human extinction, or we sense that we live in the age which Jewish mystics have called *Athalta D'geula*, "the beginning of redemption."

Year-Round Messianism in the Liturgy

The Jewish people is the Messianic people. This means not only that according to Biblical, Jewish as well as Christian, teaching (John 4:22: "Salvation is from the Jews"), the person of the Messiah will come out of the midst of and primarily act upon the Jewish people, but also that it is the history of the Jewish people which essentially determines whether, when and how God will send the Messiah. Thus it stands to reason that in our time we have had to try to understand the doctrine of the Messiah in the light of the historical experience which we have undergone. This does not imply that Jewish history itself determines his advent; it may merely constitute the condition under which God, in His own wisdom and time, will consider "the days fulfilled." It also does not imply that any event in history is itself the Messianic fulfillment, for example, the establishment of the State of Israel; it may merely be "the beginning of redemption." But the historic development that we prayerfully look upon as such a "beginning of redemption," the survival and restoration of the Jewish people after it had been pushed to the very edge of the abyss of total extermination, is surely described correctly in the words of the prophet Zechariah (3:2): "This is a brand plucked from the fire"; therefore, the prophet goes on, though it may still be dressed in filthy garments, whoever rebukes it is a "Satan," for he does not carry out God's order to exchange these for pure robes and a pure mitre.

These phrases come from a section of the Book of Zechariah which Jewish tradition has assigned as the prophetic lesson for *Hanukkah*.⁴ *Hanukkah* is only a semi-holiday in Jewish law, and it has usually been regarded as merely an historic commemoration until, in our time, with the rise of Zionism and the establishment of the State of Israel, it gained new meaning. In fact, if properly and profoundly understood, *Hanukkah* is a grand Messianic celebration. He who thoroughly fathoms *Hanukkah* has heard the first steps of the coming of the Messiah.

An old calculation proves that the motto of *Hanukkah* (*Naes Gadol Hayah Sham*—"a great miracle happened there") inscribed on the *dreidel* refers to the Messiah, for both the Hebrew word "Messiah" and the initials of the motto have the numerical value of 358. The famous *Hanukkah* hymn *M'aoz Tzur* actually speaks very little of the Hasmoneans: the first stanza prays for the Messianic and enduring restoration of the Temple; the hymn then goes on to trace the course of the Messiah through Jewish history, in the paradigm of redemption in Egypt (second stanza), the pattern of the return from exile in Babylonia under Zerubabel (third stanza), the defeat of the enemy of Jewry, Haman (fourth stanza), and the Hasmoneans, after they triumphed over Antiochus Epiphanes, who is conceived as the Messianic enemy Gog (fifth stanza). In short, *M'aoz Tzur* proclaims that Messianic redemption will consist of the synchronism of liberation, return, triumph and rededication. Little wonder that (probably in the sixteenth century) the Messianic past was once more projected forward toward the final consummation of *Hanukkah* in an additional sixth stanza: "Oh stretch forth the hand of Thy holiness; bring near the end of salvation; execute the retribution of Thy servants upon the evil kingdom. For the hour has lengthened, and to this evil there seems to be no end . . ."

The fullest and most magnificent explication of the Messianic meaning of *Hanukkah*, and therewith of the Messianic doctrine itself, is, however, offered in the prophetic lesson of *Hanukkah* from Zechariah. To taste its flavor would really require a verse-by-verse, word-by-word interpretation. Many of the classic Jewish commentaries, and even more the modern students of the Bible, have tended to cover up its Messianic significance by concentrating too much on the historical background out of which this prophecy emerged; they are too parochially "scientific" and go on endlessly telling us that Zechariah lived at the time of the Babylonian return under Zerubabel, of whom he spoke. They forget that the Bible and Jewish tradition (like the *M'aoz Tzur*) conceive of Zerubabel as a descendant of David and thus as a link in the chain which binds us to the future Messiah.[5] Still, as we shall see, there have always been enough eschatological hints in the exegesis of Zechariah to make this one of the *loci classici*— if a neglected one—a catechism, as it were, of what Judaism teaches about the Messiah. We can only summarize it here.

That the Zecharianic passage is Messianic is put beyond doubt by verse 3:8: "Behold, I am sending my servant *Tzemah*." The commentary *Metzudat David* points out that the "name" *Tzemah* refers back to Jeremiah 23:5 where *Tzemah*, "Flower," is a name for the Davidic redeemer: "Behold, days are coming, says the Lord, when I shall raise a righteous *Tzemah*-flower of David, and a king will reign wisely who will do justice and righteousness in the earth. In his days Judah will be saved, and Israel will dwell safely; and this is the name by which he will be called: 'The Lord of our righteousness.' " *Tzemah* is, of course, also an allusion to the Messianic prophecy of Isaiah 11:1 ff.:[6] "A *shoot* will go out from the stock of Jesse, and a branch will blossom from its roots. Upon him will rest the spirit of the Lord, the spirit of wisdom and understanding, the spirit of counsel and might, the spirit of knowledge and of fear of the Lord . . ."[7] Furthermore, the cue-words "on that day"—the well-known, special day when the Messiah will arrive—introduce Zechariah 3:10, the self-same words which introduce almost all great Messianic prophecies, like Amos 8:9 and like Zechariah 14:8 ff. itself, with which we close every Jewish worship service: "It shall be *on that day* . . . the Lord will be King over all the earth. *On that day* the Lord will be one and His name one." The fact is that the entire book of Zechariah is permeated with Messianism from beginning to end, stimulated, no doubt, by the events surrounding Zerubabel but referring far beyond them. For that reason the gospel according to Matthew uses Zechariah repeatedly, thus satisfying itself that Jesus is the person of the Messiah: Zechariah 9:9 ff. becomes the story of Jesus entering Jerusalem on a donkey, and Zechariah 11:13 becomes the story of the thirty pieces of silver.[8] Above all, the final fourteenth chapter of Zechariah—a tremendous apocalyptic vision of the end of history—has in turn been set aside by Jewish tradition as the prophetic lesson for the first day of the Feast of Tabernacles, because *Sukkot* is the festival of the Messianic unification of all mankind. On *Sukkot* seventy sacrifices were brought into the Temple as acknowledgment of God's sovereignty over all the seventy nations of which mankind was believed to consist.

What, then, does the *Hanukkah Haftarah* teach about the Messiah? When the Messiah arrives Israel will rejoice, for God will again dwell in its midst (Zechariah 2:14). "Many nations will be joined to the Lord on that day. They will be My people, and I shall dwell in your midst" (so reconstituted by the gentiles who will have accepted the truth) (2:15). Israel will be restored to its Holy Land (2:16). Then follows the episode in which the Messianic people is called "a brand plucked from the fire," and its shabby past is exchanged for a beautiful everlasting present (3:1-6). So that its stage of purification may lead to the enduring Messianic fulfillment, Israel must implicitly obey God's law. Then, indeed, will Israel "walk among the angels" and be "men worthy of the miracle" (3:7-8). Again emphasizing the universalistic aspect of the rule of the Messiah, the foundation-stone of this new kingdom is pictured as inscribed on seven sides, corresponding to the seventy nations which constitute humanity (3:9).[9] Then every man will sit safely "under his vine and under his fig-tree" (3:10). The prophetic lesson for *Hanukkah* ends with the splendid vision of the golden candelabrum (no doubt the immediate cause for the selection of this lesson for *Hanukkah*) overhung—literally—by an olive-tree on each side from which, without human help or hindrance, oil drips directly into its seven branches. Zechariah is puzzled, but an angel explains: "Not by might nor by strength, but by My spirit, said the Lord of hosts" (4:6). It is an almost incredibly ironic and daring lesson for *Hanukkah,* the festival of the heroic and militant Hasmoneans. In Messianic perspective, God's kingdom will not be brought about by human exertion, however moral and progressive, but alone through God's intervention in human history.[10] No power will be able to resist the Messiah once he has begun to manifest his might. "Grace, grace," not power will rule forever after (4:7).[11]

The chief features of the belief in the Messiah can then be summarized: 1) his rule of truth and goodness will extend over all mankind; 2) Israel will be restored to its pristine glory and security; 3) his sovereignty will be ushered in by God's enactment, not by human achievement; 4) the Messiah will be a single human person through whom God will perform the ultimate miracle.

This proclamation of the Messianic faith of Judaism could, point for point, be duplicated by similar passages from all sections of the Bible, Talmud, prayer book and throughout Jewish sacred literature. They would, in a sense, be appropriate for literally every single occasion during the Jewish year, not *Hanukkah* alone. We have seen how the prophetic lesson for *Hanukkah* is one end of a bridge that ends on the other side with the prophetic portion taken from the same prophet for the first day of Tabernacles, thus pointing from the national liberation of Israel to the universal redemption of mankind. Passover is, of course, another grand paradigm of the ultimate triumph over human slavery: on the "Passover of Egypt," as Jewish tradition calls it, Israel experiences an historic and, therefore, only inter-mediate salvation, one which it underwent fleetingly and pass-ingly: "For in haste you went forth from the land of Egypt" (Deuteronomy 16:3); the ultimate salvation of "the Passover of the Messiah" will endure, for when the Messiah comes "you will not go forth in haste, and you will not go in flight, for the Lord will go before you, and the God of Israel will gather you in," as the prophet Isaiah puts it, in direct counter-statement to the Deuteronomic text, in one of his most classic Messianic prophecies (Isaiah 52:12). Therefore, Elijah, the herald of the Messiah, is invited at the *Seder* table. On the Festival of Weeks, the Book of Ruth with its genealogy of David, the Messianic king, is read. The universality of the High Holy Days is replete with Messianic expectations: the "Adoration," taken from their liturgy, ends with the Messianic prayer of Zechariah that looks forward to the "day when the Lord will be one and His name one." And the central insertion in the *Amidah* pleads for the unification of mankind under God's universal rule.

But the Messianic note in Judaism is not only struck on annual holy days. Every Sabbath is a Messianic celebration. For twenty-four hours a foretaste of the Messianic kingdom is savored by the Jew in peace and security and spiritual concentration. If at its end the Messiah still has not come Jews conclude it with pleading songs invoking at least his herald, the prophet Elijah. The Messianic calendar could be continued indefinitely, for literally every single day in the year is suffused with Messianic expectations, prayers and preparations: fifty days lead from the Messianic Passover to the Messianic Feast of Weeks—and every day may turn out to be the last before the advent: never ask on what day the bell tolls; it tolls today.[12] This is the meaning of the phrase which we quoted at the outset from Maimonides: "he may come on any day."

Messianic expectation is thus literally the daily and even hourly posture of the Jew. The word *Tzemah*, like musical motifs in Wagner's operas, is a widely dispersed recurring theme-word which, each time, causes the Jew to snap back into this posture. Three times a day, on every weekday, it looms up right in the very heart of the "Eighteen Prayer" (*Amidah*), the core-piece of Jewish worship: "The flower-*Tzemaḥ* of David, Thy servant, cause Thou soon to flower (*tatzmiaḥ*), and raise Thou his horn through Thy salvation, for upon Thy salvation do we hope all the day. Praised be Thou, O Lord, who causes the horn of salvation to flower (*matzmiaḥ*)."

We are back at the same stand. No fewer than three times is the cue-word *tzemaḥ* employed, as if to make certain that none can miss the point.[18] And that we hope for God's salvation "all the day" is, of course, simply another formulation of Habakkuk 2:3, which Maimonides also cited in his Twelfth Principle in the phrase "I shall await him (the Messiah) on every day on which he may come."

We are here dealing with the fifteenth of the benedictions that constitute the thrice-daily "Eighteen Prayer," but we are not dealing with it only for its own sake. If it were merely a matter of this particular benediction, then the expectation of the Messiah as here expressed would be only one among many more or less similarly significant Jewish doctrines. The fact is that this fifteenth benediction must be recognized as the peak of the mountain: all the benedictions before it are in turn thoroughly Messianic prayers which step by step rise to this peak, and all the benedictions after it are equally Messianic in character and gradually descend again to the foot of the mountain. To change the metaphor, the fifteenth benediction is the angle from which the best perspective can be obtained on the entire "Eighteen Prayer," and once this perspective has been taken the entire Jewish liturgy appears in a different and transfigured, namely in a Messianic, light.[14] We cannot, of course, here subject the entire prayer to a close analysis from this point of view—e.g., how the first benediction actually spells out its petition for the coming of the "redeemer," the second gives thanks for the Messianic resurrection, and so on.

Let it merely be pointed out that the string of benedictions immediately surrounding the one with which we are primarily concerned, i.e., benedictions ten to seventeen, are a continuous Messianic invocation in which literally all the themes that make up the ultimate Messianic symphony are struck. Benediction Ten, "Blow the great (Messianic) *shofar* . . ." prays for the perfect freedom and for the ingathering of Israel under Messianic auspices. Benediction Eleven, "Return our judges . . . ," prays for the establishment of perfect justice and grace and the total elimination of human sorrow at the hands of the Messiah. Benediction Twelve, a somewhat later insertion into the *Amidah*, was originally directed against the "heretics" (*minim*), not against the "slanderers" as the text now has it, who proclaim a false Messiah. Benediction Thirteen spreads the benefits of the Messianic fulfillment to all "the righteous and pious," the teachers in Israel no more than to "the sincere proselytes" who will, in the day of his advent, join us. "Mercy" (grace) and *ḥelek* (share, i.e., "our share in the world-to-come") are the Messianic cue-words in this paragraph. The next benediction explicitly prays for the restoration of the Temple and the Davidic throne (alluding to Zechariah 8:3), thus leading to the ultimate and climactically Messianic passage, the fifteenth. The full statement of the eschatological worship having been exhausted, the "Eighteen Prayer" now slowly ebbs from this crescendo again: the sixteenth benediction asks that the previous prayers be accepted and fulfilled, the seventeenth details the hope for the restored Temple in the components of sacrifice and prayer. It is no happenstance that it is into this benediction that the special prayer for the Holy Days is inserted; for the New Moon Day and the pilgrimage festivals, it spells out the Messianic plea in the words: "May the memory (of Thy promise) . . . of the Messiah, the son of David, Thy servant, arise before Thee . . . in grace, lovingkindness and mercy . . . and save us . . . for Thou art a royal, gracious and merciful God."

Thus, as the special occasions of the Jewish year spread their Messianic wings over every weekday, so also the weekday imperceptibly blends into the festal Messianic spirit. The "Eighteen Prayer" is seen to rehearse all the significant Messianic themes: perfect human freedom, the ingathering of Israel, perfect justice, the elimination of human sorrow, God's universal reign in justice and grace, universal acceptance of Jewish truth, and the restoration of Zion, the Davidic rule and the Temple.

Without wishing to impugn in the slightest degree, then, the legitimacy of any Jew who earnestly seeks to find God, it is difficult, in the light of this all-pervasive belief in the eventual coming of the Messiah, to see how one can be a believing Jew while abandoning this doctrine.

The Person of the Messiah

Who is this Messiah whom Judaism awaits?

He is, in the first place, a human being, not a divine person—a descendant of the royal family of David. "There shall come forth a shoot out of the stock of Jesse, and a twig shall grow forth out of his roots" presages the prophet Isaiah (11:1). To be sure, this man who is the Messiah will carry out a special divine mission, and for this mission he will be endowed with the necessary special powers and qualities, but then there have been other messengers of God throughout history who performed tasks of which other men were incapable and who possessed the unique qualifications required for their purposes without being considered superhuman or divine. Moses redeemed Israel at the beginning of its history as the Messiah will redeem it "in the end of days," and the Bible most emphatically asserts Moses' humanity. The prophets, one and all, revealed God's will, as will the Messiah, but they were born, lived and died like all other men. Indeed, Maimonides says:[15] "The Messiah will die, and his son and his son's son will reign in his place. God clearly announced his death in Isaiah 42:4: 'He will not weaken nor crumble until he will have established righteousness on earth.'"

It has often been pointed out, and quite rightly, that a basic disagreement between Judaism and Christianity concerns the coming of the Messiah: Christianity holds—indeed, this is its central dogma—that the Messiah has already come, whereas Judaism still awaits him in the future. More fundamental even than this disagreement about the time of the arrival of the Messiah is the disagreement about his nature. While, as we have seen, Judaism awaits a Messiah who is a human person, delegated by God, Christianity maintains that the Messiah who has come was, though human, also completely divine, himself God, one of the persons in the trinity that is God. To Jewish sensibility such a doctrine is a profoundly jarring infringement on absolute monotheism: nothing and no one that can be seen are God, though everything and everyone are His handiwork.

The thoroughly human nature of the Messiah is further deepened by the conception that he is the "suffering servant of the Lord" (especially Isaiah 52-53, ironically used in Christianity as a pre-eminent Christological text). The royal scion, while awaiting the hour of redemption, undergoes all the pains of human existence, most specifically the prototypal human pains of Jewish existence:

> He had no form nor comeliness, that we should look upon him,
> Nor beauty that we should delight in him.
> He was despised, and forsaken of men,
> A man of pains, and acquainted with disease,
> And as one from whom men hide their face:
> He was despised, and we esteemed him not.
> Surely our diseases he did bear, and our pains he carried;
> Whereas we did esteem him stricken,
> Smitten of God and afflicted.
> But he was wounded because of our transgressions,
> He was crushed because of our iniquities:
> The chastisement of our welfare was upon him,
> And with his stripes we were healed.
> All we like sheep did go astray,
> We turned every one to his own way;
> And the Lord hath made to light on him
> The iniquity of us all.
> He was oppressed, though he humbled himself
> And opened not his mouth;
> As a lamb that is led to the slaughter,
> And as a sheep that before her shearers is dumb;
> Yea, he opened not his mouth . . .
> And they made his grave with the wicked,
> And with the rich his tomb . . .
> Yet it pleased the Lord to crush him by disease;
> To see if his soul would offer itself in restitution . . .
> And that the purpose of the Lord might prosper by his hand:
> Of the travail of his soul he shall see to the full, even My servant,
> Who by his knowledge did justify the Righteous One to the
>   many,
> And their iniquities he did bear.
> Therefore will I divide him a portion among the great,
> And he shall divide the spoil with the mighty;
> Because he bared his soul unto death,
> And was numbered with the transgressors;
> Yet he bore the sin of many,
> And made intercession for the transgressors.
>
> (Isaiah 53:2-12)

This theme is elaborated upon throughout Bible and Talmud: the Messiah will appear humbly riding into Jerusalem on an ass (Zechariah 9:9)—he waits sitting in front of the gates of Rome, the incarnation of the enemy of Israel, binding up the wounds with which his body is covered, among the outcasts of society (*Sanhedrin* 98)—above all, again and again, he suffers without guilt!

A number of traits are thus discernible in the figure of the Messiah as Judaism envisions it: he represents the epitome of poverty and humility as well as the fate of the Messianic people of Israel; he, therefore, presages redemption from these very experiences when he will appear in his glory to assume dominion.

Hermann Cohen, the great Jewish theologian of the beginning of this century, has formulated the human and social meaning of this dimension of the person of the Messiah in classic words:

> Thus the Messiah becomes the representative of suffering, and in this capacity he throws the clearest light on human history. Poverty is the moral defect of all past history. The poor are recognized as the pious. And the pious are the heralds of the Messiah. The representative of suffering brings this truth to the world—and thus founds an ethical concept of history: all eude- monistic appearance is but illusion; the true value for the history of all nations resides in moral ideas, and this true value can, then, only be formulated by people who are authenticated as bearers of such ideas . . . Jewish history, considered as history and, there- fore, as the realization of moral ideas, is a continuous chain of human and national misery. "Despised and pierced" these servants of God have always been, and "cut off from the land of the living." And although people have never ceased marveling at the survival of this peculiar people, nonetheless what the Isaianic text expresses so wondrously always remains true: "and in his time, who has considered this?" The Messianic people suffers as the representative of human suffering. This view is not an exaggera- tion of the mission of Israel if it be true that the Messianic realiza- tion of monotheism is the historic task of the Jewish religion. . . . All injustice in the history of the world is an accusation raised against mankind. Thus, the misery of the Jews has at all times leveled a terrible indictment at the other nations. But from this Messianic point of view a new theodical light is cast on the Jewish puzzle of history. It is true that eudemonistically the suffering of the Jews is a misfortune. But the Messianic vocation of Israel illumines the history of the Jews in the world differently. As in the mind of the prophetic poet Israel suffers for the idolators, so Israel suffers to this day as the representative for the inadequacies and violations which always again halt the realization of mono- theism.[16]

The Messiah will come in God's own time—and that will then turn out to be "the end of time," the conclusion of human history as we have known it—to establish God's kingdom. Under God's kingdom there will be no more war, poverty or falsehood; His law will reign supreme, and all mankind will acknowledge and abide by His will as He has revealed it to Israel through the Torah. Israel in turn will be reconstituted as a holy people in its land, the priest-nation of a mankind united in the service of the true God. The prophet Isaiah described the conditions which will prevail when the Messiah will have done his work in a famous passage:

> And it shall come to pass in the end of days,
> That the mountain of the Lord's house shall be established as the
>   top of the mountains,
> And shall be exalted above the hills;
> And all nations shall flow unto it.
> And many peoples shall go and say:
> "Come ye, and let us go up to the mountain of the Lord,
> To the house of the God of Jacob;
> And He will teach us of His ways,
> And we will walk in His paths."
> For out of Zion shall go forth the law,
> And the word of the Lord from Jerusalem.
> And He shall judge between the nations,
> And shall decide for many peoples;
> And they shall beat their swords into plowshares,
> And their spears into pruning-hooks;
> Nation shall not lift up sword against nation,
> Neither shall they learn war anymore. O house of Jacob, come
>   ye, and let us walk in the light of the Lord.
>
> (Isaiah 2:2-5)

Implied in this conception of the Messianic age is the recognition that God will cause something to be brought about that ought to be and must be brought about which, however, human beings by themselves cannot bring about. If man could achieve the goal of the perfectly good life by himself, God's intervention would not be needed, and if the goal were not desirable and even imperative—then God would not need to bother. Man left to his own devices cannot attain the fulfillment that God has set for him: his lusts overpower his virtues; his vainglory makes him hate and combat his fellow; the limitations on his understanding and wisdom misdirect him past his destination or even away from it. In the Garden of Eden, in his original, primordial existence he actually possessed the conditions intended for him, but from the outset he abused the very divine-like qualities given to him for immoral and impious purposes. Ever since, God has offered man the means with which to reconstitute himself and his environment so that he will conform to the image which he was meant to present and which he himself senses to be his ideal condition. The means offered to him to achieve this goal is God's law, but the defects in his character which caused his original deviation continue to disable him for fulfilling the law. At best man is limited and fallible, and at worst sinful. If man's destination, on the other hand, is perfection, this perfection cannot, therefore, in its nature, be brought about by man. It must be accomplished by God. To say this is simply a somewhat circumlocutory way of saying that human salvation is a miracle, something which by the laws of nature and logic is impossible. That a single human person should be the instrument through which this miracle is to be performed is simply another way of underlining its miraculous nature. In any case, is it not much more "miraculous" and illogical that a great number of people should be able to accomplish the humanly impossible than that only one man should? The modern rebellion against this doctrine of "salvation by grace" is the source of the besetting evil of our time. ("Salvation by grace" has a Christian ring to most Jewish ears in our time. Let it, therefore, be pointed out that the English word "grace" is meant to correspond to the Hebrew terms *ḥesed* and *raḥamim*, usually translated as "loving-kindness" and "mercy"—but when ascribed to God they mean, of course, beneficences which God bestows upon us without our merit, and this is precisely what is meant by "grace.")

The desire for perfection in the life of this world and the belief that it could be attained only through human endeavors characterized the spirit of the nineteenth century. Liberalism put its faith in gradual but rapid progress made by man.[17] Thus, apart from being profoundly disappointed by the course of events, it also disqualified itself to cope with human evil and irrationality whenever and wherever it ran into them, even within itself; faced by Marxism, fascism, technology and the social "death-drive" it all but collapsed. Marxism itself put its faith in progress through convulsions: the convulsions came—in part brought about by itself—but the progress not only failed to come; it was actually brutally reversed. Nationalism, international enlightenment, technological advance—these and other forms of nineteenth-century humanism all share not only the confidence that man can procure his own complete salvation but also the reliance on social, collective endeavor. When all these delusions came to a bloody end in our time, the pendulum began to swing in the opposite direction, and there has been a "failure of nerves": all hope for social improvement was abandoned, all belief in enduring ethical norms dissolved, and individual nihilism together with social "stand-pattism" took their place.

The Messiah proclaims the partial truth and the partial falsehood of both extremes. Man must, indeed, work at *Tikun Ha'olam*, the increasing reparation of the world. But this work can succeed only if it complies with the law of God. Furthermore, man's greatest and most effective exertions will never suffice to reach the goal of salvation. We do not know precisely where the limits to his effectiveness are drawn; everyone who predetermines them interferes with God's plan: Reinhold Niebuhr, the pessimistic Protestant theologian, when he claims to be able to predict the outermost boundary of feasible social advance, and Karl Marx, the optimistic spokesman for this-worldly man, who is sure that the kingdom will come about if purposive and ruthless policies are pursued. As the Rabbis put it: "When here below we do a little (as much as possible), God above will complete it." The best human beings are capable of is not the guarantee but the condition of God's intervention—even as, according to Maimonides, man can adequately "prepare" his own prophetic endowment, but God reserves the right to bestow or to veto it. (This also detonates the frequent accusation that Messianism induces a passivism which sits back and waits for God to do the work.)

That it is a person who is the Messiah rather than an "idea" or a "movement" or an "historical development" is important to realize in order to be fully aware of the divine, miraculous events of which we speak when we talk about "redemption." This is also important, however, in order to reassert the supreme place of the individual in an age in which collectivities increasingly usurp all values and loyalties. Not only society but also religion are rapidly being depersonalized. The optimists of the nineteenth century did not oppose the concept of a Messianic consummation of history but insisted that nations or all of mankind together would attain this goal; therefore, they jettisoned the belief in a personal Messiah. The humanists of the nineteenth century did not reject the belief in established moral values, but they shrank back from the idea that a personal God was their author; therefore, they gave their allegiance to "philosophies" and "principles." The social reformers of the nineteenth century were far from foreswearing the goal of human happiness and security, but they did not hold out any hope that an individual could attain them by himself, and they, therefore, subordinated the individual and his fate to the destiny of the group. Thus, we entered the twentieth century shorn of the persons of God, the Messiah and of ourselves: we were digits in a world of digits. Along comes the Messiah and announces: salvation still comes from the individual to the individual; all truth is and remains human and personal. This is not to be taken in any politically reactionary sense so as to oppose the increased social consciousness of our age; it merely, but significantly, reasserts the concept to which much lip-service is paid, the centrality of individual persons. Thus it turns out, paradoxically but not surprisingly, that the very doctrine which embraces the divine and miraculous in human history is also the doctrine which may rightfully claim the name of "humanism." (Connected with it appears, therefore, also the doctrine of resurrection, *T'ḥiyat Hametim*, which affirms the unique "psychosomatic" integrity of the human personality.)

Resurrection is, of course, the doctrine that, "in the end of days," God will restore the human person in its complete integrity, i.e., the body and the soul, and "re-vive" it. Despite all evasive translations, this is the clear content of the second benediction in the *Shmoneh-Esreh*—an essential pillar of all classic Jewish teaching—and expressed in manifold ways throughout the prayer book: "There is none but Thee, oh our Redeemer, even in the days of the Messiah, and there is none comparable to Thee, oh our Savior, (who is capable of bringing) about the resurrection of the dead" (Sabbath Morning Service). To interpret *T'ḥiyat Hametim* in a "spiritual" sense, in any sense other than that which ascribes to the physical, crassly material body of human beings ultimate, divine and eschatologically imperishable value, is to denature the doctrine not only of its unmistakable meaning but also of its value, for then we would again fall prey to the Greek denigration of matter as being evil, or at least less endowed with divine dignity than the "spirit." The quotation from the prayer book states the connection of resurrection with Messianism very well: the arrival of the Messiah will put an end to human history as we have known and thought of it; resurrection is then part of the work of the Messiah (as a tool of Him who is "incomparable"), i.e., it obviously takes place outside the framework of "normal" history. To try to specify the nature, time and place of resurrection beyond these statements would be to try to fathom the mysteries of the Godhead against which Maimonides warns us. Resurrection is one of the features of the Messianic kingdom, and Maimonides logically climaxes his Thirteen Principles of Faith in the doctrines of the Messiah and of resurrection—in that order.

In the social dimension of Messianism there has always been a tension between those who believed that they themselves could bring about the utopia (pseudo-Messianists, humanists, etc.) and those who regarded such an attitude as arrogant and advised passive patience awaiting God's action (quietists, passivists, etc.).[18] The established classic Jewish solution to this problem seems a compromise without being one. It declares that men can hasten —not force!—the advent of the Messiah through their virtuous actions but they cannot delay it, for even in the absence of human merit God will bring about His redemption in the time which He has set for it.

This is not the middle position between the two extremes which it sounds. (Divine truth is not the result of collective bargaining.) What this doctrine really states is that, either way, redemption always remains in the hands of God and is undeserved by imperfect men. But men do play a significant part in the drama of salvation, and they can affect its *dénouement* by their lives. Thereupon various Messianic courses of action are followed: vegetarianism, socialism, pacifism—the characteristics of the Messianic kingdom are regarded as commandments for daily living; they, as it were, anticipate the world-to-come in this world and try radically and piously to "transform the world in the image of the kingdom of heaven." [19]

The belief in the Messiah, rather than in Messianism, also safeguards us somewhat against the facile distortions and abuses of modern pseudo-Messianism. Jewish, like Christian, history has thrown up a number of false Messiahs, some sincere, others malicious; they range from Jesus of Nazareth through Shabbetai Z'vi and beyond. All of them failed, and all of them will continue to fail until the one true Messiah, "the Messiah of our righteousness," appears. Failure is itself the final arbiter of a Messianic claimant's authenticity. That is to say, if history goes on—as it has always gone or differently, but history nonetheless —the Messiah has not come. This was understood by the *Hasidic rebbe* who, on hearing in his study the sounds of the *shofar* being blown on Mount Zion by someone who wanted "to force the end"—instead of running to see who the man was—looked out the window, saw people continuing to haggle in the market, and quietly turned back to his books to pray for the future coming of the Messiah. And Jesus belongs in this line of (Jewishly seen) false Messiahs: his or the church's claim to divinity is, as we have seen, beyond discussion; his Messianism is refuted by the world and by the normal lives of his own adherents. Pseudo-Messiahs, of course, also differ from one another: they exert good or bad moral and religious influences on their followers in different degrees—and this, then, is a question which one can discuss as a matter of history and ethical evaluation—but their fundamental claim to divine delegation puts them all equally under the onus of the Deuteronomic classification of false prophets (Deuteronomy 18:21 ff.). When sincere, they thought they could "force the end," pin down God's hands, as it were, to remedy the sufferings of Israel and mankind; instead they brought delusion and disillusionment, excess and death. Gershom Scholem, in his new standard study of Shabbetai Z'vi, therefore, asks the profoundly disturbing question: "What price Messianism?" [20] Many answers have been essayed to that question in the course of time. One answer is—and it seems the most relevant answer in our time—that pseudo-Messianism is not the product of Messianism but of non-Messianism, as superstition is not the product of faith but its antagonist.

When belief in the personal Messiah faded in the nineteenth century, men replaced it with the belief in progress which they called Messianism. But one cannot detect progress in human history; one can only discern movement. To be able to determine whether that movement is progress or chaos, or—for that matter—regression, one would have to know the goal of history, for progress is movement in a known and fixed direction. For this reason the inebriates of progress also had to stipulate a final end, and since they could define it only in terms of their own experience this end invariably loomed very near. (Our catastrophic age may be assumed to have refuted once and for all the simple-minded belief in linear, inevitable progress. Here again the Jewish Messianic doctrine, had it only been taken seriously, could have prevented much heartache. Does not *Mishnah Sota* 9:15 describe our experience? "In the footsteps of the Messiah impertinence will increase . . . the country will slip into heresy, yet there will be no scolding, the assembly [of the sages] will degenerate into whoring . . . The face of that generation will look like the face of a dog: a son will put his father to shame. . . . On what, then, can we rely? On our Father who is in heaven.") When they acquired power they thought the end had come, and they regarded themselves as entitled, therefore, to impose their views and policies with divine finality. The experience of Soviet Russia is altogether relevant to this problem: Communists are constantly discussing whether they have yet advanced from the stage of Socialism to that of Communism, respectively their pre-Messianic and Messianic eras—and "the cult of personality" which they now claim to have discarded arose quite logically in direct reversal of the religious order: they deceived themselves into believing that "social progress" had produced the soteriological personality, whereas Judaism asserts that the redeeming person will produce the moral society.

Nor has the Jewish people in our time been completely spared this experience. Some have been tempted to confuse the *Athalta D'geula* of the establishment of the State of Israel with redemption itself. They, too, "hastened the end." When they then looked at the reality of the State and, of course, discovered that, human institution that it is with all of its achievements and inadequacies, it is far from perfect, they sometimes threw up their hands in despair and, because they did not get the whole loaf, threw away the slice of bread. Alternatively, like David Ben-Gurion, they continue to talk about "Jewish Messianism," make ultimate, eschatological demands; but because they are not awaiting the person of the Messiah they are only riding for more falls in the future, when their Messianic expectations and promises will again frustrate those whom they succeeded in firing with their enthusiasm.

The Jewish doctrine of the Messiah declared that the end of history is in the hands of God not only in the sense that only He can bring it about but also in the sense that only He knows its nature: "The hidden things belong to the Lord our God; only the revealed ones to us and to our children forever: to do all the words of this Torah" (Deuteronomy 29:28). In the words of Maimonides:

> Concerning these things and others of the same kind, none knows how they will be until they occur. For the prophets veil these things, and the sages have no tradition concerning them save what they have deduced from the Scriptures, and so herein their opinion is divided. At any rate, neither the order of this event nor its details are the root of faith. A man must never ponder over legendary accounts nor dwell upon interpretations dealing with them or with matters like them. He must not make them of primary importance, for they do not guide him either to fear or to love God. Nor may he seek to calculate the end. The sages said: "Let the spirit of those breathe its last who seek to calculate the end." Rather let him wait and trust in the matter as a whole, as we have expounded.[21]

If we have the strength to wait for "the Messiah of His righteousness" neither Marxist nor Zionist nor liberal-democratic counterfeits of God's kingdom will be able to mislead us. All will be relativized by God's Sinaitic society. The Deuteronomic verse really says it all: ours is the task to fulfill God's law—and He, not we, will bring His anointed.

FOR FURTHER READING

COHEN, Gerson D., *Messianic Postures of Ashkenazim & Sephardim* (New York: Leo Baeck Institute, 1969). A leading medievalist, and former chancellor of The Jewish Theological Seminary, reviews the messianic consciousness of the two main units of medieval Jewry.

KATZ, Jacob, "Israel & The Messiah" *Commentary* Vol. 73, (January 1982). Israel's leading modern Jewish historian reflects on the meaning of messianism vis-a-vis the State of Israel.

NEUSNER, Jacob, *The Messiah in Context* (Philadelphia: Fortress Press, 1984). A new review of classic sources.

PATAI, Raphael, *The Messiah Texts* (Detroit: Wayne State University Press, 1979). A basic collection in English translation of key sources on Jewish messianism drawn from classic texts.

ROSENAK, Michael, "The Mitvoh, the Messiah, & the Territories." in *Tradition* Vol. 10 (Spring 1969). A critical evaluation of the messianic self-consciousness of religious groups in contemporary Israel after the 1967 war.

SCHOLEM, Gershom, *The Messianic Idea in Judaism and Other Essays* (New York: Schocken Books, 1971). A brilliant revision of the understanding of messianism by the outstanding Jewish scholar of our time.

A TRADITION
IN TRANSITION

Every generation regards its own era as the "modern times." And the "modern times" of each generation are beset with pressing problems. To paraphrase a Biblical verse: problems shall not cease from the land. But the problems of the mid-twentieth century are far more complex than those of any previous generation.

The challenge of our age derives from today's lightning rapidity of change, too rapid for normal, comfortable adjustment. Never before did man face such vast problems as the possession of atomic power, automation and race tensions. Never before were such deadly forces balanced against each other so delicately and so dangerously. Within this worried and frightened world are to be found the scattered remnants of a decimated people which, according to the Bible, is "the fewest of all peoples." Yet this tiny people, the Jews, plays a remarkably important role, altogether out of proportion to its size. It shares the massive world problems with all humanity, but, in addition, it faces weighty problems of its own that spell survival or extinction.

Having encountered death in the Nazi extermination camps, the Jewish people is once more threatened with possible annihilation. The Jewish community in the Holy Land is surrounded by mortal enemies. The Russian Jewish community, the second largest in the world, is being condemned to slow death. And the largest Jewish community, that of America, is threatened with a "natural death" through the forces of assimilation or the so-called "tide of disintegration." To be sure, there are counterforces that give hope of successful resistance. And there is the historic Jewish will-to-live which may yet tip the balance in favor of survival and creativity.

The religious divisions of American Jewry—Orthodoxy, Conservatism, Reform and Reconstructionism—are earnestly groping for answers to the problems of our day. Organizations and movements, national and international, are promoting programs of action. Fundraising agencies proclaim the crises of the day, demand support and promise definitive solutions. The thoughtful Jew is obviously confused. He wants a rational presentation of the problems, an objective analysis of their significance and an evaluation of possible programs with which to meet the threat of this generation.

Part Four is designed to do just that. The authors face the issues that challenge the modern Jew; they analyze the complicated problems with candor and courage, and present the suggested programs with sympathy and understanding. But they do not prescribe definite lines of action. Their primary aim is to stimulate thinking and encourage serious study and discussion.

15 . Challenges of Modern Times

IRA EISENSTEIN

THE RELIGION of the Jew has always been inextricably interwoven with the Jewish people. In fact, as many have pointed out, there is no word in the traditional vocabulary for "religion." The idea conveyed by that word was represented in Judaism by participation in the life of the Jewish people. That meant knowing its origin, accepting one's part in its ongoing life, submitting to the disciplines of its Torah, and identifying one's life with the role of the Jewish people in history and with its ultimate destiny. The traditional Jew could not conceive of himself as achieving his salvation or self-fulfillment outside the Jewish people.

Until the late eighteenth century, all Jews shared a common idea about the origins of the Jewish people, its relation to God and to other nations, its role in history and its ultimate destiny. That common idea was based on the Bible's account of Israel's history and on the literature which grew up in post-Biblical times.

It is remarkable to what extent Jews concerned themselves about that image. Indeed, it may be said that no other people was as preoccupied with the meaning of its own existence and the significance of its past and future. For the Jew believed that the Jewish people occupied the very core of all creation. Just as the world for the traditional Jew was the center of the universe, so Israel was the center of the world. What happened to Israel affected the course of all human history. Israel was conceived as having cosmic significance. To be an integral part of the Jewish people was to occupy a strategic place in the drama of life.

In that traditional image, the Jewish people began with a special act of creation performed by God when He selected Abraham. With the patriarch and with his descendants God entered into a covenant by which He would be their God and they His "peculiar treasure." The purpose of that covenant was to establish a people with a purpose, to live by God's Torah and thus teach that Torah to the world. If Israel were to live by the covenant, it would enjoy peace and prosperity on its land. If Israel were to sin, it would be exiled from the land. This exile (during the past two thousand years, the *second* exile) was to come to an end when God would have considered the sins expiated. Then would come redemption and the return to the land with the advent of the Messiah. All the nations would recognize the spiritual hegemony of Israel and the sovereignty of the God of Israel. Then would come the initiation of the world-to-come followed by the resurrection of the dead and the final judgment.

Challenges of Modernity

Modern times arrived for the Jews approximately at the end of the eighteenth century and the beginning of the nineteenth century, with the advent of "enlightenment" and "emancipation." That combination brought about the weakening of the syndrome of ideas and concepts about the world and the Jewish tradition which produced a crisis of belief and practice in Judaism.

"Enlightenment" refers to the impact of new learning upon Jewish belief in the validity of the traditional Jewish image of the Jewish people, its Torah, its history and its ultimate destiny. For example, scientific discoveries revealed that the Biblical account of the origin of the world and its place in the universe were based upon myth and legend. Astronomers showed that the earth is by no means the center of the universe; indeed, this universe itself is only one of many universes. Geology proved that the earth is much older than the Bible's description indicated. Later, the theory of evolution threw grave doubts upon the Biblical conception of how man came into being (i.e., created by God in a special act, unrelated to the other creatures).

The "humanities" in their turn seriously challenged traditional thought. The science of history accounted for the rise and fall of nations in terms of political, economic, social and cultural causes—and not, as Jews had always believed, in terms of reward and punishment of Israel. For the traditional Jew, the rise of Assyrian strength, for instance, was part of God's plan to punish Israel for her sins; Assyria was the "rod of God's anger." The Babylonians, the Greeks and the Romans were all pawns in the hands of God. Persia under Cyrus was believed to be beneficent to Israel because God wished to effect the return of the exiles to their land. A naturalistic interpretation of history was bound to conflict with this theological interpretation.

The scientific study of the Bible, too, involving "higher criticism" and archeology, comparative philosophy and comparative religions, all contributed to the general acceptance of the idea that Judaism was one of the several cultures which had grown up in the Middle East during the second millennium before Christianity; and that much of Jewish thought and practice had been borrowed or adapted from neighboring civilizations. This did not necessarily down-grade the uniqueness of Jewish culture; but it did weaken the traditional basis for Orthodox Jewish belief in the special revelation which God was believed to have made to Israel.

Effects of Emancipation

"Emancipation" refers to the revolutionary change in the political, cultural and social conditions of the Jews resulting from their desegregation, their release from the confinement of the ghetto and their integration into the total life of the nations among whom they dwelled. That integration was never perfected; anti-Semitism intervened in many places and often to a tragic degree. But the overall effect of Emancipation has been to liquidate the autonomous, segregated Jewish community and to relate individual Jews to their national states as citizens enjoying civil rights by law.

This had the effect, first, of challenging the age-old conception Jews had of themselves as living in *galut*, as members of a nation in exile. Now as French, German, English or American citizens, they identified themselves with their respective national states, surrendering (except for the purposes of far-off Messianic fulfillment) any notion that they were holding themselves in readiness for the coming of the Messiah who would gather them up for reunion in the Land of Israel.

Becoming citizens meant, further, giving up the practice of governing themselves by Jewish law. Thereafter, all litigations between Jews were not to be brought to the rabbi but to the civil courts. Marriages were now registered by the state; divorces were governed by the state. Contracts were made according to civil law.

Emancipation meant, further, entrusting to the state the basic education of the child. Jewish education, which theretofore had constituted the very source of Jewish literacy, was now made a voluntary and secondary experience. Thus the very process of communicating the tradition was seriously impeded; it was accorded marginal time and enjoyed only ancillary status.

With the multiplication of economic, political and cultural opportunities came the desire to be accepted socially by non-Jews. This required conformity to gentile ways and adjusting to prevailing patterns. Thus *Shabbat* and Jewish holidays were widely disregarded once Jews found themselves living by the calendar of the majority culture, which gave no recognition to Jewish sacred occasions. Having to eat with non-Jews as part of the process of doing business with them led many to abandon traditional dietary regulations.

In previous generations when Jews were confronted with the conflict between the Jewish way of life and their worldly interests, they often sacrificed those interests and sometimes even their very lives rather than yield to the alternative which many Jews now adopted. The intellectual foundations of Jewish faith were weakened by the enlightenment, and opportunities that were being offered were eagerly accepted. The concepts of revelation, covenant, *galut*, Messiah, resurrection, final judgment, the world-to-come—all these had been so affected by the new scientific outlook that for many Jews—not all—the very value of Judaism, of further resistance against the forces of assimilation, of rejecting conversion were exposed to serious doubts.

Contemporary Theological Responses

Jews loyal to Judaism and capable of mounting a counterattack, on an intellectual basis, upon the forces of enlightenment have used all the ingenuity at their command to stem the tide of disintegration which has set in during the last 150 years. They have taken account of the findings of the sciences and have sought, through interpretation and adaptation, to reconcile Jewish traditional concepts with those current in Western civilization, with which they are now familiar and of which they feel themselves a part. In some instances no conflict has been acknowledged and hence no "reconciliation" has been deemed necessary. In others, cognizance has been taken of a genuine conflict, but it has been felt that much of the tradition—certainly the essence—could and should be salvaged.

The various contemporary approaches to the problem of reconciling tradition with modern thought were brilliantly analyzed by Milton Steinberg, in a memorable and in some respects historic paper presented to the convention of the Rabbinical Assembly of America in 1949. He found that the philosophers who responded to the challenge in the first half of the twentieth century divided themselves into three distinct groups: the fundamentalists, the modernists and the post-critical revelationists. He describes each of these types as follows:

1. . . . where modernity has made inroads, it (revelationism) takes the form of fundamentalism, that is to say, a perseverance in faith in the literal validity of the Scriptural text, but a faith now deliberately and effortfully maintained.

2. The second revelationism, the modernist or critical, recognizes the relevance of scientific inquiry into the Bible and accepts its conclusions, all professedly without surrendering the doctrine of Scriptural inspiration. Not the letter of Scripture, it holds, nor the text nor the details are divinely given, but the spirit, the central intuitions, the core assertions. So apparently one investigates the Bible freely, and at the same time retains faith in its authority and validity. But only apparently. For among modernists, as those of us who are of this stripe will admit in moments of candor, truth is determined not by the Bible, but by reason and experience. Scripture is accepted as binding only in so far as its assertions conform to conclusions derived from other sources, ultimate reliance reposing not in the Bible as God's word, but in the powers of human thought.

3. And now alongside of these two older forms of revelationism a third has appeared which, in contrast with the other two, may fairly be termed post-critical. Here one encounters neither

Orthodoxy's antagonism to criticism or modernism's capitulation. Unlike the former, post-critical revelationism sets up no resistance against free, scientific exploration into the Bible. To the contrary, it may join in the enterprise. Only it insists that true and interesting as the outcome may be factually, it must be irrelevant to essential religion.

Against the modernist, in the other direction, the post-critical position assigns a cognitive role to Scripture. That is to say, it looks to it for the truth necessary to man's salvation, in advance and independent of the disclosure of it by other disciplines, indeed, beyond their reach altogether. In a word, the new revelationism, without withdrawing its hand from Higher Criticism, still holds to the Bible as the supreme, indeed unique, source of religious truth.[1]

First Type: Orthodox

The first type which Steinberg describes—the fundamentalists —may be found among the so-called Orthodox, "so-called" because their spokesmen frequently reject the designation. Their opponents, however, often refer to them as "neo-Orthodox," or *new* Orthodox to distinguish them from the traditionalists who have never been exposed to the challenge of modernity—or who deliberately protect themselves from such exposure by rejecting all secular learning.

Second Type: Modernists and Liberals

Among the second type—the modernists—may be found men like Kaufmann Kohler, one of the leading spokesmen for the classical Reform position. For example, in discussing the concept of the "chosen people," Kohler writes,

The Jewish people had, amidst oppression and persecution, the peculiar mission assigned to them of being "witnesses" to God in His absolute unity and sublime holiness. And to be witnesses meant, as the Greek translation "martyrs" suggests, to testify to the truth held forth by them by offering up their very lives in martyrdom for it.

Above all he remained ever conscious of the mission assigned to Israel as "the kingdom of priests and a holy nation." He led a consecrated life; in the midst of a world full of profanity and vulgarity, or coarse sensuality and drunkenness he displayed the virtues of chastity and modesty in his domestic and social sphere.[2]

Thus did Kohler "reinterpret" the concept of chosenness and mission, in terms of fidelity to an ideal of personal and group holiness.

Another example of this type of reinterpretation, by a contemporary, is found in Ben Zion Bokser (identified with the Conservative movement in the United States), who writes as follows:

> The doctrine that Israel is endowed with moral and spiritual assets such as do not appear in the cultures of other people is fully consistent with this recognition of the uniqueness of men and communities . . . That the Torah had come into the trusteeship of Israel did not necessarily represent favoritism for Israel. For it was the very purpose of Israel's trusteeship to serve as the tool by which its truths were to reach the rest of mankind. And if the other peoples of the world grew to sensitivity, to see themselves and their destiny from the perspective of the universal providence of God, they would find in their own careers similar evidence of God's love. In their unique way, they too carry some tune which they can add to the all inclusive symphony of life. In their own way, they too are God's chosen, for God works through all men in their diverse capacities and interests.[3]

Speaking of the Messiah, Dr. Bokser says:

> We do not know when harvest time will arrive in human history. The Rabbis (*Sanhedrin* 98a) say this, however: The Messianic redemption will come "in its time" and as the natural climax of a long process of historical development, regardless of what men will do. But if men prove worthy, the Lord "will hasten it. . . ."[4]

Interestingly enough, a number of thinkers generally identified as "secularists"—because they were not affiliated with any of the religious movements but rather with the Zionist, nationalist movement—attempted to deal with some of these themes. For instance, Ahad Ha-am, the Hebrew philosopher and essayist, writing about the idea of the "chosen people," said:

> It is admitted by almost everybody . . . that the Jewish people is pre-eminent in its genius for morality. No matter how it happened (sic!), or by what process this particular gift was developed; it is certainly a fact that the Jewish people early became

conscious of its superiority to its neighbors in this respect. In the manner of those times, this consciousness found expression in the religious idea that God had chosen Israel to "make him high above all the nations," not in the sense of forcible domination . . . but in the sense of moral development . . . in other words, to realize through the ages the highest type of morality, and to bear for all time the burden of the most exacting moral obligations.[5]

The Labor Zionist philosopher, Hayim Greenberg, tackled the problem also:

The conclusions to be drawn from the development of Jewish religious attitudes are apparent. God is one, the world is one, and humankind is also a unity. Mankind is still divided into Jews and non-Jews, but eventually this hiatus will be bridged, and men will become one—in the religio-moral, if not the ethnical sense. This will be accomplished not by the acceptance by Jews of the faiths about them but by the Gentiles' acceptance of the Jewish Torah. Otherwise, there can be no possibility of *eschatos*, and God cannot triumph. "Thou has chosen us" must not be taken to signify a *superior race* but a *superior faith*, destined to become the faith of the entire world. Jewish religious awareness at its deepest knows of no higher and lower races or peoples; the Jew, through his faith, is merely *advanced*, while those of the Gentile world are still closed.[6]

Not a secularist, yet not in the category of those already quoted, since he is a naturalist and not a supernaturalist, Mordecai M. Kaplan may be said to represent a viewpoint only now emerging. He sees Judaism as an evolving religious civilization. Whatever may have been the Jews' conception of themselves, in retrospect they may be recognized as having made vital and basic discoveries in the realm of the spiritual life, which they called "revelation." They had a high sense of commitment to an ideal, which they expressed in terms of the "chosen people" concept. They had a dream of the ultimate perfection of mankind, which they embodied in the notion of a Messiah.

But in our time, says Dr. Kaplan, each of the traditional concepts must be re-evaluated in terms of scientific knowledge, and in the light of human needs and motivations, in order that salvation—or human self-fulfillment—may be achieved. Thus, for example, with regard to the election of Israel, Dr. Kaplan offers an alternative, the "vocation." He writes:

Jewish religion expects the Jew to live the civilization of his people in a spirit of commitment and dedication. To live thus is to live with a sense of vocation or calling, without involving ourselves in any of the invidious distinctions implied in the doctrine of the election, and yet to fulfill the legitimate spiritual wants which that doctrine sought to satisfy.[7]

Third Type: "Post-Critical" Thinkers

In the third category outlined by Steinberg, we find a philosopher like Will Herberg. He defines revelation as follows:

> There *is* a third way, not "between" modernism and fundamentalism but beyond and distinct from both. Franz Rosensweig and Martin Buber, among Jews . . . have shown how one may take Scripture with the utmost seriousness as the record of revelation while avoiding the pitfalls of fundamentalism . . . Revelation is the *self-disclosure of God in his dealings with the world.* Scripture is thus not itself revelation . . . but a humanly mediated record of revelation.[8]

Herberg quotes with approval the famous letter of Franz Rosenzweig to Dr. Jacob Rosenheim (April 21, 1927) as saying:

> Our difference with Orthodoxy consists in this, that from our belief in the holiness and uniqueness of the Torah and its character as revelation, we cannot draw any conclusions as to its literary origins or the philological value of the received texts. Should Wellhausen prove right in all his theories . . . our faith would not be affected in the least. We too translate the Torah as a single book. For us, too, it is the work of one spirit . . . Among ourselves we call him by the symbol which critical science is wont to designate its assumed redactor: R. But this symbol R. we expand not into Redactor but into *Rabbenu.* For he is our teacher; his theology is our teaching.

Herberg adds: "This view, it should be noted, implies that the work of recording, compiling and redacting that has gone into the making of the Bible is itself an instrument of the divine intent in revelation." [9]

With regard to Israel, Herberg explains that "at the very heart of Hebraic religion is the conviction that, in a special and unique way, Israel is God's instrument for the redemption of the world." [10] Why this group rather than that? To ask this question is "to demand a universal rule by which the time-bound particularities of history may be rendered rationally intelligible and the will and purposes of God justified before the court of human reason. . . . Biblical faith . . . permeated with the inexpugnable particularity of existence, takes its stand on the affirmation: 'Salvation is of the Jews.' " [11]

Israel is not a "natural" nation; indeed, it is not a nation at all like the "nations of the world." It is a *supernatural* community, called into being by God to serve His eternal purposes in history. It is a community created by God's special act of covenant . . . Apart from that covenant, Israel is as nothing and Jewish existence a mere delusion. The covenant is at the very heart of the Jewish self-understanding of its own reality . . . The covenant is an objective supernatural fact; it is God's act of creating and maintaining Israel for His purposes of history.[12]

Since Israel is a "supernatural" community, it must not expect to possess the same characteristics as other groups having a land and a national history.

The destiny of Israel *begins* and *ends* with Zion: it is the land to which, in the beginning, God called Abraham and to which he led the people of Israel from out of Egypt; it is also the land to which, in the final fulfillment of the Messianic Age, the People Israel will be restored. But *between* the beginning and the end, there is "the great parenthesis" when Jewish existence and Jewish destiny are irremediably dual, centering around *both* Zion *and* the *Galut*.[13]

Similar in general orientation is Abraham J. Heschel. Speaking of revelation, Heschel says:

Revelation is a mystery for which reason has no concepts. To ignore its mysterious nature is an oversight of fatal consequence. Out of the darkness came the voice to Moses; and out of the darkness comes the Word to us. The issue is baffling. And if you ask: what was it like when the people stood at Sinai, hearing God's voice? the answer will be: Like no other event in the history of man.

Seen from man's aspect, to receive a revelation is *to witness how God is turning toward man*. It is not an act of gazing at the divine reality, a static and eternal mystery. The prophet is in the midst of a divine event, of an event in the life of God, for in addressing the prophet, God comes out of His imperceptibility to become audible to man. The full intensity of the event is not in the fact that "man hears" but in the "fact" that "God speaks" to man. The mystic experience is an ecstasy of man; revelation is *an ecstasy of God.*[14]

The youngest and most recent exponent of this post-critical type is Arthur A. Cohen, who outlines his thinking in *The Natural and the Supernatural Jew.* According to Cohen, the role of the "supernatural people" is "to be a critic of culture to make culture the partial consummation of history and the anticipation of the Kingdom of God." [15] Mankind needs to be redeemed but it cannot be redeemed within history.

> This paradox drives us again to the unique vocation of Israel— neither committed nor aloof, neither rooted nor alien, neither of this world nor of any other. The Jews may stand astride time and eternity. Of needs he must! . . . If Israel is "chosen" it is chosen for a distinguished task—to outlast the world and its temporizing solutions, to be borne up to the end of time as His alone, to strain and winnow the pride of the world, to demonstrate that the burden of this incomplete time and this imperfect history is indeed insupportable, whereas all the ideologies of this world would render them bearable, indeed, good and sufficient. This is unavoidably an aristocratic mission.[16]

The foregoing are but a sampling of the theological reinterpretations which some contemporary Jewish thinkers have offered to adjust basic ideas of Jewish religion to the thought patterns of our time. They are offered, in a sense, to individual Jews who are groping for an understanding of the idea of God, revelation, Messianism, exile, chosenness and other traditional concepts. These men are essentially religious philosophers; they are not primarily, if at all, concerned with program; that is, they do not offer a platform for action by the Jews as a collectivity. Their ideas are not translatable (except for Kaplan, who has outlined a program for American and world Jewry) into social action.

Modern Programs for Action

Action programs there are; and they may be divided broadly in four types representing four basic approaches.

1) *Pure Nationalism Based on Statehood*

What may be called *radical* Zionism, calling for the establishment of a Jewish state and the return of all Jews to the Land of Israel, sought to deal with one of the major challenges to the Jews and Judaism, the double-edged challenge of external circumstances. On the one hand, Jews in free countries were faced with the danger of assimilation; their group existence was threatened with being killed with kindness. The tolerant attitude of non-Jews was leading to integration and ultimately to assimilation. Zionism was offered as the only solution to this problem, for by concentrating Jews in their own land, they would by their very "togetherness" preserve their historic culture and at the same time produce a new Jewish culture of their own. The effects of Emancipation upon the survival of Judaism would thus be thwarted.

On the other hand, in those countries where the Emancipation *failed* and anti-Semitism threatened the survival of Jews, Zionism provided the haven of refuge. The State of Israel since 1948 has served as such a refuge. In the eyes of many Israelis—and (still) some radical Zionists—anti-Semitism is an inevitable consequence of minority status. Helpless in the face of the majority, Jews are bound to find themselves dependent upon the grace and good will of others; their dignity is bound to suffer; they are destined for humiliation and even persecution. Exile is unnatural; the age-old dream of *kibbutz galuyot* (the ingathering of the exiles) must be fulfilled if Jews are once again to be assured of survival. So say the Zionists.

Events since the establishment of the State have not weakened this thesis: in the free nations, intermarriage grows apace; education (thus far) has proved to be "a mile wide and an inch deep"; alienation of the intellectuals has not been checked, as symposia and dialogues, in America and in Israel, have demonstrated. Although there was supposed to be a revival of religion, observers have pointed out that this has manifested itself more in the growth of synagogue membership than in attendance at religious services. The Zionist movement has declined, and even the Jewish philanthropies have begun to discover that motivations for supporting Jewish communal institutions have begun to weaken. On the other hand, in democratically less developed countries—and of course, in those under dictatorships—anti-Semitism has by no means abated. Jews are subjected to discrimination in the Soviet Union, where their religious and cultural life is throttled; Jews in the Arab countries are under constant threat of liquidation; Jews in Argentina have been subjected to anti-Semitic attacks.

The Zionist "thesis," hence, contends that, for the survival of both Jews and Judaism, return to the Land of Israel is the only solution.

2) *Holy Community—Centrality of Torah*

Those who adhere to the idea that Jews should constitute themselves a holy community wherever they may live do not deny that it is a *mitzvah* to settle on the soil of *Eretz Yisrael*. But they take the realistic view that Israel cannot possibly contain all the Jews of the world. Hence, Jews who live in the Diaspora must continue to live in accordance with the traditional codes of Jewish law, to study the sacred books, and to achieve their communion with God through worship, learning and the observance of *mitzvot*.

In this view the Jewish people is, in a sense, an abstraction. They do not require a full Jewish people, an *actual* people in order to fulfill themselves as Jews. A "saving remnant" (*sh'erit ha-p'letah*) would be sufficient to keep Judaism alive. The adherents of this concept of the centrality of Torah continue to accept the ideas handed down by tradition; but how *literally* they accept the idea of exile, redemption and Messiah is difficult to assess.

3) *Synagogue or Temple—Centrality of Religion*

Without denying that a Jewish people exists or without ceasing to support the building of the State of Israel, the members of this group conceive of Judaism as basically a *religion:* they therefore believe that the normal and proper unit of organization is the synagogue or temple. All activities must radiate out from the central institution of worship and study.

In the United States, this group has enjoyed the greatest growth. According to some sociologists, this is due to the prevailing pattern of American life which calls for differentiation along the lines of religion, and integration along all other lines.

The synagogue or temple is therefore the logical place (psychological and sociological, perhaps, more accurately) for Jews to congregate. The rabbi, as spiritual leader of the congregation, is to be regarded as the proper spokesman for the Jews.

Many well-informed members of this group, however, are conscious of the fact that "religion," in the accepted American sense of that term, does not adequately describe Jews. Many Jews are unaffiliated with synagogues; and among those who are affiliated many absent themselves except on the High Holidays and other special occasions. On the other hand, organizations like Hadassah, B'nai B'rith and American Jewish Congress bring Jews together for legitimate Jewish purposes which are not directly related to the program of congregations. Certainly, fund-raising, one of the major activities of American Jewry, is largely conducted outside the auspices of the synagogue.

Nevertheless, those who adhere to this program believe that all these activities are corollaries of religion, and should constitute in a sense the secular arm of the synagogue. The direction of these activities should be predominantly in the hands of the "religious" leaders, since the central motivation and inspiration for the conduct of these communal tasks come from—or should come from—Jewish religion. They realize that Jewish "peoplehood" would not be understood by non-Jews who generally judge Jews by their own standards. As they themselves are Christian by religion, they tend to regard Jews as Jews purely by virtue of a religious affiliation.

4) *Jewish Peoplehood—Organic Communities— Zion as Core*

In this group are to be found those who believe that Jews have always constituted a people, the bearers of a religious civilization. They contend that Jewish peoplehood today must have its nucleus in Zion, that is, in the Jewish community of the State of Israel, where Jewish civilization is primary. Throughout the Diaspora, however, Jews should organize themselves into organic communities, reflecting the broad spectrum of interests which bind Jews to one another. The pursuance of these interests, involving mutual moral responsibility, constitutes the religion or the spiritual life of the people. Cultural activities, philanthropic work, education, worship—whatever Jews undertake in the spirit of enhancing their ethical and spiritual estate would form the regimen of *mitzvot* for our time.

This group comprises for the most part those who accept the Reconstructionist program, and those neo-Zionists who see in such a program the fulfillment of the second segment of the Zionist platform, the first being the establishment of the State of Israel.

Recapitulation and Summary

Beginning at the end of the eighteenth century in Western Europe (and somewhat later in the Eastern European countries) with the desegregation of the Jews from their ghettos and the suspension of discriminatory legislation directed against them, Jews experienced a revolutionary change in their status and world outlook. From an autonomous though second-class nation in exile, they were transformed into a group of individuals enjoying citizenship and equal rights. Before this emancipation they had lived a life remote from the main currents of Western thought and culture. After Emancipation they participated fully in the political, cultural and economic life of the nations among whom they lived.

Before Enlightenment they shared a conception of God, of Torah and of themselves as Israel which had come down virtually unchanged since the beginning of the Christian era. After the Enlightenment they were divided into numerous fragments, some rejecting altogether their identity as Jews, others adapting, revising, reinterpreting, reconstructing traditional concepts and values in the hope that they might reconcile tradition with modern science, modern philosophy, modern psychology, modern sociology.

The age of faith has given way to the age of questioning and challenge, with philosophers striving to build a new intellectual and spiritual structure on the foundations of the old, and with others devising practical programs to save the Jews from disintegration.

The challenge has been taken up by serious-minded Jews of the mid-twentieth century. If no one philosophy or program has yet emerged as the dominant one, comfort can be taken in the thought that, though no consensus has been achieved, the very

efforts to meet the challenges—social, cultural, intellectual—
have provided whatever vitality American Jewry has displayed.

FOR FURTHER READING

BULKA, Reuben, *Dimensions of Orthodox Judaism* (Hoboken, NJ: Ktav, 1983). A significant investigation of the current structural divisions i.e., Reform, Conservative, Orthodox, in contemporary Jewry.

FISCH, Harold, *The Zionist Revolution* (New York: St. Martin's Press, 1978). A revised, highly theological account of the meaning of Zionism and the re-creation of a Jewish state. A challenge to the secular, humanistic, understanding of these seminal factors in contemporary Jewish life.

LANDES, Daniel, editor, *Omnicide* (Los Angeles: Simon Wiesenthal Center, 1985). An important anthology of Jewish views on the nuclear question.

MAYER, Egon, *Intermarriage and the Jewish Future* (New York: American Jewish Committee, 1980). A detailed study of the nature and implications for the American Jewish community.

RUBENSTEIN, Amnon, *Zionism Dream Revisited* (New York: Schocken, 1984). An important critique of certain tendencies in the State of Israel, so central to American and World Jewry.

SIDORSKY, David, editor, *The Future of the Jewish Community* (New York: Basic Books, 1973). A collection of essays with an eye towards the future by leading figures, on all aspects of the contemporary American scene.

SKLARE, Marshall, editor, *Understanding American Jewry* (New Brunswick, NJ: Transaction Books, 1984). A valuable anthology of essays which review almost all of the fundamental sociological issues facing American Jewry. A very good place to begin any investigation into this side of the American Jewish community.

WAXMAN, Chaim, *America's Jews in Transition* (Philadelphia: Temple University Press, 1983). The newest recent, extended and interesting study of the changing face of American Jewry's sociological profile.

16 . Is the Jew in Exile?

ARTHUR HERTZBERG

F o r the last two centuries, as Jews have been entering the life of Western society, they have wanted two antithetical things: to be like everybody else, and to be quite different. Each of these desires has in its turn given birth to a swear word in the Jewish lexicon: "assimilation." This word is in such bad odor today that it has had to be replaced among Jews by a blander and more academic term, "acculturation." Leading theorists in contemporary American sociology have been laboring to define a difference between these two concepts, but Jews have shifted from one term to the other for reasons not to be found in the writings of the scholars. Those who are for "acculturation" regard themselves, unlike the classic assimilationists, as "positive Jews." In actual practice this means that they would like to be culturally and spiritually just like everybody else, but they want to bar the door to intermarriage.

On the other hand, it is almost equally daring and even offensive to say to Jews in Western countries, and particularly in America, that they are in *galut*, i.e., exile. The presumption of Israeli leaders, headed by the most redoubtable of them all, David Ben-Gurion, in maintaining this point, has led to notable and bitter interchanges between him and various American Jews. Even American Zionist leaders of the front rank have joined in expressing outrage at such a presumption. This estimate of the condition of the Jew outside of Israel denies the great dream of a new liberal world, in which the Jews participate as equals. Did not our ancestors come to America in order to experience that which could be found "only in America," the blessedness of enjoying a society of "Americans all"? For anyone to say to American Jews that they are, in any sense, in exile, therefore means to many of his hearers that he is calling the American experience a self-delusion. That they react with anger to so threatening a thought is understandable.

The life of the Jew in democratic society is, therefore, characterized by a paradox. Wanting to be just like everybody else, he devotes himself to battering down every wall of exclusion erected against him. Once all the walls, or most of them, begin to fall, he refuses to accept the implications of such events in the lessening of family and communal ties. The uniqueness of the Jew is thus not merely a creation of the exclusion that is directed against him. When it is gone, he continues to stand somewhat apart from society, by choice. The real question is not whether this is true as a fact, for that needs no demonstration. What needs to be discussed is the meaning of this stance.

"Exile" and "assimilation" are both words that describe a relation. In this case, it is the relation between a majority and one specific minority. Whether the Jews can and ought to assimilate, or whether they are in exile, cannot be considered in terms only of Jewish will and Jewish needs. We are inevitably involved in an estimate of what is America and in some projection of the probable future of American culture and society. Clearly the Jews who remain in Yemen are in exile. Most Jews believe that this is true at this very moment of the Jews in Russia. Certainly the American situation is different from both of these—but what *is* the American situation?

The "Melting Pot" Approach

We can define four stages in the evolution of a new, twentieth-century vision of America—and each of these visions has been, revealingly, constructed largely by Jews. At the turn of the century, in the midst of the last great wave of immigration, the accepted image of the country was that of a "melting pot"—the phrase is Israel Zangwill's; it was the title of a play in 1908 which was the forerunner of the more famous *Abie's Irish Rose*. The enemies of Americanism were the hyphenated Americans, who were attacked by Theodore Roosevelt, among others, for continuing to cultivate in the new land loyalties which reached back into their pre-American past. In the stage of Americanization, of losing their blatant and hampering foreignness and of learning the language and manners of the country, most Jews participated in this vision. Several factors, however, acted to make it clear, and not entirely to Jews, that this definition of America was too narrow. Other groups, too, were made uncomfortable by a view of America that was really an extension of the self-image of the then dominant white Anglo-Saxon Protestant community.

In part, disillusionment set in as it became apparent that even being melted down successfully did not guarantee one's acceptance, at least socially, by the oldest elements in America. A newer image of America was therefore suggested in the second decade of the century, and there, too, the thinker who defined the new concept was a distinguished Jew, Horace M. Kallen. He proposed the notion of cultural pluralism, i.e., a society within which there were to be sub-groups, each of which would continue in some part of its life the heritage that it had brought with it. This was to include the language and culture of its ancestors and some considerable concern for the country of its origin. All of these groups would meet together in the larger dimension of American cultural and political life, which they would share in common.

Cultural Pluralism

This theory of cultural pluralism has recently been refurbished by Nathan Glazer and Daniel P. Moynihan in a study of the minorities of New York City, *Beyond the Melting Pot*. These writers argue, quite convincingly, that not only the Negroes, and now the Puerto Ricans, but also the Jews and Irish continue to remain recognizably different communities, even into the third and fourth generations. The implication of this argument, perhaps even its concealed major premise, is that America is becoming a confederation of minorities whose behavior is comparable and can be explained on the same basis.

The vision of cultural pluralism had the merit, historically, of helping to turn the corner away from the presumption that what colonial America had been was, of right, the continuing rule of its existence. It emphasized that many cultures and several religions had gone into the making of America. It began the naturalization of cultural differences as valid on the American scene. It has not, however, succeeded in achieving its very patent "Jewish" purpose, to reorganize America in such fashion that all of its various communities would so live their lives that the Jews could, in the very act of being themselves, be just like everybody else. There are two keys to the failure: politics and culture. In both dimensions the Jews have acted uniquely and not like any of the other minorities.

During World War I there seemed, on the surface, to be a considerable similarity in political behavior among the minorities. Before 1917, the immigrants of German origin, for example, pressed for neutrality and, comparably, there was considerable pro-German sentiment in all divisions of American Jewry. Jews from Germany tended to be super-patriots of their old country; newer immigrants from Russia had little initial enthusiasm for the Allied cause because they detested the Czarist regime. Nonetheless, such similarity in conduct did not last. Pro-Germanism remained a political force in America into the 1930's; it has been demonstrated that Midwestern isolationism before America's entry into World War II was related to the German origins of a major segment of the population of that region. However, the contemporary heirs of such isolationist politics are not German-Americans of the third and fourth generation. Some have indeed, as individuals, disappeared into earlier American families and now form part of the human material to be found in the John Birch societies and comparable groups, but the tone of these groups is more nearly akin to the Daughters of the American Revolution. It came quite as a matter of course that the commanding general in America's war against Germany, Dwight D. Eisenhower, and several of his leading colleagues, were themselves of quite recent German origin. Any remaining loyalties to Germany to be found in the United States today would require those who have them to be internationalist in stance. There are no such German-American organized politics on the present scene.

The Irish in America are another case in point. There was considerable emotional involvement, and practical support as well, in the battle for freeing Ireland from the British. This played some role in American politics, especially during the Wilson years. The traditional hatred of the British predisposed

Irish-Americans to neutrality in the early months of World War II. Ireland ltself remained obstinately neutral throughout the war, but this was entirely irrelevant in America on the morning after Pearl Harbor. Some specific flavor remains to Roman Catholic politics, which means largely Irish Catholic politics, in contemporary America. This community is considerably more anti-Communist than any other group, but even this is lessening. The Vatican itself has been moving toward coexistence with the Russians. Within America the younger generation produced an intellectual and internationalist like John F. Kennedy rather than a local satrap like James J. Curley as the newest version of an Irish Catholic politician. It is fair to say that in "foreign policy" Irish Catholic politics are rapidly losing their uniqueness.

There are, to be sure, marginal elements of "foreign policy" in the ongoing struggle of the Negro. The identification with Africa and occasional expressions of Negro neutralism in the cold war do betoken something of the anger of the Negro at his being kept apart in America, but these moods are secondary. The essence of the Negro revolt is in his unrelenting struggle for equality in education, jobs and housing on the domestic scene. This is equally true of the Puerto Ricans. Puerto Rican nationalism does exist in America, but, as in the case of the Black Muslims, each of these groups represents a far-out element, not the prevailing tone of opinion within the Negro or Puerto Rican communities.

Jewish politics are precisely in reverse. For themselves, on the domestic scene the Jews have no major bastions left to conquer. No one really cares much about the continued existence of social exclusion in country clubs and some of the town clubs. There is indeed some emotion about economic exclusion of Jews by some of the largest corporations. Despite the noise that is occasionally made about it, however, the economic profile of the contemporary Jewish community is such that these practices, though hateful, are not really very threatening. Bright young Jews, fresh out of college, can find many places in which to work, even if they are not allowed in any significant number into the bureaucracies of the public utilities. Since the Jews were a have-not group as recently as one generation ago, the memory of their travail and of the battle against it still influences Jewish political behavior to a general sympathy with the dispossessed.

The Jews do remain predisposed to the Democratic party and to the politics of the New Deal, but Republican strength is slowly rising among them.

A comparable process is taking place before our very eyes on the issue of race. The top leadership and all the major organizations in the Jewish community are unequivocally enlisted on the Negro side. Many Jews are indeed still personally close enough to their own deprived past to sympathize. For appropriate leaders to demonstrate and sit in on behalf of the Negro, side by side with comparable dignitaries of the churches, is even in some minds one of the most positive forms of being "at home" in America. The taking of such action demonstrates that the Jews have really arrived at their own equality. For a variety of reasons it is therefore fair to say that, despite certain unhappy economic encounters between Jews and Negroes, the Jews have been and still are more nearly pro-Negro, in action as well as pronouncement, than any other white group. Nonetheless, there is considerable evidence that this commitment is not absolute. On the local level, all Jewish institutions are not rushing to open their doors on an interracial basis—in large part, to be sure, because of their own concern for cultivating the integrity of Jewish identity as distinct not only from Negroes but from all other American Christians. In candor, it need be added that the Jewish masses appear to be moving toward a position on race less liberal than the views of their leaders and more akin to the outlook that is conventional in comparable segments of the gentile community.

The processes of acculturation are thus eroding the distinctiveness of Jewish politics in domestic affairs. What remains of this element is not an expression of an existing need; it is sympathy. Jews no longer battle for social reform in their own name; they do it together with and generally for others. The fights the Jews continue to have with other Americans, the issues for which they hurry to Washington with delegations and for which they marshall their maximum resources for the persuasion of others, include the suffering of the Jews of Russia, an unceasing effort to liberalize American immigration policy and, above all, the defense of the State of Israel.

It is necessary, and even useful, to re-emphasize here that other groups in America have before, and will again, put pressure on the rest of the country in the area of foreign policy to achieve results which are of more concern to themselves than to the majority. But the point here is that minorities in America (whether their motivation is ethnic or religious) have stayed in the political business, indeed in the business of being minorities, in the long run in order to fight their own immediate domestic battles. Thus the Germans as an organized group are well nigh gone because they have no such battles left to fight.

Irish Catholic behavior has so much in common with the Jewish that the difference between the two is particularly revealing for our present purpose. These two groups have recently been colliding semi-overtly over liberalism (especially in the McCarthy years) and openly and directly over church and state. The key distinction between the two communities is, however, not in their disagreements but in the importance to each of its investment in these issues. The second is vital to the largely Irish-dominated Catholic community. It remains in the political arena because of one great domestic issue, parochial schools, which still divides it from others. It is fighting for tax support with the emotion of a group doing battle for something that it regards as essential to its survival in its own terms. The Jews have no comparable domestic concern, not even in ending prayers in the public schools, for they could have afforded the loss of that battle. The one battle that, in their own terms, they cannot ever lose is in "foreign affairs." American Jews may, in the future, cut loose from the rest of the Jewish world, but no one who knows them can doubt for a moment that this will be the surest sign that the American Jewish community is beginning to disappear. So long as there is a serious Jewish presence in America, it will be marked by a continuing, unique kind of politics.

There is an equally striking difference between Jews and the other minorities in the area of culture. The grandchildren of the Italians, the Slavs and the rest have become completely assimilated culturally. Only the Chinese have made a serious attempt to teach their traditions, through supplementary education, to their descendants in America into the third and fourth generations. The other European immigrants of the last century have failed to provide Jews with parallels for their devotion to some continuity for their own sub-culture. To be sure, as Glazer and Moynihan have pointed out, there is still some specific

socio-economic and even intellectual flavor to several of the
minorities, but all of them have translated themselves into
variants of the American idiom. The nearest parallel is the Irish,
in whose case, too, the memory of oppression, religious difference and ethnic uniqueness have gone together. Nonetheless,
even they have not labored to perpetuate Gaelic in the way that
many Jews continue to fight for at least some Hebrew.

Religious Pluralism

A new formula, therefore, needed to be found to naturalize
what differentiated the Jew, and to find valid analogues for these
differences on the American scene. In its turn, the Jewish third
generation needed its vision of an America so explained as to
make it comfortable. This was supplied, again, almost inevitably,
by a Jewish writer, Will Herberg, in his famous book of a decade ago, *Protestant—Catholic—Jew*. Herberg propounded the
thesis that regardless of their origins Americans had lost, or were
in the process of losing, all cultural and political differences
which were based on immigrant heritages. The only divisions
among Americans that would be recognized as legitimate in the
future were religious ones. The ultimate meaning of the changes
that had been taking place in the last century is that America
had ceased being a white Anglo-Saxon Protestant country,
essentially by having broadened the definition of religion to include the three major faiths. Indeed, to be a good American
meant to be identifiable within one of the three communions.

From the Jewish point of view, this definition has much positive merit. It surrounds the Jews with the aura of American respect for religion, in place of what remains of American distaste
for "foreigners." As a religion, this small minority is suddenly
translated by this formula to the estate of one-third of America.
Much of what Jews do corporately can be explained, to themselves and, more important, to others, as a natural expression of
religion.

Jewish supplementary education is easiest to define in these
terms. It has in the last generation become almost entirely a function of the synagogue, and so nothing seems more obvious than
that it is just like Christian education. Local federations of Jew-

ish charities are presented as the peer group for Catholic and Protestant charities, and the United Jewish Appeal becomes the counterpart of Catholic and Protestant overseas endeavors. As we shall see, all these explanations are forced, but they can at least be made to work on the surface. What cannot be explained on this principle is the unideological but deep and patent concern of Jews for other Jews all over the world. A century ago Abraham Geiger, one of the founders of Reform Judaism in Germany, attempted an explanation of Jewish identity in that country that was comparable to Herberg's definition. It led him, by its inherent logic, to declare that he was much more interested in how many Jews were admitted as equals to the professions in Prussia than in the battle against pogroms in Russia. Geiger was among those who declared that Berlin was now his Jerusalem; so Herberg has recognized the inherent meaning of this stance by having turned ever more anti-Zionist in the years since the appearance of his book.

Jewish motivations and self-definitions are, however, less important than the estate of America as a whole. There is, indeed, considerable evidence for the presumption that America's definition of itself has been moving away from the identification of the country's official establishment with Protestantism. For example, in the last several inaugurations of Presidents of the United States, rabbis have been participating in the greatest of state occasions along with Protestant divines and Catholic bishops. The famous victories of the last several years in the battle for the separation of church and school have also tended to confirm the idea that all religions are now on an equal footing. It can be said with considerable truth that before the national government Judaism is today the equal of the Christian denominations. This is less true in various local jurisdictions, especially in the South, with its small Jewish population and its Bible-belt tradition, where Protestant Christianity remains pretty much the state religion.

The real nub of the issue, however, is not in the relationship between Jews and Judaism and the state; it is in the estate of American society and culture, as distinct from the state. There can be no denying the proposition that American society, for all its secularization, is not neutral. It is Christian. For all the matters that are crucial to the actual experience of the individual Jew, as Jew, within America, the tempo of life as such has inevitably to favor Christianity and to act against Judaism.

Jewish Alienation

We are by now so accustomed to this mode of living that it usually does not even occur to us to identify it for what it inevitably is, an experience of alienation. The day of rest is Sunday. No matter how successful we may be in getting some legal redress for Sabbath-observing Jews, as a matter of social experience the Jewish Sabbath costs every individual Jew who is mindful of it an act of will. The majority of Jewry has abandoned the Sabbath, under pressure of its inconvenience in a society which is attuned against it. What is this if not a phenomenon of exile? Nor is this an economic compulsion, rooted in the need of the Jews to make a living. From the very beginning of public school, field trips, parties, dances and football games all take place on Saturday as the most convenient time. The Jewish child either participates or abstains; in either case he experiences his radical otherness. For that matter much of the weight, or lack of weight, that is being given to Jewish holidays is related to the pressure of a majority culture. A prime example is, of course, *Ḥanukkah*, which has now become that which it was never intended to be, the Jewish equivalent of Christmas.

The distinction is therefore clear. It is possible for the Jew to maintain within our democracy that he is no alien to the state. He could make the same claims about society only if a new order were created in which it would be equally comfortable, or uncomfortable, to be a Jew or Christian. It cannot be emphasized strongly enough that this situation is essentially beyond change. The kind of reorganization which might alter our society enough to bring the Jew into new relation with the majority would have to be more radical than the Communist revolution. The creation of such a new order would produce one of two results: if it were successful, it would homogenize all identities, after the death of both Judaism and Christianity; if it failed to produce a complete new order, as Russian Communism has failed (and as all of the preceding revolutions since 1789 have failed), the alienation of the Jews would forthwith reappear.

Jews say that they are like all other Americans; they even fervently hope that the others will believe them. The gentile majority in America, including its own Negro minority, knows that this is not so. It knows that the Jews are different because they are alien to the Christian history and style of the majority, in all its components. But do the Jews as an organized community really act (apart from talking) on a different assumption? What they are doing, insofar as it contributes to that fervently hoped-for value, "Jewish survival," is very clearly based on an unexpressed assumption of unique apartness. It is just as clear that this apartness, as it exists, does not fit into a conventionally religious definition of the Jew.

One of the keys to understanding the situation is the battle against intermarriage. It is conducted among Jews more bitterly, and with relatively greater success, than among any other group in America. It makes no difference whether Jews believe or do not believe in any version of the Jewish tradition; they battle with equal fervor against the threat of the intermarriage of their children. Certainly one would be shocked to discover non-believers of Catholic or Protestant extraction fighting comparably with their own children. What comes to expression in the Jewish attitude is an implicit assumption of Jewish identity as quite unique. Indeed, paradoxical though it may seem, more of the brooding mystery of what it means to be a Jew is to be found, in all its nakedness, in the anguish of the unbeliever, facing the threat of the end of his family's Jewish identity, armored only with an outcry of pain, than is present in the glib rationalizations of the members of synagogues who give conventional arguments about religion and the home and religious differences as the breeding ground of divorce.

This *sui generis* peculiarity shows in every other area of Jewish life. Jewish charitable endeavor is largely the "synagogue" of unbelievers. The United Jewish Appeal is clearly a different kind of affair than the Catholic Bishops' Fund or the various Protestant denominational appeals for aid to missionary activities overseas. Here too, the mystery incarnate in Jewish existence is most apparent in negative phenomena. For example, the rabbis, as guardians of the tradition, have on many occasions reacted with outrage to business meetings, overt or semi-disguised, held by some of our national organizations on the Sabbath. The occurrence of such a problem among the supposed Christian counterparts of these bodies is inconceivable. It cannot be explained away by maintaining that the Jews are here behaving not like a religious denomination but rather like an ethnic minority. The circles guilty of such conduct are usually led by the most "American," least culturally different from the majority, of all Jewish groups. These are the people who shout the loudest, in a well-bred way, of course, that they are just like everybody else. It is their disobedience of the tradition, rather than their devotion to it, which is the indwelling sign of their existential attachment to Jewish uniqueness.

Even the synagogue itself is not in today's America a primarily religious phenomenon. Affiliation is very high, but going to synagogue or believing in God is lower than among any communion on the American scene. This can be explained only on the presumption that this generation is safeguarding the mystery of Jewish identity, while being "absent with leave" for what it regards as its inconvenient details, such as religious faith, worship and piety.

The Jewish education of the young has become overwhelmingly an affair for the synagogue, but the reasons motivating parents to send their children in many cases are not religious. In an undefined but strong sense the intent is to root the young in a feeling of wanting to continue the enterprise of being Jewish, though what that enterprise means is really undefinable, at least by the Jewish mass mind.

Here too, in considering the attempt to define Jews as a religion, what radically refuses to fit is the actual state of the relationship to the international Jewish community and to Israel. Precisely because national political identities are so exclusive in the twentieth century, much Jewish ink has been spilled in defense of the notion that Jews owe no dual loyalties and that their emotion about Israel is really exactly like that of any other group in America about the place of origin of its ancestors. This makes useful defensive argumentation against those Jews who would really like the ties that bind the international Jewish community together to be severed. We are so super-conscious of what anti-Semites have done and can do with the term "international Jewry" that we are constrained to use arguments to deny something that is patently true, i.e., that there is a Jewish identity that transcends national and even cultural boundaries. Parenthetically, is there not an element of *galut* in this very fear of proclaiming it aloud?

This loyalty to an international Jewish identity can and does involve Jews, and not only enrolled Zionists, in stretching the definition of what is politically permissible to a special minority. Jews who are not opting out of the community expect of themselves and of each other that this concern will, at least in crisis, be well nigh paramount in their lives. In the battles of 1947 for the creation of the State of Israel, for example, a quite estranged Jew, Bernard Baruch (and he was not alone), was expected to lend his large influence—and he did. The contemporary American Jewish community no longer excommunicates anyone for religious aberrations, but it has come close to doing precisely that with the more vehement elements of the anti-Zionist Council for Judaism. This attitude does lead to conflict, not only in the public arena but within the individual Jew's soul. It is the presence of the problem, rather than the various solutions that each Jew may have for himself, that is a positive mark of Jewish uniqueness.

The Newest Self-Definition

The Jew remains in America what he has always been in the history of the West, a co-founder who is yet a resident alien. In religion, he may have lost faith to a greater degree than the Christian majority, but an enormous distance remains even between those who never go to synagogue and those who never go to church. The more committed majority among Jews represents a uniqueness in both culture and politics, an apartness from all other Americans, that they both will and choose. The bourgeois Jew, nonetheless, insists that the Jews are just like everybody else. Since this is patently false, it is not surprising that this idea is presently being denied by some of the younger Jewish minds in America. The chic word among the best Jewish writers today is "alienation," which is a way of recognizing the truth that the Jew is irretrievably different. Writers like Norman Mailer and Leslie Fiedler, and a host of others, have the merit of seeing that this fact continues to exist even where Jewish learning or active commitment has evaporated. They may no longer know why, and they may deny those reasons that they do know; yet these writers proclaim that the Jew in his very existence is alien to the world.

Nonetheless, this newest self-definition of the Jew is vitiated because it too is being used for self-delusion. Most of those who speak of the alienation of the Jew add that this alienation is indeed the essential condition of modern man as a whole. In other words, the young literati rebelling against their bourgeois parents are really standing the bourgeois Jewish myth on its head. The Jew is not becoming like everyone else, they say; it is that everyone worth mentioning is really becoming just like the Jew.

There is some superficial truth to this assertion at a moment in American life when so much of its literature is being written by Jews. It seems all the more believable because the new hero of the more advanced literati is the Negro. Jewish writers are leading the parade toward identifying with the Negro's alienation —and with his supposed sexiness. Norman Mailer, for one, can thus both castigate white America in the name of justice for the Negro, and defy his own chaste and inhibited Jewish ancestors in the name of salvation in the bedroom, which is supposedly to be learned from the true children of nature, the men and women of African ancestry. A significant part of today's intellectual scene in America is thus an alliance among three elements. It consists of Jews who are alien to their own past, at least in terms of conscious knowledge, and who yet know that their Jewishness has something to do with their feeling of being critical outsiders, even pariahs, in society. A second element is a collection of several kinds of gentile intellectuals who regard themselves as outsiders, many because they are sexual deviates. The third group consists, of course, of a number of Negro writers and artists. This new anti-establishmentarianism appears cohesive, alienated and therefore "Jewish." The Jewish intellectuals who act as its spokesmen think that they are more at home among the very best non-Jews, the wave of the spiritual future, than any Jewish businessman has ever felt at a Community Chest dinner.

Here too what is crucial is not the self-image of these Jews but what is really developing on the larger American scene. It is becoming ever clearer that some white intellectuals may be casting the Negro for the role of the alienated man, but that is not his own desire for himself. "I want what you've got" is not the slogan of a group which finds virtue in standing permanently outside of society. On the contrary, the very bourgeois suburban respectability which Philip Roth finds shallow is the present end-value of most Negroes; nor are their intellectual leaders, including even some of the most radical among them, really so contemptuous of this middle-class world. The Negro revolt is not a plea for a new heaven and a new earth, for the building of a new America on different spiritual and cultural foundations. The Negro is quite simply fighting for the opportunity to enter the bourgeoisie, accepting it as it is. We are thus confronted by a paradox: the white intellectuals, especially the Jewish ones, who have banged the door on middle-class culture to join the Negro in his alienation, are enlisted in a campaign to help him attain the very situation they have just abandoned.

The tension inherent in this paradox is already beginning to strain the alliance between the largely Jewish devotees of alienation and the Negro. He is becoming ever more impatient with and contemptuous of those who would cast him for a role that he has not chosen for himself. The most important negative figure in current Negro writing is no longer the white oppressor or the Negro Uncle Tom; it is the white (often Jewish) intellectual who is an amateur Negro.

Basically, however, the Negro is a side show for the "alienated." They may even forgive his present drive to become part of the majority and think of it as a necessary but temporary affair. It can be argued that once the Negro attains his immediate goals, he will then be free to recognize the true condition of modern man. It is to this situation that forward-looking Jewish intellectuals are supposedly speaking, in concert with the best gentile voices. But are these Jews and these gentiles really sharing in a comparable alienation?

True, Jewish and gentile writers are both alienated from middle-class culture—*but in radically different, indeed antithetical, directions.* Unlike the Jews such alienation among the gentiles has not always been revolutionary, in the name of some new realm of the spirit yet to be born. It has often been conservative, looking back to an earlier age, before Western man was vulgarized by democracy. Too often to be an accident, and equally among conservatives and radicals, alienation has been coupled with anti-Semitism, sometimes of the most virulent kind. In gentile minds, to be alienated has not meant merely to withdraw from middle-class culture; this hated word has generally been identified with the Jews.

There is all too much evidence for these assertions. In an earlier generation Henry James and, later, T. S. Eliot chose to live in England, hating American rawness—and the Jews. Theodore Dreiser stayed home, to speak for the poor—and against the Jews. Ernest Hemingway, in his Parisian exile, was not much kinder to the one Jew about whom he wrote, and Henry Miller, who is presently the high priest of the beat generation, has written some nasty pages of anti-Semitism. The tale of Ezra Pound is too well-known to need repeating. Nor is this phenomenon confined to American letters. The great and alienated French writer, Louis Céline, was, even under Hitler, a Jew-hater of the most vicious kind. In the Nazi years the alienated André Gide coolly wrote his journal in which there was little sympathy for those millions who were being killed. It was the not alienated François Mauriac, the greatest voice of the liberal Catholic spirit in France, who suffered with the victims.

The "alienated" Jews have, in essence, agreed with the gentile attack on middle-class culture; they have even quite openly accepted the identification of this unlovely world with the Jewish bourgeoisie. What they have produced as a defense of themselves, in their own persons, is the plea that they stand apart from and in criticism of the main body of Jewry.

To understand correctly the relationship between alienated Jews and these alienated Jew-haters, we must review one element of modern Jewish history. All this has happened before. A recurrent and tragic motif to be heard in the various attempts of the Jew to enter Western society is his acceptance of his enemy's estimate of himself. At the very beginning of the Emancipation, some two centuries ago, there were Jews to agree, though it was not true, that the Jews in general were money-lenders and economically unproductive. These individuals pleaded for their own right to equality because they personally were different. There have been Jews in the last century or so who have agreed that Jewish culture and manners are inferior;

they have merely proclaimed themselves as made over in the image favored by the majority. Are not the alienated Jewish intellectuals really the newest "white Jews"?

The world, however, has a habit of reminding Jews that there are no "white Jews." This was what Hemingway meant in his version of Robert Cohen in *The Sun Also Rises*. Cohen can try his utmost but he remains as alien to the bull-fight as to the Mass.

The question here is not whether Marjorie Morningstar and her family are really nice people, or whether it is immoral in Jewish intellectuals to be viciously critical of their own community. Marjorie is boring, and divinely appointed Jewish writers since time immemorial have been denouncing the Jews, usually at very inconvenient and very dangerous times. The essential issue is the vantage point. Does one really enter some wider cultural world by detesting Cohen and, *a fortiori*, Marjorie, as much as Hemingway did? Or is the alienated Jew still irretrievably different?

For modern man as a whole, alienation is not his ultimate condition; it is a phase through which the Western spirit has passed before. There always occurs a change of temper, some form of restoration, in which the former antagonists find that they can meet again and draw nourishment together from some ultimate resource of a culture rooted in Christianity and in Greek experience. Almost without exception, even the revolts have been battles within the larger framework of the living tradition of Western culture. Their protagonists may place themselves for a while in the posture of critical outsiders, but they are in their very being of the flesh and bone of the society against which they are revolting. No matter what their programs may say, hidden within them there is always the premise that the world will continue and that the meaning of their work will be, ultimately, to change and modify it but not to destroy it from its very roots. The most alienated gentile intellectuals can go home again; indeed they usually do.

The Modern Galut

To this home an individual Jew can indeed repair, but his own alienation is not sufficient passport. He must burn all the bridges to his Jewish past through radical conversion to the culture and, in effect, to the religion of the majority. Disraeli, Heine, Boris Pasternak and Bernard Berenson all chose this path (and paid various prices for the choice) for they knew that they could not abandon their home without entering someone else's. Limbo is only a temporary abode, except for the completely damned. For all those Jews who stop short of conversion, there must always remain a specifically Jewish sense of alienation, which is quite different from any momentary travail of Western man. It is the feeling of being not quite inside a culture even when one dominates much of its literature. It is, in short, not alienation, but exile, *galut*.

So long as anything remains of the Jew's own specific identity —it is even enough that he should merely refuse to give up that label and convert—the Jew remains unique, apart, exiled. Even today in America he has not been melted down. His politics are peculiar to himself. He does not fit into the category of either ethnic minority or religion. He remains a stranger to Christian culture. But the Jew has been battling for two centuries to overcome these barriers, not only in the world around him, but within himself. He has imagined a society which will open its doors to him and into which he can make himself fit. The nearest approach to such an achievement is in America, and it is here that the ultimate tragic paradox of *galut* is clearest.

Wherever freedom has existed for several generations without a break, the Jews have never in the last two centuries settled down to be themselves. Even in Central and Western Europe in the nineteenth century, in such towns as Budapest, Vienna and Berlin, the rate of falling-away was disastrous. In the third and fourth generation it began to approach one half. Today in America we are reaching the stage of the great grandchildren of the Russian Jewish immigrants of less than a century ago, and all the indices of disintegration are beginning to rise. Freedom is resulting, in part, in the naturalization of corporate Jewish identity in America; it is also resulting in large-scale attrition. A community which must define itself in uncharacteristic modes; which must will its survival within a society to which it is not congenial; whose continuity is most severely endangered by the very plenitude of freedom which is its most devout wish—such a community is in exile.

But do the otherness of Jewish behavior in America and the

feeling of emotional alienation really amount to exile? That depends, of course, on the definition one gives to that term. In the classic Jewish tradition exile meant, in the first instance, the notion that the Jew was outside both society and history; he was waiting for return to his own land. Meanwhile, he suffered the pain of living in a hostile environment. But, even in the medieval period, that did not mean only pogroms. It meant also being debarred from achieving one's own full identity. The radical change in our time is that environment is doing away with Jewish individuality not by attack but by openness. Hence the individual Jew, biologically, is no longer in exile in democracy; it is his Judaism, even his Jewishness, that is in exile.

In the last two centuries two radical solutions to the problem of exile have been devised. The very Orthodox have perpetuated a ghetto by choice; the Zionists have insisted on a complete end to exile. The majority of Jews have chosen neither alternative. They have continued to live on, usually pretending that the exile no longer exists, and attempting to find various palliatives for its unadmitted pains.

An over-arching answer does not exist. Perhaps our age was meant to be an age of waiting. Perhaps it was intended that we hang on as best we can, incarnating in our oft tormented ways the mystery of Jewish existence. Perhaps the beginning of the cure is in an honest recognition of our estate, as *galut*. Perhaps the great paradox of the Jewish situation is that the only Jews who are safe as Jews, outside of the homeland to which all will repair in some Messianic future, are those who know that they are in exile. Perhaps the falling-away, the personal trauma and the sheer emptiness of so many Jews are related to an underlying pervasive delusion that the exile which is specific to the Jew ends with the last pogrom. Such is the mystery of our being that a new kind of *galut* begins on the morrow.

What is to be done? The Jewish community has spent the last century or so in emphasizing its resemblances to all other groups. It has not really convinced many non-Jews, and it has been all too successful in convincing Jews and leading them out of Jewish life. The strategy of the next century should be based on the cultivation of that which is *sui generis*. That is the necessary precondition of survival. It is also the index of the faith of the Jew in the America which has given him unconditional freedom. The ultimate test of his trust in that freedom will be his willingness to be unique.

FOR FURTHER READING

BLAU, Joseph, *Judaism in America* (Chicago: University of Chicago Press, 1976). A light but useful introduction to the varieties of Jewish religious experience in contemporary America.

FEINGOLD, Henry L., *A Midrash on American Jewish History* (Albany: State University of New York Press, 1982). A provocative, diverse, highly individual account of the main ideological structural elements on the contemporary Jewish agenda.

HALKIN, Hillel, *Letters to an American Friend* (Philadelphia: Jewish Publication Society, 1977). A strong challenge to American Jewry from a classical Zionist perspective.

HERMAN, Simon, *Jewish Identity: A Social Psychological Perspective* (Sage Publishing Company, Beverly Hill, 1977). A wide-ranging study by a leading Israeli sociologist of Jewish identity. A standard work.

LIEBMAN, Charles, *The Ambivalent American Jew: Politics, Religion, and Family in American Jewish Life* (Philadelphia: Jewish Publication Society, 1973). A well-known, critical review of the uncertain, inwardly divided identity of American Jewry.

SIDORSKY, David, editor, *The Future of the Jewish Community in America* (New York: Basic Books, 1973). A series of informed essays by experts on all aspects of contemporary American Jewry.

SKLARE, Marshall and Joseph Greenbaum, *Jewish Identity on the Suburban Frontier* (New York: Basic Books, 1967). Though two decades old, its professional, sociological description of Jewish suburbia still proves informative.

WAXMAN, Chaim, I., *America's Jews in Transition* (Philadelphia: Temple University Press, 1983). An up-to-date sociological study of the dynamics in the present, highly fluid American Jewish situation. Very good on Jewish institutions and the American context in which these institutions exist.

17 . Jewish Faith and the
Jewish Future

EUGENE B. BOROWITZ

A N Y O N E who has lived through the past 25 years has seen the great constructive change which has swept over American Jewry. Together with its brother Jews in many but, sadly, not in all corners of the world, American Jewry, both leading and led, as patron and as beneficiary, has attained such Jewish self-respect that it seeks positive and creative ways of living its Jewishness. Much of its concern today is "what does it mean to live a modern Jewish life? How can we do so?"

Nothing could be more astonishing or more significant after what Jews have suffered. The disaster of European Jewry had no precedent in the long history of Jewish pain nor in the perversities of modern civilization. That one out of every three living Jews was killed for no other reason than that he was a Jew, even when he had only the most peripheral connection with Jewry, should have been enough to make the rest of Jewry resign from history. And the exterminated Jewish communities were the human source and the spiritual standard of all the other Jewish settlements in the world. What organism can survive such a loss of heart or head?

Had this destruction been the work of invading barbarians, the chance effect of an uncontrollable epidemic or natural catastrophe, the Jews might simply have endured and, the visitation past, returned to normal existence. But can there ever again be "normal" existence for Jews? The Germans were not a nation of primitive and illiterate men but among the most educated and civilized of the twentieth century. They did not kill Jews in sporadic outbursts of uncontainable rage or unaccountable accident. They killed coldly, out of mature reflection, with deliberate intent, by industrial methods and in hope of leaving no survivors. That the Germans could do such a thing is an irreducible fact of future Jewish history. And the extent to which the democratic nations might have helped but did not or would not is still a matter of research and debate.

The attitude of the non-Jewish world cannot be taken lightly. The existence of modern Jewry is dependent upon its good will. That is an obvious fact for Jewish communities like the American which participate intimately in the lives of the nations. The survival of the State of Israel is equally dependent on the active help or passive acquiescence of the great powers.

Are the nations today trustworthy? World Jewry, with its people ravaged and its confidence in educated, democratic man shattered beyond reconstruction, had every right after World War II to refuse to go on. By willful and conscious personal assimilation, by ceasing to do anything more about being Jewish, by the easiest sort of drift into the large anonymous masses of modern society, out of disgust, rebellion, exhaustion or weariness, the Jews, in a generation or two, could have quit. Hitler, though defeated, would have won. Perhaps that, in itself, is the major though unconscious reason why the Jews, once again, refused to be reasonable. The revival of world Jewry is the Jewish, morally spiteful insistence that Hitler's defeat must be complete.

Post-War Resurgence

After the war, the overwhelming majority of Jews refused to capitulate. The European survivors were an awe-inspiring example of that will-to-live as Jews. Shortly after the concentration camps were liberated, weddings were celebrated, economic enterprises begun, organizations founded, and protests and debate, that steady sign of Jewish vitality, abounded.

This was more than an animal instinct for survival. It stemmed from that deep-felt belief, fostered and ingrained by Jewish observance, that life comes from God and is good, that living is the indispensable means to holiness and that holiness is reached in life, not beyond it.

The years following the war required Jews to build a new Jewishness, to bring into being a more significant and fulfilling Jewish life than had hitherto existed. It was not the Jewish love of life alone that erupted but that fundamental Jewish sense of responsibility, that Messianic thrust, that impelled and powered them as well.

Two great accomplishments resulted which epitomize the miraculous result. A Jewish state was re-established in the Land of Israel. Years of familiarity have dulled the memory of nearly two thousand years of waiting and weeping, and fifty years of intense political and cultural effort. The great nations may have allowed the State to come into being, but it was Jewish sweat, talent and blood that created and sustained it. No communal Jewish effort since Biblical days can be compared to it.

Less spectacular but equally providential has been the extraordinary maturation of the American Jewish community. Adversity in Europe meant responsibility here. American Jewry accepted its duties and grew to new stature in fulfilling them. The record of rescue and rehabilitation, of political agitation and support, is in the noblest traditions of Jewish brotherliness. Many doubt that an instance of equally generous communal *tx'dakah* can be found in the annals of Jewish history.

These concerns for the welfare of other Jews brought a new and searching concern for the future of American Jewry itself. Working and giving for other Jews meant acknowledging one's Jewish identity and a commitment to act upon it. Increasingly that consciousness turned inward and asked what it meant to be a Jew in the United States, what should be done to make American Jewish life more meaningful and significant. That most American Jews today live in a quiet pride of Jewishness, that American Jewishness is stronger, richer, more varied in program and higher in standards than anyone would have dared estimate before World War II are measures of the startling suddenness with which what seemed barely in bud has now come into flower.

This recitation of achievement is not meant to deny the serious problems which still exist in Jewish life. To discuss Jewish hope is not to be blind to the perils of Jewish life but rather to focus on those aspects which the Jew views with some confidence.

The post-war resurgence of Jewry was not a response to a great, dramatic personality who in his person, by his deeds or speeches summoned forth all the energies left in this tried and tired people. Nor was it channeled through an intellectual movement which by its analysis so explained what had happened and so justified what yet was to be that this people, despite its physical debilitation, felt constrained to move forward. Nor was it the result of any organization whose program was so appealing that the Jews seized it as the fulfillment of their Jewish needs. This is not to underestimate the importance of either the rescue or Zionist organizations. Both did an invaluable job in Europe but they did not so much lead the people as respond to their needs, they did not create the desire for life and the will to emigrate but nobly took advantage of an opportunity. Their greatness is that they were ready and responsive to a people which had itself already made the basic decision.

The hero of the post-war period is *the Jewish people itself*. Without prophet or lawgiver, without a great book or dominant school of philosophy, without benefit of world-wide resolutions, conventions, declarations or press releases, it determined to survive Jewishly and in honor. That basic will-to-be-Jewish has characterized the Jews in the past two decades and has been responsible for the remarkable change in the content and tone of Jewish life. Because its roots are deeper than a man, a concept or an organization, because it is a widespread and pervasive phenomenon, it must be understood in proper depth. The believing Jew will approach this phenomenon with a certain awe, recognizing here another of those Exodus-experiences which characterize the uncanny history of this holy people, or, in brief, the saving hand of God.

For the moment at least, the Jewish people is conscious of and interested in its Jewishness. Discussions of the Jewish future are not hypothetical but concrete, not *whether* it will be but *what* it will be.

How Jewish life has changed in the United States in the past 25 or 30 years! Self-hatred, or at least ambivalence, dominated in the 30's, the decade of the furtive changing of names, the straightening of noses, the suppression of accents and gestures, the cultivation of non-Jewish manners and non-Jewish approval.

Though some of these symptoms are still to be found, negative attributes no longer characterize today's Jews. They are, on the whole, self-accepting. They know that they are Jewish, and assume that others know and respect them for it. And they do not hesitate to do some things, at least, that identify them with the Jewish community. Their children too are growing up with the notion that it is natural to be a Jew. They have not had the traumas most of their parents experienced in discovering their Jewish identity. (As the next decade or two brings these children to maturity their advent may itself be anticipated with hope.)

The immediate temptation in analyzing American Jewish life is to deal with its organizations and their programs. But a catalog of them would be dull and unrealistic. The great American Jewish organizations do not lead Jewish life but rather try to keep up with what the community seems to want. That is why their activities overlap and compete. Hence, an analysis of the positive patterns of Jewish existence in America is better done in social and intellectual terms, a description of what Jews in real Jewish communities in different parts of the United States are doing. To make the various possibilities clear, three major levels of activity have artifically been isolated—social, cultural and religious. This broad division reflects the author's commitment to the religious interpretation of Jewishness. No claim is made that this is the only way in which this community and its life may truly be depicted. It must also be noted that while some Jews limit themselves to only one aspect of Jewish life, many partake of all three with varying degrees of emphasis.

Social Motives for Jewish Identity

The most peripheral form of Jewish association is probably that which exists for the sake of self-defense. At one time this was a major preoccupation of American Jewry. In the 1930's anti-Semitism was open, active and supported by non-Jews of stature and influence. Though positive Jewishness meant little to many, the fear of those who hated Jews made many a Jew cooperate with his co-religionists in self-protection. The post-war era has seen a radical decline in the extent, intensity and influence of anti-Semitism. What exists openly is disreputable and lunatic fringe. Such pressure as the Jew feels today is largely social in character in terms of clubs, neighborhoods and cliques, though there is always the threat of something more serious.

Despite these changes some Jews make their appearance only when the subject of defense is involved. Their caricature is the well-known figure who is active in interfaith activities but has no real faith of his own. There are those, however, who convert the acceptance of their destiny into a moral virtue. For them the fight for Jewish rights is a means of realizing democracy. Leaving the Jewish people while it is embattled is cowardice, working with it the least a decent man can do. Such ethical self-respect is admirable but it cannot build a Jewish way of life.

More positive is the uncomplicated assertion of those Jews who like Jews, and who prefer to associate with them. No deep philosophic necessity drives them to buy a home near other Jews, to join a Jewish club, to send their children to a non-sectarian but obviously Jewish camp, or make their reservations at resorts frequented by other Jews. They feel more comfortable with Jews; they enjoy being with "their own kind." No one has ever tried to estimate how widespread this sense of Jewish sociability is, nor are there any standards by which to measure its strength. Nonetheless, the American Jewish community today would be unrecognizable without its operation. Its expression ranges through the use of Yiddish or other "inside" Jewish expressions, the enjoyment of Jewish jokes, the preference for Jewish foods, the joining of Jewish social or recreational clubs, the insistence, for reasons otherwise unclear, upon marriage within the community, up to the vague assertion that one simply prefers the Jewish style of living.

When conviviality is the honest choice of those who genuinely prefer people of similar backgrounds, standards and interests, it is difficult to deny its legitimacy. When, as still happens, Jews huddle together from an archaic, tribal fear of the outsider, the *goy*, that is a counter-prejudice, but a prejudice nonetheless and therefore deserving elimination, not preservation. Still Jewish fraternity can hardly serve as a central motive for the life of American Jewry. It arose as the by-product of a deeper unity which held the generations together in their pursuit of a great historic goal. What will create that feeling as the generations pass if there is nothing else to give rise to it but the memory of previous generations' conviviality? As democracy becomes practice and Jews are socially more welcome among their non-Jewish neighbors, what will sustain the Jewish community? Is good fellowship all that remains of the noble Jewish tradition?

Many Jews have responded to these questions by hitching their social needs to some worthy Jewish purpose in the form of a Jewish organization. This is not entirely an American phenomenon though the American mania for organizations and conventions is well known. Jews of the Middle Ages also had societies, the *hevrah*, whose function might be burying the dead, marrying off eligible but indigent Jewish maidens, the study of the Talmud, visiting the sick. Nor did they get together only to fulfill their stated goal. Their records are full of meetings, feasts and celebrations. Thus the host of organizations which may be found in even the smallest American Jewish community today has distinguished forbears. When the Jewish will-to-be-sociable is linked to "a good cause," the American Jew finds it difficult to resist.

Most Jewish organizations may speedily be recognized for what they are: "moral fronts" for Jewish enjoyment. The American Jewess apparently does not feel quite right about spending afternoons at fashion shows or card parties and her husband has a similar anxiety about spending evenings bowling, watching a magician or listening to a sports celebrity. Let these activities be connected with a worthy Jewish cause and the guilt is expiated.

Projects of mutual Jewish concern and value are pursued with devotion and accomplishment by many organizations. The most consistently praiseworthy are the local combined charity appeals, the international rescue and State of Israel aid programs. Here at least, the interminable dinners, the ego-serving awards and the social pressure to give, serve significant Jewish ends. They not only keep the American Jewish community organized and alive; they mean life or death to Jews in many another land.

In the less dramatic but equally significant work of the Jewish communal agencies at home, settlement houses and vocational agencies have more and more been replaced with personal and family counseling or services to the aging. These are but the most evident of the professionally staffed, morally oriented programs of high standard which American Jews have created and carried on for their brothers.

At this level there is surely positive reason for Jewish life and action. Jews need and want to help one another. Through a voluntary system unmatched in human history they have done so and will continue to do so. For many Jews such praiseworthy concerns with organized mutual help are sufficient reason for their active participation in and loyalty to the Jewish people.

Tz'dakah has been lauded by Jewish sages through the centuries and the American Jew has learned to practice it on a grand, international scale. No realistic Jew can cavil at its importance but questions can and must be asked about *tz'dakah* as the sole or central concern of American Jewish existence. Whence does the extraordinary concern of Jew for brother Jew arise? Whence the motive to give generously for distant and unknown souls? *Tz'dakah* may have special appeal to Jews but, like Jewish fellowship, it is but one product of a deeper sense of duty and obligation. With governments increasingly entering the welfare field, with Jews integrating more intimately into American society, the worthy practice of Jewish charity cannot alone power American Jewry but is itself in need of strengthening.

Jews by Culture and Education

A more positive foundation and indeed an understanding of all Jewish activity is offered to the American Jew by the cultural and religious interpretations of Jewish living.

The term Jewish culture once encompassed a lively array of divergent approaches to Jewish life. Today the living options are limited to two, the educational and the Zionist.

In the 1920's, when the great masses of large-city Jewry were still fresh from Central and Eastern Europe, and still in the '30's when accommodation to American culture was slowly making headway, a variety of Jewish cultural theses were propounded and lived. Jewish socialism claimed the allegiance of thousands whom it enlisted in the cause of human betterment through political action. Carried out in the Yiddish language and appealing to the historic memories and prophetic concerns of the

Jewish people, it seemed an extraordinarily worthy fusion of the Jewish past with the needs of contemporary man. Even its opposition to Zionism and religion could not dim its appeal, though little of the movement remains today (except for the Yiddish daily newspaper *Der Forverts*). Closely allied to and often indistinguishable from it was the Jewish labor movement. Here the old Jewish concern for justice and opportunity took the form of organizing unions among the Jewish working class. Since substantial numbers of immigrants were laborers, concentrated largely in the needle trades, it seemed as if a major portion of metropolitan Jewry could be involved in the struggle for social justice. Though these unions today may retain their Jewish leadership, their Jewish members are retiring in increasing numbers and have for some years been outnumbered by rural Southerners, Italian, Negro and Puerto Rican recruits.

Applying a full-scale philosophy of Judaism in its program, the secular Yiddishist or Yiddish Nationalist movement took a number of organizational forms, the chief survivor of which is the Sholom Aleichem Folk School movement. The ideology of the various groups was roughly similar: though Jewish existence could not be based on religion because of the growth of modern science, the Jewish heritage still had much to say to modern man in his search for a rich existence.

According to these secularists, the fundamental problem of modern Jewishness lies in its misinterpretation of the nature of the Jewish group. While religion had been its major concern in the Middle Ages, that had been only one part of a folk existence. The Jews survived not because of their faith but because the governments under which they had lived had always granted them a measure of autonomy. They had collected their own taxes, operated their own courts and provided their own educational system. In Eastern Europe, where this theory originated, many nationality groups lived within one state and continued their own ethnic cultures. The Yiddishists felt that though the United States government did not officially recognize such folk communities, the Jews should voluntarily create and operate their separate folk life, thus enriching the total American culture.

In opposition to the Zionists, the Yiddishists turned their backs on the Land of Israel and its language. They argued that mankind was moving toward greater unity, beyond the sovereignty of individual states and toward internationalism. The Jews were really the first cosmopolitan nation, an example of the way in which national groups should reach a trans-geographic, moral and humanistic level. Yiddish being the living, functioning language of this people, it should be fostered and extended through research, creativity and usage. The hope was that through the creation of a Yiddish-centered culture, the American Jew would be both simultaneously a man of the modern world and a significant inheritor and progenitor of the Jewish tradition.

The breadth and daring of this effort to reconstruct contemporary Judaism must still inspire respect though social developments have rendered it almost completely impractical. With most American Jews now native-born, the use of Yiddish has largely disappeared. The serious Yiddish theater is down to a week end, museum-showcase in New York, and literary creativity of quality is better found in South America where more recent immigration and Latin exclusiveness have kept Yiddish alive. Today's advertisements for the Sholom Aleichem Folk Schools in the suburbs offer a secular Jewish education to those who cannot find themselves at home in the synagogue, but also provide for a "secular Bar Mitzvah" (sic!).

Much of what remains of the once strong Jewish secularist movements now finds its outlets in that ill-defined cluster of attitudes which center about the desire "to give my child a Jewish education." This is perhaps the clearest, most self-conscious, most intense and direct Jewish concern of the American Jew.

Why the American Jew should feel so strongly about this matter is not clear even to himself. On the whole he is dissatisfied with his own Jewish education, but that paradoxically has led him to want his child to have a better one. Even if he is not religiously observant or Hebraically informed, he still wants his child to know that tradition and its language. Many parents also feel that should their children ever face anti-Semitism they should know why they are Jews.

Aside from either the Zionist or religious justifications of education, some parents and many educators take a cultural approach to Jewish schooling. At its simplest level they can speak of Jewish ethics, the importance of teaching the child that positive, activist, demanding attitude to human relations which is peculiarly the fruit of Jewish thought and experience and has been embodied in Jewish practice. Some speak of Jewish values, whose larger perspective includes such virtues as the love of life, the appreciation of pleasure, the emphasis on rationality, the encouragement of individual worth. Others speak of the Jewish way of life, embracing not only intellectual content and folk forms, but the very people and its creativity as well. Another group wishes to transmit the Jewish heritage, that great accumulation of experience and wisdom, of books and customs, of heroes and endurance.

How positive a force this is in contemporary Jewry may be seen in the variety and growth of Jewish educational institutions, or in the pervasive dissatisfaction with what was done in the past. Since World War II the most rapidly developing sector in Jewish education has been the Jewish day school, which takes in almost ten per cent of the children currently receiving a Jewish education. A similar concern with depth has been shown in both the Conservative and Reform congregational programs. The former have not only insisted with great success on a minimum three-day-a-week program but are now engaged in an effort to extend the Bar Mitzvah training to include an early start and a high school continuation for Jewish education. The Reform Jews, who have long had better continuity in their programs, are now engaged in expanding their voluntary mid-week programs, in raising the age level of confirmation and increasing the number of post-confirmation classes. Both groups have placed heavy emphasis upon summer camping and sponsor group visits to the State of Israel.

What may be the single most revealing sign of the state of Jewish education is the virtual disappearance of the "Bar Mitzvah mill." No longer will any self-respecting congregation agree to a ceremony after three months of training. Two-year requirements are becoming minimal, with many congregations insisting upon three or four years of prior study. Since there is no authority in the Jewish community to enforce such a rule, its general observance must be attributed to its endorsement by the general will of American Jewish parenthood. This is a constructive sign, which indicates how a devotion to Jewish education, for whatever reason, strengthens and supports Jewish life in America.

The desire to educate is beyond Jewish criticism except when it is presented as a full answer to the problems of Jewish existence. Such views maintain that Jewish education is an end in itself; it requires no justification, no philosophical validation. But even if the question "why educate?" is momentarily set aside, then the question "educate for what?" immediately springs forward. No school system has enough time nor its personnel enough wisdom or energy to do everything. Those who arrange its program must make decisions as to what they will and will not teach, arouse, exemplify. In these judgments a standard of Jewish values is at work. Consciously or unconsciously a philosophy of Judaism is founding and directing this plan of Jewish education. The will-to-educate cannot itself provide a criterion of judgment; all it can say is that the more education the better —a futile and unrealistic position, considering the realities of Jewish life and its continuing transition.

Jewish education is an absolutely indispensable means for the development of Jewish life. It is a major incentive for such devotion as the American Jewish community has already mustered. It must be continued in effort, enlarged in scope, deepened in mastery, intensified in effect and made the responsibility of every Jew, not just of his school or synagogue. But it can do so only when it serves a broad philosophy of Jewish life, not when it tries to become one itself.

The Zionist Approach

Two major interpretations of Jewishness, two general theories of Judaism remain active among thoughtful American Jews: the so-called "Zionist" and "religious" concepts. The term "Zionism" is still so deeply associated with the efforts to establish the State of Israel that to use it to describe a mode of Jewish living years later seems anachronistic. Because the word "religion" suffers from its close connection with the Christian, particularly the Protestant, understanding of the relationship between God and man, connoting church rather than folk, creed rather than commandment, the personal rather than the communal, it hardly seems appropriate to describe the traditional relation between God and the Jewish people. Still, the terms must be used.

Other than a frontal anti-Semitic assault, nothing so actively unifies the American Jewish community as a common interest

in and concern for the State of Israel. The older generation re-
members the bitter refugee years and the struggle to bring the
State into being. For them the State of Israel still means the excitement of its declaration, the day its flag was hoisted at the
United Nations, the arrival of the first Israeli ships in American
ports, the pictures of refugees debarking at Haifa, the victory
against Arab attacks. Though American Jewish youth lack this
personal historic depth, they easily identify with pioneering,
embattled, humanitarian aspects of a living reality which has accompanied much of their existence. The community as a whole
is still generous to causes in the State of Israel whether these be
charitable or investments. This positive concern extends to the
realm of education as well. American Jews want their children
to know about the State. There is hardly a community of size
where individuals have not already visited or are about to tour
the State of Israel.

On the everyday level, to the average American Jew, "Zionism" is the web of feeling and response noted above. Some
Zionist philosophers, however, continue to urge that Zionism
could constitute a full pattern of Jewishness for Jews outside
Israel. For implicit in the effort to create the State was a positive
and creative attitude concerning the Jewish people and its life.

According to Zionism, the Jews are not primarily a religious
group though there may be many today who wish to live a Jewish religious life. For many centuries in the Middle Ages Judaism
was limited entirely to religious activities. This contraction of
self-expression enabled the Jews to preserve their group nature
in a difficult and trying time. But the Jews were always a folk,
a people, or, in the special European sense of the term, a nation.
(Those who find this usage painful should remember that connotations change. A precisely similar species of embarrassment is
created today by the usage of the anti-Zionist Reform thinker
Kaufmann Kohler, who, in a nineteenth-century European sense,
used the word "race" to describe the Jewish group.)

Now that modern Jewry is free to be itself and since modern
men have so many doubts about the value of religion, say the
Zionists, Jews should express themselves in every normal avenue
of national expression—land, language, government. This is
what makes a state so desirable from the cultural as distinct from
the humanitarian point of view. The State will not merely save

Jews, it will save Judaism. It will do so not merely by preserving the best of the Jewish past but by creating new values, new patterns, new modes of Jewishness. And it will do so in a way that Diaspora Jews never can, for the Israeli need be true only to his Jewish self, not to some alien majority which will set his cultural standards. On its own land, speaking it own tongue, true to its own standards, the Jewish people can be truly Jewish at last.

For many European Zionist thinkers as for a substantial number of Israelis today, Zionism is the only real hope for Judaism in the contemporary world. The Jewish communities outside the land are destined to disappear either by anti-Semitic outbreak or by assimilation to the majority culture. From this standpoint the great duty of Jews in the Diaspora is to immigrate or prepare themselves for immigration. Anything less would be unworthy of a desire to lead a full Jewish life.

Such theories of Zionism have never had much sway in America, as the low level of American immigration to the State of Israel indicates. American Zionists have rarely risen above their preoccupation with rescue and rehabilitation. On such occasions, they have spoken in terms of "cultural Zionism," the hope that Jewish life in the Diaspora can continue if it bases itself upon Israeli culture. The Hebrew language is the key to this cultural influence, permitting the Jew in other lands to read the novels, plays, poetry of the gifted writers of his people. Through their essays, criticism and discussion, he can share the intellectual excitement of the Jew speaking as a Jew, confronting the basic issues of modern society. Through their concentrated research into the Jewish past, qualitatively different from that of any other center by virtue of its existence on the land of the Bible and its at-homeness with the Hebrew tongue, he can gain new insight into his Jewish past. Their crafts, music, painting and dance can adorn his life and inspire him in his own land to similar levels of creativity. He will not, for all of this, be any less a citizen of the culture of his native country, but his life will rather be enriched and uplifted by the special quality which Jewishness will add to his existence. This humanistic-spiritual bond with his brothers in the State of Israel will all the more effectively bind him to Jews in every part of the world and tie him to their common purposes. The Jewish people can live not only on its land, but through its land, elsewhere as well.

Through this concern, or something akin to it, a wide range of projects has been sponsored in the American Jewish community. Most obvious is the devotion given to the teaching of Hebrew to adults as well as to children, not just as a classic tongue but as the living language of a living people. Those trained in the old *ba, bo, be, bi* method of learning Hebrew will be surprised to find today's teachers using the full panoply of modern teaching devices from tapes and records to language laboratories and teaching machines. Some communities have experimented with teaching Hebrew via television. The Hebrew-speaking summer camp, the Hebrew high school and the teachers' college are respected community efforts and the summer, semester or year spent in Israel is common.

The broader cultural exchange has touched far wider circles in the community. Visiting Israeli artists regularly appear in most reasonably large American cities while the largest are graced by the great Israeli ensembles, the Symphony, Habimah Theatre and the Inbal Dancers. Records of Israeli folk songs are widely produced and purchased. Israeli crafts are found in many an American Jewish home. Courses and lectures on the State, its geography, politics, peoples and problems are frequent and well received. Israel folk dance groups, *halil* classes, folk song sessions are not uncommon. When these diverse cultural activities are tied to the political concern and the emotional involvement of the American Jew with the State of Israel, the "Zionist" influence furthering the maturation of the American Jewish community can be seen as a living force.

Some Zionists still believe that this incipient cultural renaissance will grow to the point of a full-scale foundation for Jewish life in the United States. The overwhelming majority of American Jews, however, seem to be moving in another direction. While the State of Israel, its people and to a lesser extent its culture, will always remain precious to them, it apparently cannot serve as the center of their Jewish existence in America. Membership in male Zionist organizations has declined drastically since the founding of the State, and what is left is neither youthful nor enthusiastic. Hadassah and Pioneer Women manage better because of their "good causes." Most Hebrew courses end with few in attendance; the number reaching a second or third year level is small indeed. American Hebraists grow increasingly rare, and most realistic American educators admit that Hebrew will, at best, be a second tongue for only a small minority of American Jewry. Thus the readers of current Hebrew literature are few, and the creators of American Jewish plays, stories and poems in Hebrew are largely an older, immigrant generation.

Zionist leaders both in the United States and abroad have admitted the depth of this problem by fitfully seeking to define a new statement of Zionist principles, one that would revitalize the movement and give guidance for Jewish life in the post-State era. These efforts have ended in futility, or in other versions of the old and tired programs of the past.

Despite such criticisms, love for and concern with Israel have a sure place in the future of American Judaism. Anti-Zionism, despite similar "spiritual" fanaticism on the part of ultra-Orthodox and ultra-Reform groups, is as unthinkable for most American Jews as the Zionist culture theory is impractical.

The Religious Interpretation of Jewish Life

In American Jewry today, it is the "religious" interpretation of Judaism which holds the decisive place. In 1925 only forty per cent of American Jewish children enrolled in Jewish schools were being educated by congregations, with most of the remainder in communal schools whose tone was largely cultural and Zionist. By 1957, over ninety per cent of children receiving a Jewish education were doing so under congregational auspices.

The phenomenon of rising religious affiliation is not confined to Jews. A similar movement has affected other religious groups in American society since the end of the war. Since the contemporary American ethos not only permits but encourages religious difference, the American Jew, whose religion is acknowledged as one of the major American faiths (an extraordinary, even providential fact), accepts religion as the chief factor in his Jewish distinctiveness. As a result, in new communities synagogues always precede Jewish recreation facilities, and then devote themselves to the stimulation of communal, familial and private Jewish living. There is almost no modern Jewish community whose congregations are not prime movers of much of its organized activity.

But a paradox lies at the heart of this situation. A truly religious Jewry, conscious of itself as a folk dedicated to serving God through His commandments, would have direction and guidance, purpose and passion for its communal and personal Jewish existence. However, for all its numbers and activity American Jews cannot be called significantly religious. Studies of synagogue affiliation and religious beliefs make abundantly clear that most Jews join congregations for everything but religious reasons. Distance, membership costs, social standing, the personality of the rabbi, the reputation of the school: these count. Attendance at services and adult study as contrasted with social events or general meetings shows how slight is the concern with God and His law. Regardless of their denominational label, most American Jews are largely non-observant, at home and in their everyday life. Ironically, it may well be that secular Judaism, which could not dominate American Judaism under its own name, now may do so under the auspices of the synagogue. Here too the pattern is not limited to Jews but has been noted in most of American religious life.

The average synagogue and the large synagogue organizations do not redeem this situation by the example of their own religiosity. Their competition for pre-eminence, their preoccupation with public relations, their inability to apply to their own organization what they tell their members to do in their lives perturb and offend the sensitive believer. The American Jew may belong, but he does not believe much. His religiosity is rarely serious or profound.

Thus the paradox emerges. If the American Jew were truly religious he would create a living American Jewish community, but though he organizes his community along religious lines, his life shows little religious belief and practice. *If he were* . . . that is the crisis of the American Jewish future and the problem which American Jewish religious leadership must meet.

For some sectors of the religious community the answer is clear. The ultra-Orthodox, for example, know that they are right, that they are doing what God wants Jews to do. While their numbers may be small they have confidence in their way of life. This security stems not only from their observant Orthodoxy but from their refusal to deviate from the full social style of their European forbears. Dressed in the *kaftan*, adorned with *peyot,* devoted to their *rebbe,* they continue steadfastly on what they know to be the one authentic Jewish path.

All other varieties of religious Jewry feel something must be done to transform European Jewish piety into a compelling American style that is yet truly Jewish. Some limit their efforts to what has been done before, perhaps trying to do it a little better. Others seize on the technical approach, utilizing better group "know-how" to attract larger crowds, more participation, greater follow-up. Still others wait for some new development in general culture to justify their work. Last year it was Judaism and psychiatry. This year race relations. Next year outer space. Equating performing commandments with keeping busy they have neither time nor reason to wonder whom they are serving. There are countless creative reasons for avoiding God and His will.

To speak seriously of the religious content of Judaism is to speak of the thoughtful few. There are such thoughtful men in every wing of American Jewry. No one point of view dominates the scene or gives promise of sweeping across American Jewry. Each demands too much for many men to be speedily yet deeply converted to its truth.

The Neo-Orthodox Approach

On first thought the modern American-style Orthodox would seem to have the easiest task. What they propose is concrete action, not foggy spirituality; authentically Jewish, not traditionally unrecognizable; conformable to America, not alien or ghetto. If one clarifies the distinction between Jewish law and the folk patterns of Poland or Hungary, the essentials of Jewish living can be distinguished from what one or another locale added to them. The appropriate use of English, short men's jackets, reasonable decorum in the service are not incompatible with a life based on *Halakhah.* True Jewish life will still make special demands on the observant American Jew but any religion which does not do so is unworthy of serious respect. The Jew who wants to be faithful to Judaism will want to observe the Law God gave on Sinai and that He has graciously allowed His sages to clarify for every succeeding generation.

The Orthodox call to the Jewish community to return to

their ancestral standards in a way legitimately accommodated to this country has met with far more response in the post-war years than most non-Orthodox thinkers anticipated. The young, fully observant Jew is no longer a stranger to American Judaism and, though many have thought religion and science incompatible, the devoutly Orthodox Jewish scientist is in plentiful evidence. The growth of human knowledge has not made the tradition meaningless for such Jewish products of contemporary education and culture. Rather, knowing the best that man has to offer, they believe that God has given man the critical guidance he needs to meet the demands of modern existence, that through God's Torah modern, as ancient, man can live in full faith, confidence and hope.

But for all its directness and unequivocation, modern Orthodoxy faces a fundamental problem. The American Jew has abandoned traditional observance. Even when he calls himself Orthodox, his observance of the Sabbath and *kashrut*, not to mention lesser laws, is generally characterized by transgression.

This lack of observance stems from the belief, unarticulated but unquestionably real, that "God doesn't really care about these details." If the modern Jew could truly believe that God Himself was outraged if he flipped an electric switch on the Sabbath, ate chicken not killed by a *shoḥet* or had less repetitive services, perhaps he would accept the holy discipline with all its benefits. But, on the whole, he remains skeptically American. He cannot imagine that God is not pleased with him when he actively seeks to be a decent human being while retaining as much of Jewish practice as he can. Orthodoxy cannot settle for such a laissez-faire attitude, but how it can bring the American Jew to revere traditional law and its observance is unclear.

Four Non-Orthodox Views

The various non-Orthodox views all grant the religious validity of the American Jew's turn from fully *halakhic* conduct. They concede that modern society requires a new statement of Jewish life, one which begins from the tradition but moves forward. What makes them liberals, in all their diversity of theory and label, is their willingness to depart from the established norms of Orthodoxy to meet the needs of a changing situation.

All of them suffer under a blanket criticism from the Orthodox, who believe there is but one Torah tradition, one genuinely
Jewish way of living. To say this is not binding is, in the Orthodox view, to create a mongrel Judaism, inauthentic and untrue.

The progressive groups have sought to counter this criticism
by insisting that Judaism has always changed and that their various means of change represent the best of the tradition facing
the best of the new world. Most American Jews have found
these arguments convincing or have been willing to accept them
as rationalizations for their new way of living.

The changes introduced have made American Jews more comfortable—but it must be granted that they have not substantially
increased the proportionate number of observant Jews even by
their less demanding standards.

Yet is there any alternative? Can the scientific, political,
esthetic, philosophic changes of the past century and a half be
met with an attitude that seeks mainly to preserve the past? Is
timidity in the face of radical change a Jewish virtue? The pro-
gressives do not enter upon their roles lightly or proceed capriciously. Theirs is a deeply serious Jewish responsibility which
they seek to meet in all its difficulty.

Four intellectual positions may be isolated from the multitude
of claims and pronouncements which regularly assault the Jewish community. These are theoretical positions, rarely to be
found in Jewish life in abstract and unalloyed form. They cut
across most denominational lines as they seek to describe what
people believe rather than which label they employ.

1) Judaism as Ethical Monotheism

One view sees Judaism as a unique religious idea preserved by
its similarly unparalleled social carrier. The idea may be termed,
too simply, "ethical monotheism," that trust in one real God
who undergirds and orders all of creation, but who is distinguished from all other gods of similar mathematical singularity
by His righteousness. For the Jew, to know God is first and foremost to be commanded to act ethically, to love one's fellow man,
to build a just society. All the wrath and comfort of the prophets, all the planning and exhortation of the rabbis, all the hope

and challenge of the Messianic idea here come into play. For mankind, despite its pretensions, does not yet understand that this is indeed who God is and what God wants. Jewish distinctiveness is founded in Judaism's conceptual superiority. The Jewish people, as the bearer of this unique idea, as the group which has embodied this belief in their communities in various cultures through the ages, thus has an insight and a unique experience which mankind today needs desperately. Jewish observance, as the means of strengthening and exemplifying this religious truth, is a necessary concomitant of a commitment to this noble historic task. The modern American Jewish community should, by deepening its Jewish roots, devote itself to making justice live, both in its private lives and in general American activity. Then not only the Jews but all mankind will appreciate the worth and value of a continuing Jewish community.

2) Jewish Peoplehood: The Social Foundation

A second view begins from a contrary premise, that there is nothing distinctively Jewish about the idea of one God or the primacy of ethics, or the two taken together. Perhaps in pre-Christian, pre Moslem, pre-Enlightenment days there was, but today these concepts belong to all thoughtful men. What remains Jewish about the American Jew when his primary concern is ethics, even with a religious grounding, is therefore difficult to see.

Why not rather begin the other way around, with Jews themselves? They are primarily an ethnic group, and like any other people have the right to exist and perpetuate their heritage. The individual is inseparable from his people, and the price of turning one's back upon it is the insecurity and rootlessness which characterize so many modern Jews. The creation of a flourishing Jewish community begins not with thinking the right ideas but in the personal acceptance of one's Jewishness.

From this decisive sociological step all else flows. Now, Jewish religion follows naturally upon Jewish healthy-mindedness, provided the content of Jewish belief is put in terms modern men can accept. Men want to believe in God; how else could they dream of self-improvement and strive to better their world?

Without faith in the universe, they cannot live constructively. When God is thought to be supernatural and other-worldly, the modern mind has no choice but to reject Him. With God rather described as a Process or Power working within nature, yet making for human self-fulfillment, scientifically oriented men can accept Him. And in consonance with the universality of ethics the concept of the Jews as God's "chosen people" is rejected. The Jews do not now need it to justify their existence, and such a view is incompatible with the brotherhood of mankind. While other ethnic groups take their own way, Jews will naturally articulate their understanding of the one God in their individual folkways as well as be creative in all the other non-religious forms of folk expression. Thus the Jewish community will grow in continual constructive evolution.

This view has had great appeal to differing groups in the Jewish community. Some culturally oriented Jews have found its primary emphasis upon the Jewish folk a vindication of their view and have been willing to accept the reinterpretation of God that accompanied it as a properly delimited theism. Some traditional Jews, disturbed by the Biblical and prayer book descriptions of God as a man complete with human emotions and attributes, have found this new view of God liberating. Others, disturbed by the clannishness and self-righteousness of the Jewish community, have been converted by its uncompromising universalism mixed with love of the Jewish people and its culture.

The position has not, however, evoked more than modest enthusiasm. Though it has for thirty years been passionately championed among the leaders of the various Jewish professions, it remains peripheral though alive. Its basic social theory has all the virtues and defects of the proto-modern sociology which is its foundation. The American Jew does not find it easy to think of himself primarily as a member of a folk, with his cultural center in the Land of Israel, and only then involved in a particular way of expressing universal religious faith in the United States. The theological suggestions have also faced serious challenge. Religious devotion is either taken deeply or is meaningless, and most men find it difficult if not impossible to become personally involved with a God who is impersonal to them. Moreover, if Jewish commandments are to be thought of as folkways, why should today's general non-observance not receive sanction and the vulgarity which characterizes much of the folk level of American Jewish life not soon become a *mitzvah?*

3) Centrality of Jewish Law

This question of the standards of Jewish life, particularly as they relate to the highest and best in Jewish law, has produced a third view. The Jewish legal tradition, it holds, has ordered and motivated the life of the Jewish people through the ages. Rules of observance both ethical and ritual, not social theories or creeds on the nature of God, have given Jews their distinct character through the ages. Today, when Jews have largely sacrificed Jewish practice for American attainment, to scrap Jewish law would be treason against the generations who held the Law sacred, who lived by it and died for it and thus rendered it indispensable. It would also be profitless appeasement of a self-indulgent generation which, in truth, desperately requires the discipline which Law alone can supply.

Not that the present state of traditional Jewish law can speak to modern man. Unfortunately, times have changed more radically than the traditional interpreters of the Law could appreciate or accommodate. But the Law is not without its inner resources to meet even these unprecedented demands. What is required today is the courage to utilize those special means by which in former times of stress the Jewish sages managed to keep the Law true to itself but relevant to its social situation. Such a renaissance of Jewish law must be left to those who are steeped in its ethos, committed to its observance and thoroughly competent in its sources and methods. Such scholars could produce a body of traditional yet modern Jewish jurisprudence to guide American Jewish life in an authentic way. While their decisions would not bind those who did not wish to accept them, many American Jews would welcome the opportunity to live under a modern Jewish law.

Opponents of this view consider it unworkable in practice and ungrounded in theory. The view has been discussed for decades now, and considerable effort has been made to put it into action with meager results. Few major questions have been treated, and several of these have ended with half the authorities remaining strictly traditional, the rest advocating a position akin to what many in the community had already reached by their private sense of Jewish responsibility. This reticence and indecisiveness have not commended the process to the skeptical observer, but have rather raised questions about the realism of the proposal. To give one example, traditional Jewish law is reasonably clearly against contraception, factors of health aside. But the American Jewish community is almost completely committed to the practice of birth control as a means to planning and pleasure. Can traditional Jewish law be made to speak on this issue other than to condemn current practice? If so, what can it do beside justify what the community is already doing and for the general moral reasons that are rather widely known?

Another species of criticism questions the justification of Jewish law today. True, it was central to Judaism in previous ages, but that was because God had revealed and still authorized it. Who or what authorizes Jewish law today? Previous usage surely cannot, for the same theory which proclaims its significance also admits that it is not altogether satisfactory, that in its present state it must be changed to have contemporary relevance. Only the Orthodox can use the argument of previous use for they intend to continue to use it as it has come down to them. Those who admit the Law must be changed must likewise admit the possibility that perhaps its previous indispensability is now moot.

4) *The Covenant: Judaism as Relation to God*

A fourth view focuses on the question of the source of Jewish law, custom and community—the relationship between God and the people of Israel. Tradition called this the covenant, and from Biblical days understood it to mean that the one God of the universe was using the Jews in a unique way to carry out His purposes in history. The covenant exists to bring the Messianic era, to create and await the Kingdom of God. This is not to deny that the Jews are an ethnic group; but Jewish peoplehood now takes its special meaning in terms of that ancient but continuing pact with God. That is why the character and history of the Jewish people through the ages took a form unparalleled in the records of other peoples or faiths. This people without its God is but a shadow of its historic self and destiny.

Jewish law then is more than ethics or folkways. It is the response of the Jewish people through its prophets and sages to the demands of the real God whom it encountered in history and sought to serve in communal and individual existence. Thus, to speak either of God or the Jewish people or the Law alone as the foundation of modern Jewish life is necessarily to minimize the other factors. Only when all are seen in a living relationship does each emerge with full traditional stature. Were the American Jew consciously and voluntarily able to take up that ancient covenant and make it the mainspring of his life, his observance of its law as a member of its folk would once again be mandated out of his personal relation to God.

This view is relatively new among American Jewry though it has antecedents in German Jewish thought. One of its strengths is the way in which it cuts across current divisions in the community. By making fundamental the relationship between God and the Jews from which the Law emerges, this concept identifies that which all Jews have in common, the relationship. That on which they differ, its implementation in law, is secondary if critical. Moreover, it clarifies what has been permanent in Judaism. The ideas and language of Jews change from generation to generation, the truth of the covenant relationship remains forever beyond full articulation, though the life of the Jewish community in history is its clearest human expression.

The sweep of this view is equalled by the problems it engenders. Expressing its unqualified faith in God, it must somehow explain to the quietly agnostic American Jew that God is truly real, a task modern philosophy and theology make hazardous. To affirm faith in the people, Israel's covenant with God requires explaining what this can mean in a modern view of history and why Jewish suffering and martyrdom are required in this service. It must also indicate how belief in the covenant can generate an authentic if modern Jewish way of life. The position has yet to prove itself.

Yet for the Jew who wants to know why his people must continue and what it must do, this view (in agreement with Orthodoxy) unequivocally affirms: God needs Jews. He still uses Jews for His purposes, and they should continue to work and wait for Him.

What Is Jewish Realism?

Any of these religious views might produce a vibrant and memorable Jewish life on this continent. But all are subject to the objection raised earlier. Jews, like most mid-century Americans, are timid in faith; they prefer their religion diluted, dispassionate, domesticated. To expect the kind of belief from them by which they will live their whole lives, by which they will restructure their communities, and by whose light they will judge their activities in every economic, political and social arena is unrealistic. Jews may become synagogue members but not saints. The sociologist with his statistics would scientifically corroborate the present lack of Jewish devotion and the growing social tides working for the dissolution of such Jewishness as remains. Despite the few modest constructive signs noted, the point of no return for American Judaism may already have been passed.

Most American Jews feel this tough-minded truth in their bones. Here arises the pessimism which permeates much sober Jewish self-reflection. At its worst, the mood leads either to the irresponsibility of despair or to the organization man's optimistic fantasy based on his newest program or budget proposal. But at its best Jewish pessimism can make the Jew recognize how hard he must work and what he may realistically expect to accomplish.

A long-honored Jewish tradition requires instruction to end with words of hope and consolation. The purpose is not to deceive but rather to encourage the transcendence of apathy for the acceptance of responsibility. A Jew ends with hope because that is the Jewish view of man and history.

What is as unrealistic as Jewish history, as unlikely as Jewish survival and creativity? Yet the Jews have lived; more, they have lived in holiness. Were the Jews of previous ages to have taken a dispassionate, objective view of their future they too would have despaired. If hard-headed social realism is the only view the modern Jew can bring to his Jewishness then he will never surmount his pessimism. For Jewish hope was and is founded on Jewish faith. The Jew knows that God keeps the Jewish people alive. He is the Master of their destiny even as He is the Lord of sociology, economics, politics, time and change. His providence guides human history surely though inscrutably. His help is the source of Jewish strength and His support the ultimate basis of Jewish dedication. For if this is a stubborn people, He is its equally patient, long-suffering, faithful God. Through and despite political upheaval, economic change, social revolution, cultural evolution, He has kept this people alive. For a Jew, the only true realism is faith in God and commitment to His service. With Him Jewish history begins and through Him it continues. And He alone knows when the end of days shall come and this great service be fulfilled, vindicated and triumphant.

FOR FURTHER READING

BERKOVITZ, Eliezer, *Faith After the Holocaust* (Hoboken, NJ: Ktav, 1973). An important attempt to respond to the Holocaust and the creation of the State of Israel through the construction of a contemporary philosophy of Jewish history.

FACKENHEIM, Emil, *To Mend the World: Foundations of Future Jewish Thought* (New York: Schocken, 1982). The best known living Jewish philosopher provides his "response" to the momentous events of our time.

HESCHEL, Israel, *Echo of Eternity* (New York: Farrar, Strauss & Giroux, 1969). Heschel's beautiful meditation on the elemental significance of the re-creation of a Jewish state.

KATZ, Steven, T., *Post Holocaust Dialogues: Critical Studies in Contemporary Jewish Thought* (New York: New York University Press, 1983). A searching critique of the main figures in contemporary Jewish thought.

SCHOLEM, Gershom, *On Jews and Judaism in Crisis: Selected Essays* (New York: Schocken, 1978). Scholem's reflections on the ambiguities of the current Jewish situation.

*About the Contributors

ALFRED JOSPE (*Chapter One*) is National Director of Programs and Resources for B'nai B'rith Hillel Foundations, editor of the Hillel Little Books, and author of *Judaism on the Campus, Religion and Myth in Jewish Philosophy* and other works.

ABRAHAM S. HALKIN (*Chapter Two*), Professor of History at New York City College, is also professor of Hebrew Literature at The Jewish Theological Seminary, and author of "The Judeo-Islamic Age" in *Great Ages and Ideas of the Jewish People* and of *Zion in Jewish Literature*.

C. BEZALEL SHERMAN (*Chapter Three*) is a lecturer and author of works both in Yiddish and English, which include *The Jew Within American Society, Jews and Other Ethnic Groups in the U.S.* and *Labor Zionism in America*.

BERNARD J. BAMBERGER (*Chapter Four*) is Rabbi of the West End Synagogue in New York City and author of *The Bible—A Modern Jewish Approach, The Story of Judaism* and numerous articles and reviews.

LOUIS JACOBS (*Chapter Five*) is Director of the Society for the Study of Jewish Theology in London, and author of *Jewish Values, We Have Reason to Believe, A Guide to Yom Kippur,* and *A Guide to Rosh Ha-Shanah*.

MORRIS ADLER (*Chapter Six*) is Rabbi of Congregation Shaarey Zedek in Detroit, Michigan, Chairman of B'nai B'rith's Commission on Adult Jewish Education, and author of *Selected Passages from the Torah* and *The World of the Talmud*.

NATHAN ISAACS (*Chapter Seven*) was Professor of Law at Harvard University Graduate Schools of Business Administration and of Public Administration, and the author of numerous essays on Jewish law in *Legacy of Israel, Jewish Library*, etc.

SAMUEL M. BLUMENFIELD (*Chapter Eight*) is Director of the Department of Education and Culture of the Jewish Agency, a faculty member of the New School for Social Research, and author of *Maimonides, the Educator, John Dewey and Jewish Education* and *Master of Troyes* (Rashi).

*The contributors are identified by their occupations at the time of the writing of the essays

LOU H. SILBERMAN (*Chapter Nine*) is Hillel Professor of Jewish Literature and Thought at Vanderbilt University, and author of articles in the field of theology in the *Universal Jewish Encyclopedia*.

LEVI A. OLAN (*Chapter Ten*) is Rabbi of Temple Emanu-El in Dallas, Texas, and author of *Rethinking the Liberal Religion, On the Nature of Man* and *The Philosophy of Liberal Judaism*.

ELIEZER BERKOVITS (*Chapter Eleven*) is Professor of Jewish Philosophy at the Hebrew Theological College of Chicago, and author of *A Jewish Critique of the Philosophy of Martin Buber* and *God, Man and History—Modern Philosophy of Judaism*.

HAROLD M. SCHULWEIS (*Chapter Twelve*), Rabbi of Temple Beth Abraham in Oakland, California, is founder and chairman of the Institute for Righteous Acts and co-author of *Approaches to the Philosophy of Religion* and *Mordecai M. Kaplan: An Evaluation*.

JACOB B. AGUS (*Chapter Thirteen*) is Rabbi of Beth El Congregation in Baltimore, Maryland, and author of *Modern Philosophies of Judaism, Guideposts in Judaism, The Evolution of Jewish Thought* and *The Meaning of Jewish History*.

STEVEN S. SCHWARZSCHILD (*Chapter Fourteen*) is Rabbi of Temple Beth El, Lynn, Massachusetts, editor of *Judaism*, and author of numerous scholarly articles on Jewish religious thought.

IRA EISENSTEIN (*Chapter Fifteen*) is President of the Reconstructionist Foundation, editor of *The Reconstructionist*, and author of *Creative Judaism, What We Mean by Religion, The Ethics of Tolerance* and *Judaism under Freedom*.

ARTHUR HERTZBERG (*Chapter Sixteen*) is Rabbi of Temple Emanu-El in Englewood, New Jersey, Lecturer in History at Columbia University, and author of *The Zionist Idea, Judaism* and *The Outbursts That Await Us*.

EUGENE B. BOROWITZ (*Chapter Seventeen*) is Professor of Education and Lecturer in Jewish Religious Thought at the New York School of Hebrew Union College—Jewish Institute of Religion, and author of numerous articles.

Notes

1 The Jewish Image of the Jew

1. Nahum N. Glatzer, *Franz Rosenzweig: His Life and Thought*, pp. 18-19.
2. "Reflections on the Jewish Question," *Mid-Century*, edited by Harold Ribalow, p. 398.
3. "Who Are the Jews?," *The Jews*, edited by Louis Finkelstein, p. 1158.
4. Kurt Lewin, *Resolving Social Conflicts*, p. 180.
5. *Ibid.*, p. 183.
6. *Kuzari*, Part I, pp. 27 ff.
7. *Das Judentum und seine Geschichte* (Breslau, 1910), Chapter Three.
8. *Dialogues of A. N. Whitehead*, 1954, p. 137.
9. By Arthur J. Lelyveld, in "The Application of Jewish Values to Creative Living for the American Jew" (mimeographed), JWB Biennial Convention, Washington, D. C., April 1958.
10. Leo Baeck, *The Essence of Judaism* (ed. J. Kauffmann Verlag, Frankfort-on-the-Main, 1936), p. 54.
11. "Crito," *Dialogues of Plato* (Pocket Library #7), pp. 55-62.
12. Mordecai M. Kaplan, *The Future of the American Jew*, p. 219.
13. *The Guide for the Perplexed*, II, 25; see also University of Chicago edition, edited and translated by Strauss and Pines, p. 329.
14. *Midrash Numbers Rabbah*, 14:10.
15. *Tanna d'be Eliahu*, p. 162.
16. *Judaism as Creed and Life*, p. 154.
17. Baeck, *op. cit.*, pp. 55-57.
18. These concepts are treated more fully in Chapter Twelve.
19. Quoted by Nahum N. Glatzer, *Faith and Knowledge: The Jew in the Medieval World*, p. xiv.
20. For an extended discussion of the Messianic idea in Judaism, see Chapter Fourteen.

2. People and Land of Israel

1. For a discussion of the history of Messianism, see Chapter Fourteen.
2. The source of the several items is in the Books of the Bible, most of which are certainly of earlier times. Only the Book of Daniel, very important for Messianism, in the view of most scholars, is of later date, appearing about 168 B.C.E.
3. For a more detailed picture of Jewish life in America, see Chapter Three.
4. For a discussion of Ahad Ha-am's life and thought, see essay by Simon Noveck in *Great Jewish Thinkers of the Twentieth Century*, B'nai B'rith

Book Series, Vol. III, Chapter One. See Volume IV of same series, *Contemporary Jewish Thought: A Reader* for selections from Ahad Ha-am's writings.

5. For a discussion of Herzl's life and thought, see essay by Marvin Lowenthal in *Great Jewish Personalities in Modern Times*, B'nai B'rith Book Series, Vol. II.

3. The American Jewish Community

1. Webster defines community as "a body of people having common organization or interests or living in the same place under the same laws."
2. Immigrants who came here to earn and save up some money, only to return to their native lands.
3. See C. Bezalel Sherman, *The Jew within American Society*, p. 61.
4. Samuel Joseph, *Jewish Immigration to the United States 1881-1910*, p. 137.
5. The old Sephardim practically disappeared as a group, and the new Ladino-speaking Sephardic immigrants from the Balkan states, Turkey, Saloniki, Syria and other Levantine countries were not in the mainstream of American Jewish life.
6. Only the extreme Orthodox groups, still largely immigrant, refuse to join in cooperative undertakings.
7. The Conservatives have recently entered the field of day schools, and there is one secular Jewish day school in New York maintained by the Labor Zionist movement.
8. Organized in 1932 to provide local communities with information on the various Jewish agencies and institutions appealing for financial support and to promote coordination in the raising and distributing of community funds, the Council of Jewish Federations and Welfare Funds now has affiliates in 218 communities.
9. Upon the disappearance, in 1840, of a Franciscan monk in Damascus, Syria, then under French protectorate, his fellow monks, aided and abetted by the French consul, charged that he was murdered by Jews for ritual purposes. A number of Jews were arrested and tortured to "confess." Later, the canard was exposed and the arrested Jews who had not in the meantime died in prison were released.
10. In 1858, a Catholic housemaid tending to a sick Jewish child in the Mortara household in Bologna, Italy, had him secretly baptized. The parents first learned about it a few years later, when a military detachment dispatched by Catholic authorities forcibly took the boy, six years old, away from them. All protests and appeals to the Pope were to no avail. Brought up as a Catholic, the son, Edgar Mortara, never returned to his parents or their faith.
11. Organized by a vicious anti-Semitic group with the active support of high Czarist officials, the pogrom in Kishinev, Bessarabia, broke out on April 6th, 1903 (Passover). In the two days that it lasted, with the police looking the other way, 50 Jews were killed and nearly 200 wounded. Some 700 Jewish homes and business establishments were ransacked, and property damage ran into many millions.
12. The only organized group in American Jewry rejecting the concept of Jewish peoplehood and dissociating itself completely from any religious or cultural identification with the State of Israel is the rabidly anti-Zionist American Council for Judaism. Repudiated by every responsible Jewish

religious and communal body, the Council claims a membership of less than 20,000.

13. For an evaluation of the attitudes toward Israel see: M. Sklare and M. Vosk, *The Riverton Study*, p. 7; M. Sklare and B. Ringer, "A Study of Jewish Attitudes toward the State of Israel," in *The Jews*, edited by Marshall Sklare, p. 437; A. G. Duker, "Impact of Zionism on American Jewry," in *Jewish Life in America*, edited by T. Friedman and R. Gordis, p. 316; C. Bezalel Sherman, *op. cit.*, pp. 213-215.

14. The term "third generation" is used in relation to the offspring of Jewish immigrants who came here since the 1880's, and who probably account for 90 per cent of the total number of Jews in the United States. Jewish immigration as a whole, has, of course, produced more than three generations.

4. *Torah as God's Revelation*

1. See Psalms 74:9

2. For a more detailed discussion of Philo, see *Great Jewish Personalities in Ancient and Medieval Times* (B'nai B'rith Book Series, Volume I), Chapter Four (by Erwin R. Goodenough).

3. Scholars disagree as to whether Philo ever uses the term "unwritten law" in the sense of Oral Torah. But it is certain that he often uses the expression with the meaning stated in our text.

4. For a more detailed discussion of Saadia, see *Great Jewish Personalities in Ancient and Medieval Times* (B'nai B'rith Book Series, Volume I), Chapter Six.

5. For a more detailed discussion of Maimonides, see *ibid.*, Chapter Eight (by Salo W. Baron).

6. For a more detailed discussion of Halevi, see *ibid.*, Chapter Seven (by Jacob S. Minkin).

7. Similarly, the Protestant Reformation rejected Catholic tradition in favor of direct reliance on Scripture, yet retained doctrines derived from Catholic tradition.

8. For more detailed discussion of Rosenzweig and Buber, see Chapters Six and Seven (by Nahum N. Glatzer and Maurice Friedman, respectively) in *Great Jewish Thinkers of the Twentieth Century* (B'nai B'rith Book Series, Volume III).

9. Among the *Hasidim* of Eastern Europe, the conversation and even the behavior of the *rebbe*—the inspired leader—were called Torah. This meant, however, that every word and act of the *rebbe* suggested or implied some religious truth; it did not refer merely to the aura of divinity that surrounded the *rebbe's* personality.

5. *Torah and the Personal Life*

1. See Exodus 23:19 and 34:26; Deuteronomy 14:21.

2. For a fuller discussion of prayer and its role in Jewish life, see Chapter Thirteen.

3. Lord Samuel (*Belief and Action*, revised edition, London, Cassell, 1953, p. 90) overlooks the balance of Jewish teaching in this matter when he writes: "Here we may find an additional cause of the loosening hold of religion, and of the perplexity of our times that has followed. For the modern mind, looking at the whole matter afresh, without feeling bound by traditional orthodoxies, sees that morality, if it is to be comprehensive, must allow that

egoism, at proper times and in proper measure, is a right motive, that it is indeed essential to welfare. When religion seems to ignore or to contradict this, common sense and religion stand opposed." In an interesting Talmudic passage (*Bava M'tzia* 33a) it is said that a man's own needs take precedence over those of others and a Scriptural verse is quoted in support: "Save that there shall be no poor *among you*" (Deuteronomy 15:4). But the same teacher who records this adds: he who strictly observes this will eventually be brought to it, i.e., one who always insists on his rights in this matter will eventually be brought to poverty.

4. Israel Abrahams, *Hebrew Ethical Wills*, pp. 94 f.; B. Halper, *Post-Biblical Literature*, pp. 171 f.
5. *The Palm Tree of Deborah*, translated by Louis Jacobs, p. 79.

6. Torah and Society

1. *Studies in Judaism,* Third Series, pp. 149-150.
2. See Chapter Nine, page 152.
3. *M'gillah* 31a.
4. *Sotah* 14a.
5. *Religion in the Making,* p. 30.
6. See also Exodus 21:2-11, 20, 21, 26, 27; Leviticus 25:39 ff.
7. See Isaiah 2:2-4.
8. *Great Ages and Ideas of the Jewish People,* edited by Leo W. Schwarz, p. 62.
9. See Jeremiah 32.
10. See entire Chapter 23. See also Micah 3:9-12 and Ezekiel 34.
11. See also Amos 8:4-7.
12. William Irwin, *The Old Testament,* p. 26.
13. Herford Travers, *The Pharisees,* p. 137.
14. *Yalkut Shimoni, Proverbs* 947.
15. *Exodus Rabbah* 31:17.
16. *Kiddushin* 17.
17. *Bava Kama* 112a.
18. *Shabbat* 63a.
19. *Mishneh Torah* VII, 10:7-14.

7. Study as a Mode of Worship

1. *Menorah Journal,* viii, p. 6.
2. See also Deuteronomy 11:19.
3. See Deuteronomy 6:8, 9; 11:18-20; 17:18-20; 20:12; 27:1-4, 8; Numbers 15:37-41. See also Exodus, passages about the teaching of sons and constituting with it the material for the theme of the Four Sons in the Passover *Haggadah* (12:26; 13:8, 14).
4. For another treatment of the importance and meaning of the *Shema* and its benedictions, see Chapter Nine.
5. I do not consider the saying of Rabbi Simeon ben Gamaliel near the end of the first chapter of *Ethics of the Fathers* as contrary to the tradition described here, although I find it translated in most versions to the effect that "not learning but doing is the chief thing." In fact, here we have the exception which, if properly understood, completely proves the rule. When Simeon was a student, another, according to the record preserved by the Christians, also sat at the feet of Gamaliel, the wordiest man of all antiquity, Saul of Tarsus. He entertained no high respect for the study of the Law,

and none for its practice. His theory was that salvation must come by faith and not by works. He preached and argued and explained and wrote incessantly on this point. Within the Christian Church he won his point, that the gentiles be admitted without making them submit to the Law, so long as they accepted a theory. In the light of this disturbance read the remarks of Simeon, the very antithesis of Saul: "All my days have I grown up among the wise, and I have found nought of better service than silence; 'Midrash' is not the thing that counts, but 'works' are; whoso is profuse in words causes sin." It is not Torah study that he relegates to an inferior position; on the contrary, that is closely related to the idea of "works," which means obedience to the Torah; it is the theorizing, the making everything turn on what we say or believe, that he finds an improper emphasis, an emphasis that involves its victim in sin.

8. "Thou Shalt Teach"

1. See Deuteronomy 33:10; II Kings 4:23; Malachi 2:7; Nehemiah 8:7-8.
2. Psalms 119:49; I Chronicles 25:8.
3. *Apion*, 1:12.
4. *Legatio* 16:31.
5. *Avodah Zarah* 19a.
6. *Hagiga* 9b; *Eruvin* 54b.
7. *M'gillah* 32a.
8. For a fuller treatment of this subject see Ahad Ha-am's essay "Imitation and Assimilation" in *Selected Essays*, translated by Leon Simon.
9. The etymology of the term *Kallah* is uncertain.
10. A student of the history of Franco-German Jewry came to the conclusion that "apart from the purely religious life, the Jews lived in a state of complete social assimilation with their non-Jewish neighbors." (L. Rabinowitz in *The Social Life of the Jews of Northern France in the XII-XIV Centuries*.)
11. For a detailed treatment by the author of Rashi's contributions in this area, see *Great Jewish Personalities in Ancient and Medieval Times* (B'nai B'rith Book Series, Volume I), Chapter Nine.
12. S. Asaf, *M'korot*, Vol. I, p. 4.
13. Cited by Beryl Smalley in *The Study of the Bible in the Middle Ages*, p. 55.
14. Asaf, *op. cit.*, Vol. I, p. 11.
15. Preface to *Mishneh Torah*.
16. *Laws on Learning Torah*, 1:8.
17. *Ibid.*, 1:3.
18. *Kiddushin* 40b.
19. *Laws on Learning Torah*, 1:3.
20. *Guide for the Perplexed*, III: 53, 54.
21. This description does not include Israel, whose educational philosophy and practice are different from those of Diaspora Jewry.

9. God and Man

1. It was Ismar Elbogen (*Der Jüdische Gottesdienst*, 1913, p. 15) who said: "The *Shema* contains the confession, the core of the faith of Judaism."
2. Deuteronomy 4:6-9; 11:13-21; Numbers 15:37-41.
3. *Sifre Deuteronomy* 329.

4. *Zur Kabbala und ihre Symbolik*, p. 176.
5. *Religion der Vernunft*, pp. 41 f.
6. See *Great Ages and Ideas of the Jewish People*, edited by Leo W. Schwarz, "The Biblical Age," p. 12.
7. The *G'mara* is the collection of interpretations, comments, explanations, stories, legends, centering around the Mishnah (the collection of traditional law arranged by R. Judah the Prince around 200 C.E.), incorporating the discussions of the Babylonian and Palestinian schools, the latter concluding at the end of the fourth or the beginning of the fifth centuries, the former continuing for another century or more.
8. *B'rakhot* 11a.
9. Schechter, *Some Aspects of Rabbinic Theology*, p. 61.
10. Leo Baeck, *Dieses Volk*, I, p. 19.
11. Franz Rosenzweig, *Jehudah Halevi*, 2nd. ed., p. 196.

10. The Nature of Man

1. *Sanhedrin* 38a; see also *Genesis Rabbah* 7.
2. Cited in Louis Ginzberg, *Legends of the Jews*, Vol. V, notes.
3. *Genesis Rabbah* 5, 8.
4. Rabbi Ben Azzai, in *Sifre Leviticus* 18; see also *Genesis Rabbah* 24.
5. *Avot d'Rabbi Natan* 31.
6. *Mishnah Sanhedrin* 4:5.
7. *Emunot v'Deot* 4:1-2.
8. *Ibid.*
9. *Mishnah Sanhedrin* 6:5.
10. Romans 7:14-25.
11. *Sifre Deuteronomy* 306.
12. *B'rakhot* 10a.
13. *Shemoneh Perokim.*
14. *Eruvin* 21b.
15. *Avot d'Rabbi Natan* 31.
16. *Hokhmah Shlemah.*
17. *Sanhedrin* 91a,b.
18. *B'rakhot* 17a.
19. *Genesis Rabbah* 9:5, 10.
20. In Ber Zin, *Vun Menschlichen Leben*, 1945.
21. *Tanhuma Buber* 4:124.
22. *B'rakhot* 61a. The doctrine of the two *yetzarim* is further discussed in the next chapter.
23. *B'reshit Rabbah* 9. See also *Mishnah B'rakhot* 9:5.
24. *Sifre Deuteronomy* 6:5.
25. *Yalkut B'reshit.*
26. Cited in Ginzberg, *op. cit.*, Vol. III, p. 113.
27. *Hulin* 7b.
28. *Ben Sira* 15:11 ff.
29. *Hilkhot T'shuvah* 5, 6.
30. *Ethics*, part II, proposition 48.
31. The role of *t'shuvah* in Jewish life is also discussed in the next chapter.
32. *Pirke d'Reb Eliezer* 3.
33. *Ibid.*

11. When Man Fails God

1. *Rosh Hashanah* 17b; *Yoma* 85b.
2. *Yoma* 36b.
3. *Ibid.*, 9b.
4. *Bava Kama* 50a.
5. *Genesis Rabbah* 33:3; *Bava M'tzia* 85a.
6. See *Sanhedrin* 74a; *Yoma* 85a.
7. *Genesis Rabbah* 38.
8. *Bava M'tzia* 59a.
9. *Genesis Rabbah* 34:12; *Sanhedrin* 91b.
10. See *Sukkah* 52b; *Genesis Rabbah* 22:22.
11. *Sukkah* 52a.
12. Midrash *Shoher Tov* 61a.
13. *B'rakhot* 61a.
14. *N'darim* 32b.
15. *Kiddushin* 30b.
16. *Yoma* 39a.
17. Midrash *Shoher Tov* 51:2.
18. *Hagiga* 16b.
19. The problem of reward and punishment is treated more fully and from a different vantage point in the next chapter.
20. *Ta'anit* 11a; *Genesis Rabbah* 33:1.
21. *Kiddushin* 39b; *Hulin* 142a. See also *Eruvin* 22a; *Avodah Zarah* 3a.
22. Midrash *Shoher Tov* 9:3: *Y. Pe'ah* 1:15.
23. *B'hakhot* 17a.
24. Cf. Maimonides' remarks on the subject in his Mishnah Commentary on *Sanhedrin*.
25. See *The Kuzari*.
26. Maimonides, *Hilkhot T'shuvah* 1:2.
27. *Yoma* 86a.
28. *Ibid.*, 86b.

12. Suffering and Evil

1. *Kiddushin* 39b. From *Hulin* 142a, the Rabbis opine that this turning away came when he saw the tongue of the scholar R. Judah Nahtum in the mouth of a dog; or that he saw Hutzpith, the interpreter, dragged along by swine during the Hadrianic persecutions and then commented in sorrowful disillusionment, "The mouth that uttered pearls licks the dust." Thereupon, he went forth and sinned.
2. "Yossel Rackover Speaks to God" by Zvi Kolitz in *The Bridge*, Vol. III.
3. See, for example, the reaction of Barry Ulanov and Elisabeth Orsten to the "blasphemy" of the Jobian stance, in two separate essays published in *The Bridge*, Vol. III.
4. *Genesis* 17:10 ff.
5. Ibn Gabirol, "The Royal Crown."
6. *Midrash Rabbah* on Lamentations, introductory poems.
7. *B'rakhot* 32a. The Moses legend is based on the text in Exodus 32:9-14; in particular, on the verse in which God exclaims to Moses: "Now, therefore, let Me alone that My wrath may wax hot against them."

8. See *B'rakhot* 32a; also *Ta'anit* 23a; also *Mo'ed Katan* 16b, where David is given the power to annul God's decree.

9. *The Kuzari*, Book IV:13.

10. Maimonides, *Guide for the Perplexed*, III:2.

11. This argument is used most effectively by Saadia, Abraham Ibn Daud and Maimonides. The intent of this argument is to keep God uninfected by contact with the physical basis of evil. The logic of separating God from matter has taken on a variety of forms, including the doctrines of demiurges, emanations, angelic intelligences which serve as middlemen or buffers between God and matter.

12. See Isaac Husik, *A History of Jewish Mediaeval Philosophy*, pp. 229 ff.

13. Maimonides, *op. cit.*, III:12.

14. The view of Christian Science and some Hindus that suffering, illness and death are illusory and unreal is foreign to Jewish belief.

15. See Gersonides, *Commentary on Job*, 41, 42.

16. Maimonides, *op. cit.*, III:22, and Gersonides, *op. cit.*, 1.

17. Maimonides, *op. cit.*, III:12.

18. *M'gillah* 25a; also *B'rakhot* 33. In *Bava M'tzia* 107, we read: "All is in the hands of Heaven except cold and heat."

19. R. Isaac declared, "Let one always pray for mercy not to fall sick; for if he falls sick, he is told, show thy merits and be quit of this disease" (*Shabbat* 32a). See also *Mekhilta* 95b.

20. *B'rakhot* 7a, where R. Jonathan in the name of R. Jose argues that this explanation was the secret wisdom God revealed to Moses.

21. From the traditional confession made on the death bed (*Vidui Sh'khiv M'ra*). A variety of justifications for "chastisements of love" are summarized by the fifteenth-century theologian Joseph Albo. See his *Sefer Ha-Ikkarim*, Volume IV, part 1, pp. 117 f.

22. See Saadia's "Book of Doctrines and Beliefs" in *Three Jewish Philosophers*, p. 135. Also *N'darim* 41a and the *Midrash Rabbah* on Lamentations, 5:1, where Akiba sees reason for rejoicing in the Temple's destruction: "If they that offend him fare so well, how much better they fare who obey him."

23. *Canticles Rabbah* II, 16:2, *Genesis Rabbah* 32:3 and 54:1.

24. *Sifre* 73b; *Ta'anit* 8a.

25. *B'rakhot* 5b. Note that R. Hiyah and R. Joḥanan, who have previously been cited in this passage as having advocated the doctrine of "afflictions of love," reject it in their suffering.

26. *Op. cit.*, III:17 and 24.

27. More explicit is the formulation of Ezekiel 18. See also *Numbers Rabbah* 19:33, where Moses is credited with "instructing" God against visiting the sins of the fathers upon the children.

28. *Sanhedrin* 74a,b. See Maimonides, *Mishneh Torah*, Y. *Hilkhot Y'sodei Hatorah* 5:4. "He who sacrifices his life for religious precepts when not required by the Law to do so is guilty of a deadly sin." See also *K'tuvot* 3b.

29. From the last chorus of the Passover song *Ḥad Gadya*.

30. *Midrash Tanḥuma*, Vargesher, section 4.

31. The mystic theorists of the old *Kaballah* and *Zohar* sometimes identified evil as existing in a metaphysical domain. Evil is here viewed as independent of man, "woven into the texture of the world or rather the existence of God": see *Major Trends in Jewish Mysticism* by Gershom Scholem, p. 236.

32. See *Sotah* 37b and *Sanhedrin* 43b, where not the "secret things" but those overt acts of sin are to be judged and punished by the community.

33. In his *Answer to Job*, C. G. Jung analyzes the Job story as a conflict between an amoral, unconscious power and a moral, conscious finite son.
34. "The Dialogue Between Heaven and Earth" in *Four Existentialist Theologians*, edited by Will Herberg, p. 203.
35. *Ibid.*
36. Martin Buber, *Eclipse of God*, pp. 60-61.
37. *Ibid.*, pp. 118 f.
38. *Ibid.*, p. 60.
39. *Ibid.*, p. 61.
40. Baruch Spinoza, *Ethics*, Appendix to Part I.
41. *B'rakhot* 33b and *Hagiga* 15a.
42. K. Kohler, *Jewish Theology*, pp. 195 f. The author deals with the personification of angels, Messiahs and Satan.
43. Idem, *op. cit.*, Book IV, Part 1, p. 66
44. George Santayana, *Reason in Religion*, p. 133.

13. The Meaning of Prayer

1. Isaiah 6:3.
2. *Kesser Shem Tov*, collected sayings of Israel Baal Shem Tov.
3. Numbers 14:12.
4. Rabbi M.M. of Kotzk, in *B'air Hahasidut* by E. Steinman.
5. *Standard Prayer Book.*
6. *B'rakhot* 9b.
7. New J.P.S. translation has "Sea of Reeds" in place of Red Sea.
8. Exodus 13-17.
9. A more exact translation would be "self-renewal." The commentators speak of new light and life coming to the worshipper and his seeing all things as if they were new.
10. Exodus 34:29.
11. "And after finishing his prayers, he should feel as if he were removed from this world, being numbered among the angels, so that it is difficult for him to turn his attention to the concerns of this world. This is why the first *Hasidim* would wait an hour after their prayers" (*Siddur Otzar Yisrael, Besamim, 'Rosh*).
12. *Standard Prayer Book.*
13. The prayer which follows the *Amidah* in the *Standard Prayer Book*.
14. *Rabbinical Assembly Prayer Book.*
15. The reinterpretation of the "chosen people" idea is well motivated in M. M. Kaplan's *Judaism as a Civilization* and in this writer's *The Meaning of Jewish History*.
16. For a fuller treatment of this subject see Chapter Seven.
17. *Guide for the Perplexed*, 3:51.
18. *Gittin* 56a.
19. *Sanhedrin* 103a, *Leviticus Rabbah* 17.
20. *Shir Hayihud* in *Standard Prayer Book*.

14. The Messianic Doctrine in Contemporary Jewish History

1. In his law-code *Mishneh Torah* Maimonides deals with the Messiah also in the very last and, therefore, climactic chapter.
2. *The Faith of Israel* (Jerusalem, 1948).

3. *Aufbau im Untergang—Juedische Erwachsenenbildung im nationalsozialistischen Deutschland als geistiger Widerstand* (Tuebingen, 1959).
4. Zechariah 2:14-4:7; also 4:12-14.
5. Cf. *Sefer Zerubabel*, Jellinek, *Beth HaMidrash*, II, pp. 55 ff. S. Baron, *A Social and Religious History of the Jews*, Vol. V, pp. 140 ff. and notes.
6. Cf. also *Targum* 4:2 and Commentaries.
7. Cf. also *ad locum Targum*, Radak, and Ibn Ezra who points out that *Tzemaḥ* is numerically identical with *Menaḥem*, "the comforter," as well as Baron, *op. cit.*, p. 357.
8. Cf. Matthew 21:4 ff., 27:9 ff.
9. Compare *Tanḥuma Yitro*, no. 11, p. 124.
10. Cf. *Metzudat David* 4:6, the commentary which most consistently traces the Messianic overtones of Zechariah.
11. Again, *Metzudat David* identifies the unnamed opponent of the redeemer as Gog, thus making the Messianic reference unmistakable.
12. Compare Midrash *Psalms* to Psalm 90:12.
13. Samson Raphael Hirsch, the great German Orthodox rabbi of the nineteenth century, in his commentary on the prayer book refers to our passage in Zechariah as proof-text.
14. For proof that the "Eighteen Prayer" is Messianic throughout cf. I. Elbogen, *Der Juedische Gottesdienst in seiner Geschichtlichen Entwicklung* (Leipzig, 1913), pp. 33-35, 40 ff.; A. Steinberg, "Messianic Movements Up to the End of the Middle Ages," *The Jewish People—Past and Present*, Vol. I, p. 330. For the following, how all the benedictions are tied together in a Messianic wreath, cf. *M'gillah* 18a and Beer's commentary to the prayer book *ad locum*. Cf. also L. J. Liebreich, "The Intermediate Benedictions in the *Amidah*," *Journal of Religion*, Vol. XLII, no. 4 (1952), p. 424.
15. *Perek Ḥelek*.
16. *Religion der Vernunft*, pp. 309, 312, 313.
17. Cf. Steven Schwarzschild, "The Personal Messiah—Towards the Restoration of a Discarded Doctrine," *Judaism*, Vol. V, no. 1, pp. 130 f.
18. Cf. *Sanhedrin* 98.
19. For a discussion of how the living *Kabbalah* makes a program of action out of Messianic belief, cf. Gershom Scholem, in his standard new study of Shabbetai Z'vi, pp. 37-40.
20. *Ibid.*, p. 11. Cf. a discussion of this in Schwarzschild, "Survey of Theological Literature," *Judaism*, Vol. X. no. 1.
21. *Mishneh Torah*, "Laws of the Kings," ch. 12; cf. *B'rakhot* 34b.

15. *Challenges of Modern Times*

1. "The Theological Issues of the Hour," *Rabbinical Assembly Proceedings*, 1949, Vol. 13, pp. 362-363.
2. From *Studies, Addresses and Personal Papers*, Alumni Association of the Hebrew Union College, New York, 1931, pp. 188-191.
3. *Judaism and Modern Man*, p. 128.
4. *Ibid.*, p. 15.
5. *Ahad Ha-am: Essays, Letters, Memoirs*, translated by Leon Simon, pp. 80-82.
6. *The Inner Eye*, p. 56.
7. *The Future of the American Jew*, p. 229. For a brief résumé of Dr. Kaplan's views, see Ira Eisenstein, *Preface to Reconstructionism*.

8. *Judaism and Modern Man*, p. 246.
9. *Ibid.*, p. 249.
10. *Ibid.*, pp. 261-262.
11. *Ibid.*, p. 264.
12. *Ibid.*, p. 271.
13. *Ibid.*, p. 276.
14. *God in Search of Man*, Meridian edition, p. 189.
15. *The Natural and the Supernatural Jew*, p. 307.
16. *Ibid.*, pp. 309-310.

Index